RADICAL HISTORY *Review*

Issue | 138

T0324631

Fascism and Anti-fascism since 1945
Issue Editors: Mark Bray, Jessica Namakkal, Giulia Riccò, and Eric Roubinek

Editors' Introduction

*Mark Bray, Jessica Namakkal, Giulia Riccò,
and Eric Roubinek*

"È questo il fiore del partigiano morto per la libertà"
—"Bella ciao"

Italy. Lebanon. Turkey. Chile. Iraq. India. And back to Italy. The anti-fascist song "Bella ciao" (1944) has become a sine qua non of the sociopolitical protests that have animated city squares throughout the globe. While certainly different in nature and objectives, those manifestations express a deep-seated frustration with the political establishment, fueled by rising inequality on the one hand, and economic stagnation on the other. "Bella ciao," while born out of the struggle against the Nazi-Fascist regime, has been able to extricate itself from both spatial and temporal boundaries.[1] Already in 1960, at the funerals of five workers killed by police forces during a strike in Reggio Emilia, the song made its first appearance outside its original context.[2] It then became further popularized during the political unrest of 1968. But the popularity of "Bella ciao" does not stop with the end of the counterculture. It echoed once again, this time in a more official setting, in 1984 at the funeral of the anti-fascist secretary of the Italian Communist Party, Enrico Berlinguer. In 2019, "Bella ciao" returned to the Italian squares and was heard, among other songs, in Bologna, Modena, Palermo, and Genoa, thanks to the newly formed anti-Salvini movement known as "6000 sardine."[3] Most recently, in early January 2020, protesters in Mumbai invoked the anthem during a protest in opposition to the passing of the Citizenship Amendment Act, a move by the reigning Bharatiya Janata Party to define Indian citizenship through religious affiliation.

Radical History Review
Issue 138 (October 2020)   DOI 10.1215/01636545-8359223
© 2020 by MARHO: The Radical Historians' Organization, Inc.

The popularity of "Bella ciao" well beyond 1945 hints that its historically anti-fascist message of freedom from oppression continues to echo at present across the globe. The existence of this song in places that have experienced neither the crises of interwar Europe nor the horrors of World War II invites us to ask whether the two political ideologies that generated "Bella ciao," fascism and anti-fascism, can exist outside Europe and after 1945. The articles collected in this issue of *Radical History Review* undertake, in one form or another, the challenge posed by the transnational and transhistorical nature of "Bella ciao," by considering what fascism and anti-fascism look like after World War II.

Contemporary media would certainly have us believe not only that fascism is alive and well today, but that it is on the rise. Political leaders from Erdoğan, Modi, and Bolsonaro to Putin and Trump have all been demonized by the media as "fascist." A Google search at the beginning of 2020 for "Trump and Fascism" returns no fewer than 10 million hits, about half of which ask whether he is one, while the others simply declare him as such. Leaders such as former secretary of state Madeleine Albright have written about the topic, as well as the (in)famous Yale historian Timothy Snyder, who has mongered fear in the form of the books *Road to Unfreedom: Russia, Europe, America*, and *On Tyranny: Twenty Lessons from the Twentieth Century*. So too—and on more solid ground—has his colleague, the Yale philosopher Jason Stanley.[4] The ease with which the F-word is employed today against people and ideas with which one does not agree is undoubtedly not what the Holocaust survivor Primo Levi meant when he cautioned that "every age has its own fascism," nor is it what we propose as fascism in this issue.[5] Like those who sing "Bella ciao" today, Levi was responding to current oppression in his time—American imperialism in Vietnam and the rise of military dictatorships in South America—more than his past experiences in surviving the Nazis and Auschwitz. The conundrum that today's global rise of the radical right presents us, then, is how to utilize the rhetorical value implicit in the word *fascism*, the word that Levi understood as capable of inspiring a reaction against oppressive forces, without, however, misusing or, worse, abusing it to the point of becoming desensitized to it. As historian Roger Griffin said of Trump, "You can be a total xenophobic racist male chauvinist bastard and still not be a fascist."[6]

How to define fascism has been a dilemma since, perhaps, the inception of the fascist movement in 1919. Even Giovanni Gentile, philosopher of the National Fascist Party (PNF) tasked with the challenge of tracing its ideological confines, preferred to avoid giving fascism any fixed contours.[7] In order to help contain the ontological nature of fascism, scholars of generic fascism have inherently viewed the geographic location (Europe) and time period (1919–45) in which fascism existed as discrete, even if there are some nuanced differences in how they define the term: Ernst Nolte's emphasis on a "fascist minimum," Emilio Gentile's three-dimensional understanding of fascism, Roger Griffin's differentiation between Fascism and a generic fascism, and Robert Paxton's emphasis on political action as much as rhetoric.[8] However, the reticence to move beyond strict geographical boundaries has created a certain definitional hierarchy that has besieged the field of fascist studies in the last decades, which excludes movements that shared enormous similarities with interwar European fascism but did not fit the time frame or the geographical limits. Only recently have we witnessed historians of fascism explore, in the words of Federico Finchelstein, the "global connections that were essential for fascist ideology to travel (or replicate itself, so to speak) from one side of the ocean to the other."[9] In Finchelstein's transatlantic analysis of Italy and Argentina in the 1920s and 1930s, fascism becomes a transnational ideology, one that "resists standard geo-historiographical categories."[10] Interestingly, as the field of fascist studies began to open to the possibility of considering movements outside Europe as fascist, the 2008 economic crisis unleashed a sense of fear and precarity that has resulted in a comeback of rhetorical strategies and political practices that the media has, for the most part, erroneously labeled as fascist. To be clear, fascism has recently reemerged as a hegemonic discourse, albeit in the form of what semiologist Umberto Eco in a 1995 essay aptly called "Ur-fascism" or eternal fascism. It is not so much that fascism returns but that fascism, due to its rhetorical infinitude, had never really ceased to be. Eco, by pointing to the limitlessness of fascism, reveals why scholars of fascism needed to circumscribe this phenomenon both temporally and spatially in order to productively study it. To that extent, the object of their works was not fascism per se, but what could be referred to as historical fascism—limited to Europe and to the years 1919–45. At the same time, the idea of an Ur-fascism allows for fascism to exist beyond those same limits. Eco acknowledges that there is a set of characteristics to be shared in order for a movement to be called fascist; but the ontological confusion lies in the fact that these elements contradict each other.[11] Enzo Traverso, for example, uses the prefix *post* before *fascism* when speaking of the rise of the radical right in recent years.[12] *Postfascism* in Traverso's analysis hints simultaneously at two ideas: first, the necessity of having a historical fascism to which we can compare today's radical right movements, and second, that despite perhaps being eerily similar to those of the interwar period, they are not *yet* fascist. Traverso's idea of a force in flux, of the possibility, not yet fulfilled, of becoming fascist, speaks to Eco's eternal fascism insofar as both accept that movements generally labeled as radical right can always become fascist, despite taking place after 1945.

This "fascist potential" in our current political climate has urged scholars of fascism to become more publicly vocal. In doing so, their views on historical fascism have become clearer and reveal that for most of these Anglo-American scholars, three features are crucial for a historical fascism to return: revolution, violence, and crisis. The first, many historians agree, has not quite happened—at least not yet. Trump may claim that "politicians are all talk and no action," but as historian Jeffrey Herf points out, Trump does not openly attack institutions of democracy or democracy itself as Hitler and Mussolini once did.[13] Paxton, Griffin, Matthew Feldman, and Stanley Payne agree.[14] Italian Fascism and National Socialism promised the end of democracy and the creation of a new "fascist man." "Payne emphasizes that fascism is 'a national project that is revolutionary and breaks down all the standards and all the barriers'"—or at least it aspired to do so.[15] Beyond revolution, the scholars above have pointed out historical fascism's focus on violence as a barometer for its return, and here, too, they remain wary of such a possibility. For them historical fascism did not just espouse and incite violence; rather, violence was a core philosophy at the heart of those regimes. The violent ideology of Marinetti's Italian Futurism or Georges Sorel's philosophy were key to the development of Italian Fascism—as was a selective reading of Nietzsche to Nazism—but no such deep claim can be made for most of the radical right today. The revolutionary violence that spawned historical fascism was the result of crisis, or more accurately, a constellation of crises. For historian Geoff Eley, we cannot understand the creation of Italian Fascism or National Socialism without the crises of World War I and its outcomes: total war, Bolshevism, revolutionary insurgency, mass trade unionism, growing communist and social democratic parties, and a wave of political democratization. In short, the nuances of history—like those that created fascism—do not repeat themselves. Or at least, notes Eley, "crises of a similar kind never mirror each other exactly."[16] With such a statement, Eley sums up much of the recent public discussion by historians of fascism on our contemporary world. Fascism was something that existed during the interwar years. It looked and acted a certain way, even if it had national idiosyncrasies. What we are witnessing today is not yet fascism per se—not "exactly." "But," as Herf notes, "there's still plenty of room for discomfort."[17]

Consequently, scholarly understandings of anti-fascism have also been subjected to the strict interwar framework and often focus on specific, European, examples, such as the Italian Resistenza.[18] However, such a rigid approach to what Zeev Sternhell has described as the ideology of an alternative modernity that rejects secular and democratic values risks diminishing the impact that fascism, and anti-fascism, have had on the political upheavals of the twentieth and twenty-first centuries.[19] While 1945 is an important watershed for dividing two supposedly different eras, it does not function as a concrete barrier, and ideas are bound to spill over. Thus, while we do recognize that there exists a set of characteristics proper to interwar fascism, which from here on we will call historical fascism, this issue of *Radical History Review* acknowledges the necessity to expand our understanding of fascism and anti-fascism beyond 1945. For rather than completely disappearing after the war, both fascism (and the far-right politics it influenced) and anti-fascism persisted over the following decades, albeit frequently in very different forms and contexts.

The historical memory of the defeat of the Axis powers has served to validate those anti-fascist struggles that came before it while simultaneously delegitimizing those that followed. If the combatants of the Spanish Civil War were dubbed "premature anti-fascists," then the absence of historical scholarship on postwar anti-fascists implicitly reduces them to the status of "belated anti-fascists."[20] Apart from a handful of studies of postwar anti-fascism in Britain by Nigel Copsey, Dave Renton, and others, the English-language literature written by professional historians on postwar anti-fascists confronting the far right is minimal.[21] More has been written about the use of anti-fascist rhetoric and symbols by postwar groups and movements that had broader agendas, such as the Black Panthers or various socialist and communist political parties, to condemn prevailing structures of power,[22] but many scholars have dismissed radical deployments of anti-fascism as gross distortions of the concept's historical meaning. Much of what exists on postwar anti-fascism focuses on issues of historical memory.[23] This lack of attention paid to postwar anti-fascism (especially that which has been directed toward explicitly far-right politics) by professional historians motivated Mark Bray (one of this issue's coeditors) to publish *Antifa: The Anti-fascist Handbook*, a transnational study of militant anti-fascism in Europe and North America.[24] Among Bray's goals with the book was to take seriously the elements of continuity that have existed between interwar and postwar fascism and far-right politics and anti-fascism (without ignoring the important transformations they have undergone) and to make an argument for the historical importance of the anti-fascist resistance of "marginal" groups and communities in recent decades. Along these lines, we offer a Curated Spaces feature from the Interference Archive that includes anti-fascist material from its collections, along with a necessary reflection on the logistics of showing politically controversial material to the public.

The anti-fascist song "Bella ciao" has shown us that its boundless power lies in its message of freedom from oppression, more so than in a circumstantial understanding of its lyrics. Similarly, although the word *fascism* carries within it an almost abysmal capacity for political oversimplification, it also possesses an undeniable rhetorical value whose function as a catalyst for action against forms of political, economic, and social oppression deserves our attention. While the self-proclaimed anti-fascism of movements protecting oppressed communities in the second half of the twentieth century has often been discarded as politically irrelevant or bombastic, due to the strict definition associated with fascism, the articles collected in this issue reveal instead its potential, even when operating on the margins. At times, those margins have been cultural, as Stuart Schrader's review essay on anti-fascism, punk, and Rock Against Racism demonstrates. Moreover, the essays of this issue explore how seemingly isolated movements have actually forged links across continents to produce incredibly diverse political alliances. By integrating anti-imperialism into the conversation about anti-fascism, Antonino Scalia's analysis of Italian Communist internationalism and Michael Staudenmaier's examination of the Latinx Left show how the tendency of scholars to isolate anti-fascism (or fascism) in discrete boxes often misses how such politics are always overlapping with other forms of struggle (and domination). Certainly, historians should never accept such anti-fascist, anti-imperialist argumentation (or any other form of argumentation) at face value, but such scholarship suggests that perhaps we can recognize the oversimplifications of some postwar anti-fascist arguments while also teasing out their rhetorical value for the purpose of making more fundamental points about the common imperialist foundations beneath colonialism—explicit fascism and postwar imperialism in Vietnam, for example. Such commonalities become evident when reading Rosa Hamilton's article on the London Gay Liberation Front and its coalition with disparate movements across Western Europe, and Cole Rizki's piece on the transhistorical alliance between Las Madres de Plaza de Mayo and *travestí* activism in Argentina. In her Intervention piece, Vivian Shaw explores how global anti-fascism is invoked in contemporary Japan, creating what she calls a culture of "liberal anti-fascism." If the common enemy of these groups had been called something other than fascist, these connections might not have materialized.

Many of the insights available to us through the study of postwar anti-fascism can be generated by tracing how the struggles of "marginal" anti-fascists and their allies can nuance our understanding of broader political dynamics concerning identity, migration, and community formation, and simultaneously how dissecting postwar radical analyses of capitalist authoritarianism that deploy notions of fascism can reveal aspects of continuity between far-right politics, imperialism, and historical fascism despite the presence of rhetorical excesses. Fascism becomes a positive category insofar as it promotes common struggles and the easy identification of a common enemy. The leaders of those movements acknowledged this and chose to use the word *fascism* in spite of the likelihood that some of them may not have believed that what they stood against was textbook fascism. Notably, the power of labeling a political force as fascist also works the other way around, as Benjamin Bland's concluding piece on the British Radical Right and its attempted alliance with Qathafi's Libya shows.

We understand that a generous understanding of fascism, once it is not temporally bounded in the ways scholars have often assumed, risks generalizing and normalizing a phenomenon that has specific characteristics. To this end, in our Teaching Radical History section, Giulia Riccò discusses rewriting Sinclair Lewis's *It Can't Happen Here* as a way for the students to bridge the gap between the oversimplification of fascism and its dogmatic sophistication. At the same time, we also recognize that *why* the movements discussed in this issue chose to self-identify as anti-fascist holds a certain value that cannot be dismissed simply because their use of *fascism* does not adhere to the one devised by academics. If before the presidential election of 2016 the thorny issue of defining *fascism* seemed to concern only the ivory tower, with the arrival of Donald J. Trump, Jair Bolsonaro, Matteo Salvini, Narendra Modi, Marine Le Pen, and their like on the international political scene, the necessity of rethinking our definitions of *fascism* and *anti-fascism* has become all the more urgent and public.

Mark Bray is a historian of human rights, terrorism, and politics in modern Europe. He is the author of *Antifa: The Anti-fascist Handbook* (2017) and *Translating Anarchy: The Anarchism of Occupy Wall Street* (2013) and the coeditor of *Anarchist Education and the Modern School: A Francisco Ferrer Reader* (2018). His work has appeared in *Foreign Policy, Washington Post, Salon, Boston Review*, and numerous edited volumes. He is a lecturer at Rutgers University.

Jessica Namakkal is assistant professor of the practice in International Comparative Studies, History, and Gender, Sexuality, and Feminist Studies at Duke University. Her research interests include histories of empire, decolonization, utopianism, and settler colonialism. She has published articles in *Journal of Women's History, Interventions: International Journal of Postcolonial Studies*, and *Journal for the Study of Radicalism*. Her first book, *Unsettling Utopia: Decolonization, Borders, and Mobility in Twentieth Century French India*, is forthcoming. She is a member of the *Radical History Review* editorial collective and coeditor at The Abusable Past.

Giulia Riccò is assistant professor of Italian in the Department of Romance Languages and Literatures at the University of Michigan. Her research and teaching interests include Italian and Brazilian literature and culture, fascism, and migration. Giulia's book manuscript, tentatively titled "Under the Auspices of Dante: Italianità in São Paulo, Brazil," explores the ways in which Italian and Brazilian nationalisms have informed each other. Her articles have appeared in *Forum Italicum, Cultural Dynamics*, and *Mester*.

Eric Roubinek is assistant professor of history at the University of North Carolina at Asheville. His research interests lie at the intersection of German, cultural, and transnational history. At present he is completing a monograph on the collaboration between Nazi Germany and Fascist Italy in planning an African empire. He is coeditor of *The Weimar Republic 1918/19* in the German Historical Institute's German History in Documents and Images. Further publications have appeared in edited volumes on Nazi science in Southern Europe and Nazi-occupied Europe.

Notes

1. For more on the song's origins, see Bermani, *"Guerra Guerra ai palazzi e alle chiese . . ."*
2. Malara, "'Bella Ciao,'" 62.
3. Balmer, "A Can-Do Challenge? Italian 'Sardines' Take On Salvini."
4. Albright and Woodward, *Fascism*; Snyder, *On Tyranny*; Snyder, *Road to Unfreedom*; Stanley, *How Fascism Works*.
5. Levi, "Un passato che credevamo non dovesse ritornare piú."
6. Roger Griffin in Matthews, "I Asked Five Fascism Experts Whether Donald Trump Is a Fascist."
7. Gentile, *Origini e dottrina del fascismo*, 41.
8. Nolte, *Der Faschismus in seiner Epoche*; Gentile, *Il fascismo in tre capitoli*; Griffin, *Nature of Fascism*; Paxton, *Anatomy of Fascism*.
9. Finchelstein, *Transatlantic Fascism*, 8.
10. Finchelstein, *Transatlantic Fascism*, 9. For another study of transnational fascism, see Hofmann, *Fascist Effect*, a study of Italian-Japanese intellectual relations between the 1920s and 1940s.
11. Eco, "Ur-fascism."

12. Traverso, *New Faces of Fascism*.
13. Herf, "Is Donald Trump a Fascist?"
14. Matthews, "I Asked Five Fascism Experts Whether Donald Trump Is a Fascist."
15. Payne in Matthews, "I Asked Five Fascism Experts Whether Donald Trump Is a Fascist."
16. Eley, "Is Trump a Fascist?"
17. Herf, "Is Donald Trump a Fascist?"
18. For example, Pavone's masterpiece, *A Civil War*.
19. Sternhell, "How to Think about Fascism."
20. Eby, *Comrades and Commissars*, 420.
21. Renton, *When We Touched the Sky*; Copsey, *Anti-fascism in Britain*.
22. Vials, *Haunted by Hitler*.
23. García et al., *Rethinking Antifascism*; Plum, *Antifascism after Hitler*.
24. Bray, *Antifa: The Anti-Fascist Handbook*.

References

Albright, Madeleine, and William Woodward. *Fascism: A Warning*. New York: HarperCollins, 2018.

Bermani, Cesare. *"Guerra Guerra ai palazzi e alle chiese . . ."*: *Saggi sul canto sociale*. Roma: Odradek, 2015.

Balmer, Crispian. "A Can-Do Challenge? Italian 'Sardines' Take On Salvini." *Reuters*, November 24, 2019. www.reuters.com/article/us-italy-politics-sardines/a-can-do-challenge -italian-sardines-take-on-salvini-idUSKBN1XY0BM.

Bray, Mark. *Antifa: The Anti-fascist Handbook*. New York: Melville House, 2017.

Copsey, Nigel. *Anti-fascism in Britain*. London: Routledge, 2017.

Eby, Cecil D. *Comrades and Commissars: The Lincoln Battalion in the Spanish Civil War*. University Park: Pennsylvania State University Press, 2007.

Eco, Umberto. "Ur-fascism." *New York Review of Books*, June 22, 1995.

Eley, Geoff. "Is Trump a Fascist?" *Historians for Peace and Democracy* 5, March 19, 2018. www .historiansforpeace.org/wp-content/uploads/2018/02/Eley-Fascism-1.pdf.

Finchelstein, Federico. *Transatlantic Fascism: Ideology, Violence, and the Sacred in Argentina and Italy, 1919–1945*. Durham, NC: Duke University Press, 2010.

García, Hugo, Mercedes Yusta, Xavier Tabet, and Cristina Clímaco, eds. *Rethinking Antifascism: History, Memory, and Politics, 1922 to the Present*. New York: Berghahn, 2018.

Gentile, Emilio. *Il fascismo in tre capitoli*. Rome: Editori Laterza, 2011.

Gentile, Giovanni. *Origini e dottrina del fascismo*. Rome: Libreria del Littorio, 1929.

Griffin, Roger. *The Nature of Fascism*. New York: St. Martin's Press, 1991.

Herf, Jeffrey. "Is Donald Trump a Fascist?" *American Interest*. March 7, 2016. www.the -american-interest.com/2016/03/07/is-donald-trump-a-fascist.

Hofmann, Reto. *The Fascist Effect: Japan and Italy, 1915–1952*. Ithaca, NY: Cornell University Press, 2015.

Levi, Primo. "Un passato che credevamo non dovesse ritornare piú." *Corriere della sera*, May 8, 1974.

Malara, Consuelo Emilij. "'Bella Ciao': La storia di una canzone di libertà nel paese della Mezzaluna." *Occhialì: Rivista sul Mediterraneo islamico* 4 (2019): 60–73.

Matthews, Dylan. "I Asked Five Fascism Experts Whether Donald Trump Is a Fascist. Here's What They Said." *Vox*, May 19, 2016. www.vox.com/policy-and-politics/2015/12/10/9886152 /donald-trump-fascism.

Nolte, Ernst. *Der Faschismus in seiner Epoche*. Munich: R. Piper, 1963.

Paxton, Robert O. *The Anatomy of Fascism*. New York: Alfred A. Knopf, 2004.

Pavone, Claudio. *A Civil War: A History of the Italian Resistance*, translated by Peter Levy. New York: Verso, 2013.

Plum, Catherine J. *Antifascism after Hitler: East German Youth and Socialist Memory, 1949–1989*. New York: Routledge, 2015.

Renton, Dave. *When We Touched the Sky: The Anti-Nazi League 1977–1981*. Cheltenham: New Clarion, 2006.

Snyder, Timothy. *On Tyranny: Twenty Lessons from the Twentieth Century*. London: Bodley Head, 2017.

Snyder, Timothy. *The Road to Unfreedom: Russia, Europe, America*. New York: Tim Duggan Books, 2018.

Stanley, Jason. *How Fascism Works: The Politics of Us and Them*. New York: Random House, 2018.

Sternhell, Zeev. "How to Think about Fascism and Its Ideology." *Constellations* 15, no. 3 (2008): 280–90.

Traverso, Enzo. *The New Faces of Fascism: Populism and the Far Right*, translated by David Broder. New York: Verso, 2019.

Vials, Christopher. *Haunted by Hitler: Liberals, the Left, and the Fight against Fascism in the United States*. Amherst: University of Massachusetts Press, 2014.

The Manifold Partisan

Anti-fascism, Anti-imperialism, and Leftist Internationalism in Italy, 1964–76

Antonino Scalia

The legendary commander Giap . . . wanted to honor the Italian Resistance
with words of grateful admiration when we entrusted him with the trumpet
banners dedicated by the General Command of the Garibaldi Brigades to "the
heroic fighters of Vietnam."
—Pompeo Colajanni

Thank you for coming to this event to honor a great partisan . . . and sorry . . .
I call him a partisan because he was a partisan like me.
—Leandro Agresti

In April 1965, the former partisan commander Pompeo Colajanni met the
Defense Minister of the Democratic Republic of Vietnam, Võ Nguyên Giáp.[1]
This encounter aimed to symbolically unite the Italian resistance, which fought
against the Nazis and Italian fascists between 1943 and 1945, with the Vietnamese
communist resistance against the US invasion and the South Vietnam state. Fifty-
four years later, Leandro Agresti, the last surviving partisan who participated
in the liberation of Florence, mourned another Florentine fighter, thirty-three-
year-old Lorenzo Orsetti, a volunteer in the ranks of the Kurdish People's
Protection Units (YPG) in northern Syria. Agresti defined Orsetti's armed volunteering and death in the war against the Salafi jihadi group Daesh as a form of resistance

Radical History Review
Issue 138 (October 2020)   DOI 10.1215/01636545-8359235
© 2020 by MARHO: The Radical Historians' Organization, Inc.

that he deemed to be essentially similar to the one in which the Italian partisans were involved in the 1940s.[2]

These two distant events show a lasting interconnection between the Italian tradition of anti-fascism and leftist internationalism and its survival across borders and political traditions. This article studies such interlinkage by focusing on the high point of Italian internationalist mobilizations between the mid-1960s and the mid-1970s. In particular, it examines how the Italian Communist Party (PCI) and the Italian revolutionary Left—born from or strengthened by the 1968 student and workers' movements—connected internationalism to anti-fascism in the main international solidarity movements that marked the Italian "Long 1968," and considers to what extent this tradition is still relevant today. This article further argues that this interconnection is rooted in additional, specific close relationships between anti-fascism and anti-imperialism. At various moments in time, and depending on the internationalist campaign, multiple leftist actors bridged the gaps between anti-fascism and anti-imperialism by relying on their particular relationships with the anti-fascist tradition. Furthermore, the actions of international and foreign individuals and organizations, including anti-fascist veterans and neofascists, as well as the context of the Italian and international political conjunctures, influenced the nature of such "bridging" and the resonance between these frames ("more or less established ideological constructs [which] are used strategically to frame a particular topic") of anti-fascism and anti-imperialism.[3]

The first section explores the origins of the "Long 1968" interlinkage between anti-fascism and anti-imperialism by focusing on developments in the early stages of the Cold War and the shift that occurred in this relationship from the mid-1950s. The following section examines the rise of leftist internationalism between the 1960s and the 1970s, and its interconnections with different traditions of communist anti-fascism. The third and final section discusses the contemporary legacies of this political culture and the findings of this research.

Most of the scholarship on the tradition of Italian anti-fascism after 1945 neglects the internationalist campaigns and mostly considers the anti-fascist framing of anti-imperialist and national liberation struggles as a rhetorical device.[4] The only relevant exception is Guido Panvini's seminal work *Ordine nero, guerriglia rossa*, which considers the international background of the fight between anti-fascists and neofascists and how they felt on the verge of a global conflict. However, Panvini does not provide a systematic exploration of this international element.[5] As far as the literature on the Italian revolutionary Left is concerned, there is no systematic study of their internationalist endeavors.[6] A large body of literature exists focusing on the foreign policy of Italian communists.[7] However, it devotes little attention to the role of anti-fascism after 1954.[8]

Studies of internationalist movements in Italy often discuss anti-fascism, but all focus on single campaigns in a limited time frame.[9] The few contributions concerning the role of foreign students in Italian mobilizations demonstrate a similar trend.[10] Few studies focus on the relations between the revolutionary and reformist Italian Left, and no scholarship by professional historians focuses on anti-fascist veterans' associations.[11] By contrast, internationally focused scholarship stresses combinations of anti-imperialism and anti-fascism as sources of inspiration for European "1968ers" and for the birth of a new revolutionary Left.[12] Furthermore, memories of the Second World War feature prominently in histories of European Third Worldism and its legacies.[13] However, as Kim Christiaens has argued, this scholarship emphasizes the role of the new Left in Third Worldism, often overlooking the relevant contribution of communist parties to internationalist movements.[14]

Leftist internationalism, at a very general level, is a heterogenous body of theories and practices sharing the belief that a worldwide struggle of the subaltern classes against capitalism and imperialism is the key to achieving universal emancipation and world peace.[15] Any anti-capitalist and/or anti-imperialist struggle, according to this ideology, strengthens the global struggle and therefore should be supported. These features represent merely the lowest common denominator of a panoply of conceptualizations characterized by deep differences concerning the role that nations and states are supposed to have in such internationalism.[16] For example, Perry Anderson defines any internationalism (including the leftist ones) as sharing the goal of transcending the nation-state, aspiring "towards a wider community, of which nations continue to form the principal units," whereas Mark Mazower defines the aim of leftist internationalism as a "post political mingling of people."[17] The former is a supranational model; the latter, a postnational one. Furthermore, states played a major role in twentieth-century leftist internationalism: communist internationalism—especially from 1924—equated the interests of the subalterns with the state interests of the Soviet Union.[18] During the global sixties, the radicalism of states such as Maoist China and Cuba fostered the return of revolutionary internationalism.[19]

Leftist internationalism, as a heterogenous body of thought, required the construction of a common identity across national borders that expressed itself in a number of campaigns of internationalist solidarity. This process required the use of common frames that, particularly from the 1920s onward, coincided with anti-imperialism and anti-fascism. Italian leftist actors often used these frames by following a "political logic—provocation, mobilization, demonization—not a historically or intellectually sophisticated one."[20] As a result, this article privileges leaflets and daily newspapers and does not systematically examine the parallel intellectual debate that flourished in leftist magazines and journals. This is because these periodicals avoided the popular anti-fascist and anti-imperialist tropes and deployed analytical rather than analogical approaches. For instance, the PCI's theoretical magazines, when addressing the Vietnam War, examined peaceful coexistence and

US strategy rather than comparing Italian and Vietnamese resistance as was common practice in Communist dailies.[21]

This article draws on the influential description of anti-imperialism found in Lenin's *Imperialism, the Highest Stage of Capitalism* (1917), whereby imperialism is in turn defined as a world capitalist system.[22] The Bolshevik leader's diagnostic framework provided both a powerful ideological tool for non-European anticolonial activists and a common language for internationalists all around the world. Similarly, this article adheres to the school of thought that anti-fascism constitutes "an ambivalent and multifaceted paradigm that was employed for different ends and purposes."[23] Italian leftist internationalist actors relied on two distinct communist historical conceptions of the political tradition of anti-fascism.[24] The first historical conception (1922–33) frames fascism as another face of bourgeois dictatorship, and anti-fascist struggle as based on the struggle of all the working class; in other words, anti-fascism is conceptualized as a united front from below. The second conception (1934–35 and 1941–45) defines *fascism* as the emanation "of the most reactionary, most chauvinistic and most imperialist elements of finance capital."[25] This understanding implies a defense of democracy against fascism and alliances with democratic parties to fight fascism; therefore, anti-fascism is here conceptualized as a popular front from above. Italian leftist internationalists practiced solidarity with foreign struggles through an anti-fascism that was in turn both a popular front from above and a united front from below, and that conceived of fascism in accordance with one or both of these frames.

This study is inspired by the transnational turn in anti-fascism studies, as it interprets the shifts in Italian political cultures as resulting from the interplay between multiple cultural flows (national, transnational, global) and the agency of national and transnational actors.[26] In light of this method, Italy is considered as one node in a web of connections and cultural transfers relating both to present struggles and the traveling memories of the past.[27] Moreover, this article considers local domestication of foreign struggle by refusing the logics of the "projection screen" and by stressing foreign actors' agency.[28] It uses daily newspapers and police files as sources to track international solidarity practices, as well as using the printed sources of the PCI and other revolutionary Left groups to explore their discourse(s) on internationalism.

The Origins of the "Long 1968" Interlinkage between Anti-fascism and Anti-imperialism (1947–63)

The "Long 1968" interlinkage between anti-fascism and anti-imperialism stems from the early Cold War conflict and the specific ways in which it reverberated in the Italian context. The fracturing of the leftist world in 1956 allowed the emergence of multiple ways of interlinking internationalism and anti-fascism.

The fundamental interconnections between Italian anti-fascism and anti-imperialism, as Neelam Srivastava argued, dated back to the PCI Theses of Lyons

(1926) and the Italian fascist aggression of the Abyssinian War.[29] Notwithstanding these antecedents, which also included the Italian volunteer forces in the Spanish Civil War International Brigades between 1936 and 1939, the global, national, and transnational early Cold War developments deeply influenced the Italian postwar anti-fascist/anti-imperialist interlinkage.

Significantly, the breakage in the early Cold War of global anti-fascist unity fostered a narrative of anti-fascism as unfinished business on the global level. The ideological conflict between the USSR and the United States entailed that each player defined the other as similar in nature to Nazi Germany.[30] As far as internationalism is concerned, the "two camps doctrine" of 1947 was influential. This Soviet doctrine divided the world between "anti-Fascist forces" (the USSR and its allies) and an imperialist camp championed by the US that supported "reactionary and anti-democratic pro-fascist regimes and movements."[31]

This global split echoed in Italy. Anti-fascist unity dissolved when the PCI and the Italian Socialist Party (PSI) were excluded from the Italian government in 1947. This put an end to a period of anti-fascist cooperation that had started with partisan war. At this time, in a context marked by national liberation struggle, civil and class war, the leftists joined a unitarian National Liberation Committee (CLN).[32] In 1944, with the so-called Salerno turn (*la svolta di Salerno*), the PCI secretary Palmiro Togliatti accepted entering the government led by the former fascist Marshal Pietro Badoglio, temporarily renouncing an anti-monarchist prejudice. After 1944, the communists—and the socialists, more erratically—participated in the CLN and unitarian governments until 1947.[33]

The exclusion of the leftists from the government transformed anti-fascism into a culture of opposition since, until the early 1960s, there was no national official "memory" of partisan resistance to fascism.[34] This exclusion and deliberate forgetting fostered a leftist reading of Italian history as a narrative of "betrayed resistance" that the Italian revolutionary Left reconceptualized and transformed in the 1960s. According to the PCI and PSI reading, the 1947 removal of the leftists from government was a "coup" supported by the same forces that promoted fascism in 1922. In accordance with this interpretation, the above-mentioned forces founded the postwar state on "monopoly profit and speculation."[35]

These global and national narratives of fascism as unfinished business overlapped with other transnational flows such as those coming from France, where the start of the Indochina War led to a widespread use of comparisons between Nazism and French colonial politics.[36] As a result, the Italian pro-Soviet internationalist front between PCI and PSI started to define anti-Americanism as the logical consequence of the anti-Nazi-Fascist resistance. These narrations characterized the protests against the North Atlantic Treaty Organization (NATO) in 1949.[37] Afterward, the campaign against the Korean War (1950–53) established a set of parallels between Nazi-Fascists and the US Army, on the one hand, and Italian partisans and North Korean popular troops, on the other.[38] Leftist internationalists represented all subsequent national liberation wars and anti-dictatorial struggles, from Algeria to Spain, in a similar fashion. In particular, the leftist internationalists compared any anti-dictatorial struggle to the anti-fascist struggle, since any dictatorial regime was, in their eyes, analogous with fascism. Consequently, any national liberation struggle was held to be equally analogous with the Italian one, since any foreign occupation was compared with the Nazi occupation of Italy and its war crimes. Extending the analogical thinking, Italian leftists viewed any "puppet state" (such as the South Vietnam state) through the prism of the Repubblica Sociale Italiana installed by the Nazi occupation in northern Italy in 1943.[39]

As a result of these analogies, Italian leftists used to stage international solidarity and pro-Soviet peace mobilizations on Italian sites of memory linked to the experiences of war and resistance. One notable example was the village of Marzabotto, where Nazis and fascists killed 770 civilians as part of the larger slaughter of Monte Sole, which claimed 1,676 lives in 1944.[40] At Marzabotto in 1951, a rally issued an appeal against "the imperialists attempting to rearm Germany and Japan . . . a tinderbox for the war against the free countries of socialism and peace."[41] The Cold War antagonisms had already divided Italian veterans' organizations by this time. The leftist anti-fascist Italian veterans cohered in the National Association of Italy's Partisans (ANPI) born in 1944 and were at the forefront of the pro-Soviet peace mobilizations, which were directed by the organization known by the evocative name of Partisans of Peace.[42] On the other side of the divide, Italian neofascists organized in a party called Movimento Sociale Italiano (MSI), established in 1946, and were split between a pro-Atlantic and a nonaligned position.[43] At this stage, in the late 1940s, the veterans of the Repubblica Sociale Italiana were not yet the perfect embodiment of the identification between fascism and imperialism.

The decade between the mid-1950s and the mid-1960s formed a caesura. The changes included considerable growth in the Italian internationalist leftist groups and activity and several significant shifts concerning the public discourse on anti-fascism. These factors, together with the irruption of decolonization, modified the way internationalism was interlinked with anti-fascism. First, pro-Soviet internationalism broke up following the 1956 Soviet invasion of Hungary and the 1962 formalization of the Sino-Soviet split. The PSI turned to neutralism in the Cold War in 1956, contributing to the radical internationalist splinter of the Italian Socialist Party of Proletarian Unity (PSIUP) in 1964.[44] Secondly, the Sino-Soviet split fostered the creation of pro-Chinese Marxist-Leninist parties such as the Communist Party of Italy (Marxist-Leninist) in 1966.[45] Finally, this conjuncture originated a multiform new Left that lived at the periphery or outside the official political parties and often revolved around innovative theoretical magazines such as *Quaderni Rossi* or *Quaderni Piacentini*.[46]

At this time, anti-fascism become politically and socially relevant once more, as a phenomenon both in mass movements and in official discourse. Indeed, the significant mobilization of July 1960 in response to Ferdinando Tambroni's Christian Democratic (DC) government's reliance on neofascist votes implied the rebirth of grassroots anti-fascism. The combination of two main factors provoked this wave of violent and widespread anti-fascist mass mobilizations. On the one hand, this first instance in postwar Italy of neofascists playing a significant role in the formation of a government fostered general public indignation. On the other hand, the MSI's specific provocation of hosting its congress in the strongly anti-fascist city of Genova also contributed to generating a widespread sense of anger. As a result, urban guerrilla warfare irrupted in the city itself, and repression of the anti-fascists prompted a chain of mobilizations throughout Italy. The police severely repressed these protests with a final death toll of eleven casualties.[47]

The anti-Tambroni movement shed light on the emergence of new forms of political activism by workers and young people, which, according to Guido Crainz, turned the crisis of "centrism"—the phase marked by the coalition between the DC and other minor parties—into an irreversible trend.[48] Indeed, the failure of the Tambroni experiment brought about the center-left coalition between PSI and the Christian Democratic Party. The center-left, as this form of government was called, carried out only a part of its ambitious reformist program, including the nationalization of the electrical industry and the institution of a compulsory system of schooling until the age of fourteen. The coalition did not implement the most daring part of its program, which included the introduction of economic planning and the rationalization of the construction sector. This was mostly due to the interference of invisible and visible centers of power that ranged from the General Confederation of Italian Industry to the obscure environment that plotted for a coup (known as Piano Solo, 1964) in which the operative forces would be the carabinieri, a portion of the security forces.[49]

As for anti-fascism, the coalition between Christian Democrats and socialists led to the celebration of an official memory of anti-fascist resistance.[50] This, according to Andrea Rapini, caused a polarization of the discourse around resistance between a focus on its celebration and a focus on its betrayal.[51] Indeed, the emergent revolutionary Left, primarily the Marxist-Leninist factions and some other socialist groupings, revived and rewrote the myth of betrayed resistance. According to their reading, the real betrayers were the leaders of the PCI, since the aforementioned *svolta di Salerno* entailed a renouncement of revolution and the abandonment of the partisans' aspirations for a socialist Italy. At the same time, a significant section of the new Left started to challenge the alleged revolutionary character of the Italian resistance. These groups claimed that this anti-fascist tradition, with its acceptance of a united front from above, was one of compromise rather than rebellion.[52]

These developments were interlinked with the irruption of anticolonial struggles that were simultaneously supported by anti-fascist environments, read through anti-fascist paradigms, and marked by the emergence of a multidirectional memory that combined contemporary phenomena with the memory of the world war.[53] This framing was shared also by Catholic former partisans such as Enrico Mattei, the president of the Italian National Hydrocarbon Authority (ENI).[54] This convergence between the Left and the Catholic world would grow stronger during the anti–Vietnam War campaign and undoubtedly contributed some degree of shared ideological foundation to the "Historic Compromise."[55]

Notwithstanding the proliferation of leftist internationalist factions, the PCI maintained its political, organizational, and discursive hegemony in leftist mobilizations until 1967. In 1958, the party drove the creation of the Comitato Anticoloniale Italiano, comprising a considerable number of leading leftist anti-fascist personalities and partisans, which subsequently promoted many anticolonial campaigns.[56] The most relevant anticolonial battle was the one in solidarity with the Algerian War of Independence against the French state. One of its key figures was Giovanni Pirelli. He was a socialist former partisan and intellectual with a rich background of involvement in many important cultural initiatives concerning the preservation of Italian anti-fascist memory and internationalist solidarity.[57] Pirelli's participation in internationalist initiatives included collaboration with a small clandestine web to support the Algerian revolution—in the form of French deserters and Algerian fighters—across Milan, Genoa, Turin, and Rome.[58]

The PCI cultivated the interlinkage between anticolonialism and anti-fascism by comparing their mythologies. For example, in 1963 some communist demonstrators dressed the commemorative plaque honoring the anti-fascist martyr Giacomo Matteotti with a laurel crown on which was written "yesterday Matteotti, today Lumumba."[59] The strength of this analogy provoked a rearticulating of temporalities: an article in the communist children's magazine *Il pioniere* claimed that the Algerian nineteenth-century anticolonial Emir Abdelkader was a precursor of European anti-fascist resistance.[60] Across Italy, leftist students organized several events supporting the Algerian people.[61] Moreover, Italian neofascists, after an initial fascination with Algerian nationalism, chose to support the French colonizers.[62] This created a perfect identification between fascism and colonialism and became the occasion for physical fights between anti-fascist and neofascist students driven by internationalist ideals.[63]

The High Point of Italian Leftist Internationalism (1964 to 1976): Vietnam and Greece

Leftist internationalism reached its climax during the years between the mid-1960s and late 1970s. These internationalist mobilizations were more pluralistic in essence than those of the preceding decade. This was due to the strengthening, verging on a rebirth, of a revolutionary Left around 1968. Indeed, this new revolutionary Left archipelago comprised historical and recent Marxist heretic groups, such as Trotskyists and Maoists. The participation of the new generation that was recruited during the 1968 and 1969 student and workers' movements, as well as the groups that were born after these mobilizations, such as Lotta Continua (LC) and Potere Operaio, strengthened the revolutionary front.[64] The high point of internationalism coincided with the pro-Vietnamese and the pro-Greek campaigns.

PCI and revolutionary Left anti-fascist and anti-imperialist discourses and practices shared some common traits but fundamentally differed in essence. They had in common the daily, often physical confrontation with neofascists, as well as shared support for the same anti-dictatorial and national liberation struggles. Nonetheless, they deeply differed in their relationships with the anti-fascist tradition, as well as in their conceptualizations of anti-fascist unity against contemporary fascist threats. Furthermore, they had conflicting views on the prospects for world revolution and therefore profoundly disagreed about which strategy to pursue on a global scale.

During this period, the PCI retained its support for the restoration of anti-fascist unity and reworked its positioning on internationalism. Specifically, the PCI invoked the renewal of CLN unity, primarily against the threat of an authoritarian turn in Italy, and brought forward the proposal of a coalition government between the DC and the PCI, which eventually became known as the "Historic Compromise" and was theorized in 1973.[65] This political strategy promoted cooperation between the two parties during the 1970s. However, in 1978 the leftist guerrilla organization Red Brigades (BR) kidnapped and murdered Aldo Moro, president of the DC. This event severely undermined the Historic Compromise, and Italian communists eventually abandoned it in 1980. At the same time, PCI internationalism was marked by the endorsement of the Soviet doctrine of peaceful coexistence and was further characterized by an intense activism in internationalist solidarity with non-European people.[66] This overlapped with an ideological emphasis on democratic socialism that appealed to allies in Europe—under the aegis of Eurocommunism—and resulted in an attempt to limit the party's dependence on the USSR.[67]

The multiform revolutionary Left maintained a complex relation with the anti-fascist tradition. A prominent faction of the revolutionary groups—for example, the Marxist-Leninists and the Milan-based Movimento Studentesco—supported the narrative of a red resistance betrayed by the reformists. On the other hand, the workerist (*operaisti*) groups such as Potere Operaio refused the 1940s anti-fascist tradition, since it entailed unity between capitalist and working-class reformism.[68] As for the possibility of a fascist coup taking place in Italy, a part of the revolutionary archipelago argued that the return of fascism was still a viable option for the Italian bourgeoisie, whereas other groups disregarded it as an obsolete weapon. Rather, groups such as Potere Operaio asserted that reformism was the principal tool of control chosen by Italian capitalists.[69] In terms of internationalism, the revolutionary Left was united in supporting groups that challenged peaceful coexistence and engaged in armed struggle against capitalist and imperialist powers.

Both the revolutionary and the reformist Left supported the pro-Vietnamese campaign, which was arguably the most popular campaign in the period. The mass appeal of these mobilizations was grounded both in global phenomena, such as the widespread dissatisfaction with the postwar order, and in national elements. Among these national elements, one of the most significant was the dominant age of collective action. The latter was driven by the massive societal transformation that Italian people experienced between the mid-1950s and the mid-1960s. Nonetheless, the capillary PCI organizational network was also crucial for the success of this internationalist movement.

The Italian mobilizations started shortly after the landing of US troops in South Vietnam and turned quickly into a campaign with rallies, vigils, and demonstrations throughout the country.[70] From 1967 onward, the emergent revolutionary Left started to challenge the PCI leadership in the campaign, often provoking clashes in an attempt to reach embassies and consulates.[71] The 1968 student movement participated in mobilizations and heatedly discussed the Vietnam War in teach-ins.[72] Finally, after 1968, the anti–Vietnam War campaign became a permanent site of mobilization, with many ups and downs. This rebirth and the strengthening of the revolutionary Left implied a significant growth of events, and often but not always the multiplication of separate events and committees.

The anti–Vietnam War campaign demonstrated a strong anti-fascist/anti-imperialist commitment by PCI, which was reinforced by the actions of Vietnamese representatives, anti-fascist veterans, and neofascists. At the same time, the campaign displayed a weaker use of the anti-fascist trope by the revolutionary Left. The PCI's use of the European cultural memory of the Second World War was mirrored by the contemporary experience of the Russell Tribunal, which was led by Jean-Paul Sartre and by the same Vietnamese communists. The guerrilla diplomacy of the latter began in 1962 with a visit to "several WW2 sites, including former Nazi death camps" in order to denounce the threat of a new Vietnamese holocaust.[73] They used anti-fascism as cultural code more able to facilitate communication on the international plan rather than the domestic one, since the memory of the Second World War in Indochina "produced no resistance heroes, no collaborators with the Japanese and no outright villains."[74] Nonetheless, the Vietnamese communists explicitly acknowledged the Vietnamese-Italian resistance comparison: a Vietnamese representative in Milan claimed that the Italian anti-fascist resistance had taught how no organized war machine is capable of stopping people who are fighting for freedom.[75]

On the one hand, the PCI anti-fascist framing of Vietnamese solidarity was inspired by the urgent need to vernacularize and to legitimize an unfamiliar struggle.[76] On the other hand, it was inspired by the temporal overlap of the start of the Vietnam campaign and the twentieth anniversary of Italy's liberation from Nazi occupation and the fall of the Repubblica Sociale Italiana. The PCI attacked both Nazism and the United States on the same grounds and in the same terms—labeling them as "aggressive imperialisms"—and simultaneously drew positive comparisons between Vietnamese and Italian resistance movements.[77] The linkage through analogy of the Nazi occupiers and the American imperialist forces in Vietnam was achieved through a comparison of war crimes, such as the use of gases in Auschwitz and Dachau, and the use of chemical weapons by the United States in Vietnam. Conversely, Vietnamese and Italian resistances were positively paralleled through the active work of living, breathing human symbols of Italian resistance and their encounters with their Vietnamese counterparts.[78] For example, Alcide Cervi, the father of the Cervi brothers—seven anti-fascist martyrs executed in 1943—was interviewed in 1965 about Vietnam, and declared that there were "many Cervi brothers all over the world."[79] Similarly, the PCI delegation that left Italy for Vietnam in April 1965 aimed to consecrate the identification between the Italian and the Vietnamese resistance. Beyond the medals brought by Colajanni to Giáp, the delegation brought as a gift the flag of the 144 Garibaldi Brigade "Antonio Gramsci." This was then donated to the soldiers of the Tenth Vietnamese Anti-Aircraft Brigade, which was personally chosen by Ho Chi Minh.[80] This comparison was confirmed by the MSI official newspaper that claimed the Viet Cong were cowards similar to the Italian partisans, as they would shoot their opponents in the back.[81] Indeed, during these years the MSI started to conjugate fascist doctrine as "Atlantic anticommunism," recalling and strengthening the old Cold War discourse that already conflated fascism and US imperialism.[82] Clear confirmation of this is found in the fact that, in October 1968, two young neofascists burnt a paper puppet holding a sign that read "Vietcong bandit=communist partisan." This language recalled the "bandit" label used by Nazis against Italian partisans during the Second World War.[83]

In contrast, the Italian revolutionary Left compared US aggression and Nazism but tended to avoid drawing any parallel comparison between the Vietnamese and Italian resistance.[84] This was likely because the latter was conceptualized as a defeated resistance in essence, either because it was "betrayed" in its socialist aspirations or because it was insufficiently revolutionary due to its cross-class character. Conversely, revolutionary groups such as Avanguardia Operaia considered the Vietnamese struggle as the principal front of the global war against imperialism whose victory would pave the way to global revolution.[85] The Italian resistance, even if now being rediscovered in its true red character, still paled in comparison with such a watershed in human history.

The anti-dictatorial solidarity campaign with the Greek people entailed a similar but different combination of anti-fascist and anti-imperialist framings. This campaign was deeply internalized by Italian society, and the dialectic within the Greek community held enormous significance for the Italian Left. Moreover, the PCI and the revolutionary Left somehow both managed to frame the campaign in different ways while also proving capable of acting together, especially against the Greek neofascists. Nonetheless, it was a minor campaign and had much less myth-making power when compared to the contemporaneous Vietnam and Chile solidarity campaigns. Finally, the Greek leftists themselves framed their anti-dictatorial struggle in anti-fascist terms, since Greek anti-fascist and anti-Nazi resistance had been rediscovered in Greece in the late 1950s.[86]

The revelation of an attempted coup in Italy in 1964 (Piano Solo) and the simultaneous peak of the anti–Vietnam War mobilization heavily influenced the Italian response to the Greek military coup of 1967. These two elements shaped the conceptualization of the Hellenic dictatorship as an immediate threat to Italian democracy. In addition, the Italian leftist labeling of the coup as a *vicenda greco-americana* (a Greek-American story) functioned to rhetorically position it as a fascist regime.[87] This rhetoric, deployed by both the PCI and Italian revolutionary organizations, invoked the idea that the fascist regime was backed by imperialism. The internationalist mobilizations in solidarity with Greece increased between 1967 and 1970, then declined from the early 1970s onward. Yet even at its two peaks, as marked by the coup itself and by the student occupation of the Athens Polytechnic in November 1973, the Greek issue was subordinated to other international priorities such as the Vietnam War and the Chilean coup of 1973.

From April 1967 onward, the Italian communists, together with many anti-fascist forces including the PSI, instigated an anti-fascist revival that drew upon a great number of anti-fascist veterans.[88] The former partisan Ferruccio Parri led the interparty Solidarity Committee with Greece, and former partisans also played a vital role in assisting Greek students.[89] In March 1969, Paolo Castagnino, a partisan in the Greek and Italian resistances, saved the Greek actress Melina Mercouri, a potent symbol of opposition to the Colonels, from a bomb threat at a venue in Genoa where she was expected to speak in a public meeting.[90] The fascist "strategy of tension" which "tried to use bombs and other acts of violence to undermine democracy and the left" led both the PCI and a part of the revolutionary Left in Italy to include the Greek question in their "black intrigues narrative."[91] This narrative envisioned Italian and Greek neofascists, the Greek junta, and the Italian secret service all cooperating to pave the way for an authoritarian turn in Italy.[92] However, the PCI and the revolutionary Left differed in terms of a solution: the PCI called for a united front from above, whereas the revolutionary Left claimed that the front needed to be organized from below, as—so they argued—every boss is a colonel and bourgeois democracy did not differ significantly from dictatorship.[93]

As for the Greek campaign, foreign agency and neofascism both had important roles. The Greek coup and its resistance exerted even greater influence on the political and social tensions in Italian society, as Greeks made up the majority of foreign students in Italian universities, accounting for 1,953 out of 5,563 foreign students in 1966–67 and 11,963 out of 20,803 between 1973 and 1974.[94] These students were themselves divided between support for and opposition to the dictatorship. The Greek far right presence in Italy was linked to a center of control and intimidation through which the dictatorship installed in Greece in 1967 attempted to silence anti-fascist students. The Greek far righters in Italy were naturally supported by Italian neofascists, who welcomed the Greek coup as a "healthy and essential" last resort.[95] The Greek junta acted against anti-fascist Greek students in Italy through threats of revoking the postponement of military service, canceling passports, or blocking checks sent to students by their parents. This climate of threat and tension reached its height with the self-immolation of Kostas Georgakis, a Greek student who had been recalled for the draft as a retaliation for an anonymous interview in which he had denounced two of the Colonels' agents.[96]

The thin line between the Colonels' agents and Greek far right actors combined with the escalation of violence carried out by Italian neofascists in "the most serious offensive ever attempted in Republican Italy."[97] This articulated both the encapsulation of the Greek question inside Italian militant anti-fascism and the extension of Italian anti-fascism on a global scale, confirming its close link with internationalist movements. This resulted in a minor civil war on Italian soil produced by the clash between right- and left-wing Greeks, each backed by their Italian counterparts. This clash in turn contributed to the "militarization of political struggle" that fueled more political violence during the 1970s in Italy.[98] The violence peaked after 1970 when a deliberate strategy shared by Greek and Italian leftist organizations, reaching across the cleavages between the reformist and revolutionary Left, forced most of the Colonels' followers living in northern and central Italy to relocate.[99] In response, these pro-junta neofascists settled in cities in which the Greek anti-fascists were few and disorganized, such as Messina and Perugia.

The High Point of Italian Leftist Internationalism (1964 to 1976): Palestine and Chile

The final anti-fascist campaigns that this article considers are the Palestine and Chile solidarity campaigns. Both outlived the chronology covered by this article, but their offshoot movements in the 1980s and beyond differed from what occurred in the 1970s, within a particular context marked by widespread internationalist mobilizations and the dialectic between the PCI and the revolutionary Left.

The Italian-Palestine solidarity campaign, during the period of 1967 to 1976, never spurred on mass mobilizations comparable to those of the anti–Vietnam War or Chilean campaigns. Moreover, among all the solidarity campaigns here considered, this was the hardest to frame in terms of the anti-fascist/anti-imperialist model employed in other instances. Nevertheless, the PCI constantly contributed to material solidarity with the Palestinian cause, and the Palestinian guerrilla was highly relevant to the imaginary of the revolutionary Left.[100] According to Arturo Marzano and Guri Schwarz, the Palestinian cause was not popular during this period. It became popular only after the 1982 Israeli invasion of Lebanon, and even more so following the Sabra and Shatila massacre by Christian Lebanese militias between September 16 and 18, 1982.[101]

The global leftist Palestine solidarity movement was born in 1967, when the nationalist and Marxist Palestinian groups—through the act of engaging in guerrilla warfare—joined the Third Worldist front in the wake of the Six-Day War.[102] The PCI, in line with the Soviet Union, chose to support the Palestinians, in spite of bitter divisions within Italian left-wing movements caused by symbolic links between anti-fascism and Israel.[103] The former Italian partisans were very much troubled by this choice, and until 1976, the ANPI opted for a neutral position in the Arab-Israeli conflict. After the outbreak of the Six-Day War, the ANPI issued an official statement that explicitly stated the impossibility of adopting an anti-fascist frame in relation to Israel-Palestine. Their position stated that this conflict was comparable neither to the Vietnam War nor to the internal oppression under fascist regimes such as Portugal and Spain.[104] Italian partisans began to support the Palestinian cause only after the siege of the Tel al-Zaatar Palestinian refugee camp in Lebanon in 1976. At this moment, the ANPI magazine presented an empathetic connection between the Italian anti-fascist resistance and the Palestinians on the basis that both were groups who had fought for the freedom to have their own country.[105] Despite this, the ANPI reached the point of comparing the Israeli state to Nazis only after the massacre of Sabra and Shatila.[106]

The mobilization of the European memory of the Second World War was a decisive legitimizing tool for Palestinians, who deployed this strategy from October 1968 onward. This was the moment when the Palestine Liberation Organization (PLO) composed a series of letters to the United Nations, drawing explicit parallels between its struggle against Israel and the Second World War European resistance movements.[107] Similarly, Palestinian students in Italy compared Zionist Jews to Nazis on the basis that Zionists justified the extermination of Palestinian Arabs as a price due for the crimes perpetrated by the Western world against European diasporic Jewry.[108] Whereas the PCI press was more cautious in evoking the memory of the Second World War anti-fascist resistance movements when framing the Palestinian cause, the revolutionary Left was much more prone to using such discursive strategies. For example, Lotta Continua (LC) claimed that Israel was a fascist state that used Nazi instruments of oppression and extermination, specifically concentration camps, gas, and torture.[109] As a partial strengthening of this complex object for anti-fascist framing, the MSI took a pro-Israeli stance, in contrast to other, smaller far-right extra-parliamentary groups.[110] In 1967, the Roman provincial secretary of the MSI offered the protection of neofascist activists to the Jewish community against potential communist attacks.[111] In this context, one of the sons of Benito Mussolini praised the Israeli military performance during the Six-Day War as a perfect example of the blitzkrieg practiced by Nazi generals Heinz Guderian and Gerd von Rundstedt.[112]

Finally, as far as the Palestinian students in Italy were concerned, their relationships with fascism and anti-fascism were more complex and controversial. In particular, recent scholarship relying on oral sources claims for the Palestinian organization the "tacit approval of the Italian extreme-right's solidarity."[113] However, contemporary police documents seem to provide an alternative, although complementary, account. Just as the Palestinian Fatah drew a parallel between Palestinian guerrillas and the European resistance movements of the Second World War, Arab students in Italy compared Zionism with Hitler's race-infused theory of lebensraum.[114] More importantly, in Perugia, one of the Italian cities with a significant organized Palestinian presence, the Palestinians were involved in the practice of militant anti-fascism and in multinational political feuds encompassing Italians, Greeks, and Arabs.[115]

In contrast with Palestinian solidarity, with its inherent contradictions, complexities, and asymmetries, Italian solidarity with Chile was much more deeply embedded in Italy's own internal questions, and therefore triggered what might be described as a mirror game between the representation of foreign struggles, forms of solidarity, and domestic political strategies. Here, we will focus on the first phase of the Chilean solidarity campaign, where the centrality of the struggle over the meaning of anti-fascism was paramount. It should be noted that this analysis does not take into account the Chilean exiles, who started to reach Italy only after 1974.

The Chilean political system was perceived as fundamentally similar to the Italian one, comprising a dominant Christian Democratic (DC) party, a left-wing party excluded from power for a significant period of time, and reactionary forces ready to prevent the possibility of any such return.[116] As a result, internationalist campaigns against Augusto Pinochet's regime became simultaneously and analogously campaigns about Italy and the best ways to fight the internal threat of fascism. The PCI and LC, one of the revolutionary Left's largest organizations, propagated two divergent understandings of internationalism and anti-fascism, both claiming to be the intellectually and politically correct conclusion to be drawn from the Chilean lesson. The PCI claimed that the Pinochet coup illustrated the necessity of unifying all popular forces and realizing a united front from above capable of crushing any authoritarian attempts at gaining power, backed by foreign imperialist interests. This was the theory adopted by the Historic Compromise between the PCI and the DC that, in the 1970s, reconstituted the lost anti-fascist unity that had broken up in 1947.[117] PCI internationalism consequently supported the unity of all the components of Chilean opposition, successfully welcoming Chilean exiles to Italy, while internalizing the Chilean question as an Italian question.[118] The revolutionary Left proposed another interpretation. Their assertion was that the only way to prevent fascism and defeat imperialism was to arm the masses, and the only way to overthrow Pinochet was through armed struggle. As a result, LC started the campaign for *armi al MIR* (weapons to MIR), in support of Movimiento de Izquierda Revolucionaria (MIR), an armed Chilean Guevarist organization. LC's argumentation presented a novel understanding as to how to prevent a fascist coup, according to which moderate governmental forces (Unidad Popular/ PCI) represented the best terrain in which to accumulate armed forces for the proletariat and the vanguard (LC/MIR).[119] As a result, the anti-fascist internationalist motto in this struggle became "weapons to the MIR"; by contrast, the slogan for Italy was "the PCI for government."

The anti-fascist frame of the pro-Chilean campaign was essential. A mass demonstration took place in Turin on November 21, 1973. Attendance estimates varied from the conservative police figure of 60,000 to the organizers' own tally of 150,000.[120] One of the day's official speakers was the socialist anti-fascist veteran and future president of the Italian republic Sandro Pertini, who claimed to intervene as an "old antifascist militant and friend of freedom."[121] The LC campaign was strong, raising more than eighty million lire in two months (approximately £5,471,945 in today's money) and received a testimonial from the famous anti-fascist personality Franco Antonicelli.[122] Conversely, MSI neofascists regarded Pinochet as a positive model, just as they had viewed the Greek coup in 1967.[123] The primary neofascist criticism was directed at the Italian Christian Democratic party for discussing its historical compromise with PCI. The neofascists argued that the communists were determined to follow the path laid out by Salvador Allende: whereas once they had wanted revolution in order to take power, now the communists wanted to take power in order to bring about the revolution.[124]

Conclusions

In the second half of the 1970s, the PCI—in the context of the Historic Compromise—turned its revindication of the restoration of anti-fascist unity into a rhetorical and campaigning platform for the active defense of the Italian state against the segment of the Italian revolutionary Left promoting and engaging in armed struggle.[125] Whereas the armed fringes of the revolutionary Left were defeated by the early 1980s, internationalism was profoundly transformed. This was, on the one hand, the result of the painful soul-searching fostered by the Vietnamese boat people fleeing socialist-liberated Vietnam from 1975 onward, and by the outbreak of the Vietnamese-Cambodian War in 1978. On the other hand, the so-called Years of Lead in Italy engendered a national debate characterized by a widespread refusal of violence.[126] This debate intersected with the moderate and pragmatic Italian peace movements of 1981–83, which proved to be the last mass mobilization before a long decline in collective action in Italy.[127] New internationalist activism was thenceforth defined by a prevailing discourse of peace, by a reference to anti-fascist ideals rather than anti-fascist armed struggle, and by the primacy of concrete solidarity over demonstrations and violent activism such as the case of the work brigade in Nicaragua.[128] Nevertheless, the last two decades have also been marked by a palpable resurgence of Italian anti-fascist discourse and its interconnection with international solidarity, as epitomized by contemporary international support for volunteering in northern Syria. A younger generation has rediscovered Italian anti-fascist identities and traditions in response to the constant attacks on the values and legacy of partisan resistance led by Silvio Berlusconi's governments (1994–95, 2001–5, 2005–6, and 2008–11).[129] Furthermore, the Palestine solidarity mobilizations that followed the Second Intifada (2000–2005) relaunched a set of comparisons between national liberation struggles and Second World War resistance.[130]

More recently, the global resurgence of the far right and the existence of a transnational hub in northern Syria to oppose what its fighters conceive of as fascism, specifically in the form of Recep Tayyip Erdoğan's Turkish government and the Salafi organization Daesh, has sparked a rediscovery, through its engagements and affinities with Italian political movements, of the interconnections between anti-fascism and internationalism. The contemporary legacy of this lengthy story of interlinkages suggests the long-lasting impact of the early Cold War communist discourses. Indeed, the anti-fascist and anti-imperialist frames adopted by the internationalist fighters in Syria are composed of elements similar to those employed during the internationalist campaigns in the 1960s and 1970s. For example, Kurdish actors mobilize the memory of global and Italian anti-fascism to frame their own armed struggle. One Kurdish representative has recently compared the YPG alliance with the United States against Daesh with the "tactical" anti-fascist unity between the United States and the USSR during the Second World War.[131] In Italy, the Kurdistan Information Office actively promoted celebration of the anniversary of the Italian liberation from fascism and Nazism on April 25, implicitly connecting that past fight with their own.[132] Finally, Italian anti-fascist veterans—such as Leandro Agresti—have publicly consecrated the Kurdish resistance as a continuation of the resistance movement they engaged in during the years of Italian and European fascism.

Nonetheless, this article, while detailing a history of similarities, also aims to offer a history of difference. Demonstrably, the interlinkage between anti-fascism and internationalism varied, depending on each campaign and according to different leftist political actors within the same campaign. It could be argued that the PCI's Vietnam solidarity campaign resembles a sort of "pure model" of the bridging between these frames, exhibiting some key features: the Italian communist use of the memory of fascism and anti-fascism to frame their struggles was reciprocated by

Vietnamese actors who used such tropes to communicate on the international scale; Italian leftist anti-fascist veterans almost unanimously supported the campaign; and Italian neofascists strengthened the interlinkage, since they cheered on US military action against communist "subversion." In contrast, the PCI's Palestine solidarity campaign represents a weaker embodiment of this anti-fascist/anti-imperialist interconnection, in large part because it divided the anti-fascist world and lacked the official support of key anti-fascist veterans' organizations until the late 1970s. Finally, the communist pro-Greek and pro-Chilean campaigns were marked by distinctive overarching dimensions, as they were both framed as campaigns that were primarily about Italy and the danger of a domestic fascist coup backed by imperialism. The proximity, at least in affective terms, of the threat, was made all the more striking by the connections between the Italian neofascists, their Greek peers, and the Colonels' regime, on the one hand, and the perceived similarities between the Italian and Chilean political situations, on the other hand.

Most pertinently, this article has shown how the highly heterogenous revolutionary Left differed from the PCI in articulating and deploying the interlinkage between the anti-fascist tradition and the internationalist campaigns. These differences were grounded in profoundly different relations with the history of partisan resistance, considered variously as a betrayed promise to turn Italy into a social progressive state (in the eyes of the PCI), a betrayed revolutionary epic (according to the Marxist-Leninist groups), or a cross-class waste of revolutionary energies (in the opinion of Potere Operaio). As a result, most of the revolutionary groups avoided comparing the victorious Vietnamese resistance to their own national memory of defeat. LC proposed, during the Chilean campaign, an anti-fascist united front that included the PCI as well as the revolutionary Left but excluded the DC, constituting a distinct moment of rupture with the CLN anti-fascist unity rhetorically evoked by the Historic Compromise. Finally, the revolutionary Left groups were much more prone to using the anti-fascist discourse as a frame for the Arab-Israeli conflict, perhaps because of their relative indifference to the breakup of the broader anti-fascist unity vis-à-vis leftist support for the Palestinians.

Antonino Scalia is a PhD candidate in political science at the University of Catania, Italy. He completed his master's in transnational, global, and spatial history at the University of St. Andrews, UK, as well as a master's in contemporary history at the University of Catania. He is currently working on a doctoral thesis about Italian leftist internationalism between the 1960s and the 1980s.

Notes

An early draft of this essay was presented at the Institute for Transnational and Spatial History (University of St Andrews).
I am grateful for the helpful comments made by all the participants and especially by
Drs. Clémentine Anne, Adam Dunn, Konrad M. Lawson, Siavush Randjbar-Daemi, and
Konstantin Wertelecki.

1. Colajanni, "Vo Nguyen Giap."
2. "L'ultimo saluto dei Partigiani a Lorenzo Orsetti - Firenze, 23.06.2019."
3. Lindekilde, "Discourse and Frame Analysis," 200.
4. Rapini, *Anti-fascismo e cittadinanza*; De Bernardi and Ferrari, *Anti-fascismo e identità europea*; De Bernardi, *Fascismo e anti-fascismo*; Marano, "La cultura politica dell'anti-fascismo."
5. Panvini, *Ordine nero, guerriglia rossa.*
6. Giachetti, *Oltre il Sessantotto*; Ventrone, *Vogliamo tutto.*
7. Galeazzi, *Il PCI e il movimento dei paesi non allineati*; Pappagallo, *Verso il nuovo mondo*; Riccardi, *Il problema Israele*; Riccardi, *L'internazionalismo difficile.*
8. Two scholars focus on the interlinkage between anti-fascism and anti-imperialism during the 1940s and the 1950s: Guiso, *La colomba e la spada*; Mariuzzo, "Stalin and the Dove."
9. Montessoro, "Il mito del Vietnam"; Taviani, "L'anti-americanismo nella sinistra italiana al tempo del Vietnam"; Soave, *La democrazia allo specchio*; Marzano, "Il mito della Palestina"; Santoni, *Il PCI e i giorni del Cile*; Quirico and Lomellini, "Italy: The 'Chilean Lesson.'"
10. Kornetis, "Una diaspora adriatica"; Raftopoulos, "La dittatura dei colonnelli in Grecia"; Falciola, "Wearing a Keffiyeh in Rome."
11. Taviani, "PCI, estremismo di sinistra e terrorismo"; Casini, "La sinistra extraparlamentare"; Cecchini, *Per la libertà d'Italia.*
12. Mark, Townson, and Voglis, "Inspirations."
13. Kalter, *Discovery of the Third World*; Mausbach, "Auschwitz and Vietnam"; Davey, *Idealism beyond Borders.*
14. Christiaens, "Europe at the Crossroads of Three Worlds."
15. Historian Akira Iriye describes "socialist internationalism" as "promoted by those who believed that world peace must be built upon the solidarity of workers everywhere" (*Cultural Internationalism and World Order*, 3). See also Galissot, "Internationalisme"; Bracke, *Which Socialism?*, 17; Dogliani, "Fate of Socialist Internationalism."
16. Schwarzmantel, *Socialism and the Idea of the Nation.*
17. Anderson, "Internationalism: A Breviary," 5; Mazower, *Governing the World*, xiii and xiv.
18. Pons, *Global Revolution*, 43–101.
19. On the People's Republic of China, see Lovell, *Maoism: A Global History.*
20. Mercer, "Spectres of Fascism," 124.
21. Pajetta, "La contro-rivoluzione."
22. "Imperialism is capitalism in that stage of development in which the dominance of monopolies and finance capital is established; in which the export of capital has acquired pronounced importance; in which the division of the world among the international trusts has begun; in which the division of all territories of the globe among the biggest capitalist powers has been completed" (Lenin, *Imperialism*).
23. Bauerkämper, "Marxist Historical Cultures."
24. Groppo, "Fascismes, anti-fascismes et communismes."
25. Dimitrov, "Fascist Offensive."
26. García, "Transnational History."
27. Kornetis, "'Everything Links'?"; Erll, "Travelling Memory."
28. Slobodian, *Foreign Front*; Wu, *Radicals on the Road.*
29. Srivastava, *Italian Colonialism.*
30. Engerman, "Ideology and the Origins of the Cold War, 1917–1962."

31. "Zhdanov and the Cominform."

32. Pavone, *Una guerra civile*.

33. Barbagallo, "La formazione dell'Italia democratica."

34. Ridolfi, "Rituali della memoria e linguaggi dell'anti-fascismo."

35. De Bernardi, *Fascismo e anti-fascismo*, chap. 6, "Fascismo e anti-fascismo nella memoria pubblica repubblicana."

36. Kalter, *Discovery of the Third World*, 31.

37. Guiso, *La colomba e la spada*.

38. Mariuzzo, "Stalin and the Dove."

39. Taviani, "L'anti-americanismo nella sinistra italiana al tempo del Vietnam," 169.

40. Magni, "La strage di Marzabotto nel cinquantennio repubblicano."

41. *L'Unità*, "I sopravvissuti di Marzabotto."

42. Alcalde and Seixas, *War Veterans*; Cecchini, *Per la libertà d'Italia*, 21; *L'Unità*, "I partigiani si batteranno alla testa del popolo per la pace."

43. Conti, *L'anima nera della Repubblica*, 4–5 and 7.

44. Nencioni, "Tra neutralismo e atlantismo"; Agosti, *Il partito provvisorio*.

45. Niccolai, *Quando la Cina era vicina*.

46. Chiarotto, *Aspettando il Sessantotto*.

47. Cooke, *Luglio 1960*.

48. Crainz, *Storia del miracolo italiano*, 188–89.

49. Ginsborg, *History*, 254–96.

50. Cooke, *Legacy of the Italian Resistance*, 86.

51. Rapini, *Anti-fascismo e cittadinanza*, 79.

52. Marano, "La cultura politica dell'anti-fascismo," 109.

53. Rothberg, *Multidirectional Memory*. Already in 1950 the Martinican intellectual Aimé Césaire traced Nazi crimes back to European colonialism. Cf. Césaire, *Discours sur le colonialisme*.

54. Panvini, "Third Worldism in Italy," 292–93.

55. Lomellini, "Prove di pacifismo."

56. Galeazzi, *Il PCI e il movimento dei paesi non allineati*, 52–53.

57. Malvezzi and Pirelli, *Lettere*.

58. Scotti, *Vita di Giovanni Pirelli*.

59. *L'Unità*, "Migliaia di cittadini hanno manifestato contro l'assassinio di Patrice Lumumba."

60. Galletti, "Algeria Eroica."

61. *L'Unità*, "Calorosa manifestazione."

62. Mammone, *Transnational Neofascism*, 94–120.

63. *La stampa sera*, "Scontri fra studenti dopo un convegno a Milano"; *Corriere della sera*, "Tafferugli tra estremisti all'Università di Bologna."

64. Ottaviano, *La rivoluzione nel labirinto*.

65. Pons, *Berlinguer e la fine del comunismo*, chap. 1, "Il tempo della distensione e l'invenzione dell'eurocomunismo."

66. Galeazzi, *Il PCI e il movimento dei paesi non allineati*.

67. Balampanadis, *Eurocommunism*.

68. Bologna, "Fascismo in Europa."

69. Ventrone, *Vogliamo tutto*, chap. 3, "Dalle riviste ai movimenti."

70. *L'Unità*, "Imponente la marcia della pace a Milano"; Montessoro, "Il mito del Vietnam," 279–85.

71. Taviani, "L'anti-americanismo nella sinistra italiana al tempo del Vietnam."

72. Tolomelli, *L'Italia dei movimenti.*

73. Molden, "Vietnam, the New Left, and the Holocaust"; Brigham, *Guerrilla Diplomacy*, 23.

74. Chandler, "Legacies of World War II in Indochina."

75. From Questore Allitto to the Italian Ministry of the Interior, Milan, January 18, 1972, Central Archive of the State (Rome), Interior Ministry, Cabinet, 1971–75, folder 73, file 11020/115, Milano e provincia manifestazioni pro-Vietnam.

76. Kalter, *Discovery of the Third World*, 166.

77. *L'Unità*, "Crimini di guerra: Ieri e oggi"; Pajetta, "Il coraggio di dire di no."

78. *Vie nuove*, "Se questo è l'uomo."

79. Marzullo, "Papà Cervi."

80. Occhetto, "Ho ci Minh."

81. La Mangusta, "Pajetta."

82. Conti, *L'anima nera della Repubblica*, 35; Sorgonà, *La scoperta della destra.*

83. Martellini, *All'ombra delle altrui rivoluzioni*, 26–27.

84. *Lotta continua*, "Hitler vive a Washington."

85. *Avanguardia operaia*, "La guerra di popolo in Indocina."

86. Mark, Townson, and Voglis, "Inspirations," 82.

87. Jacoviello, "Dal Vietnam alla Grecia."

88. Soave, *La democrazia allo specchio*, 11.

89. Soave, *La democrazia allo specchio*, 97–107.

90. From Prefect of Bologna to the Italian Ministry of the Interior, Bologna, March 7, 1969, in Central Archive of the State (Rome), Interior Ministry, Cabinet, 1967–70, folder 49, file 11010/107; *L'Unità*, "Con lo sciopero anti-fascista Genova risponde all'attentato."

91. Foot, *Archipelago*, chap. 3, "Blood and Reform: Institutional Change and Violence in the 1960s and 1970s."

92. Giannuli, *La strategia della tensione*, chap. 14, "La svolta stragista."

93. Panvini, *Ordine nero, guerriglia rossa*, 39.

94. ISTAT, *Annuario stastistico dell'istruzione italiana* 1968 and 1976.

95. *Secolo d'Italia*, "Estremo rimedio."

96. Paputsis, *Il grande sì.*

97. Crainz, *Il paese mancato*, 452.

98. Panvini, *Ordine nero, guerriglia rossa.*

99. For instance: From Prefetto De Vito to the Italian Ministry of the Interior, Florence, March 26, 1973, in Central Archive of the State (Rome), Interior Ministry, Cabinet, 1971–75, folder 425, file 15121, Studenti greci in Italia.

100. Riccardi, *Il problema Israele*; Riccardi, *L'internazionalismo difficile*; Marzano, "Il mito della Palestina."

101. Marzano and Schwarz, *Attentato alla Sinagoga*, 54.

102. Chamberlin, *Global Offensive.*

103. Molinari, *La sinistra e gli ebrei in Italia*, 28–45; Di Figlia, *Israele e la sinistra.*

104. Segreteria Nazionale dell'ANPI, Roma, June 9, 1967, in Central Archive of the State (Rome), Interior Ministry, Cabinet, 1967–70, folder 82, file 11080/93, Partigiani affari generali.

105. Tartaro, "Troppi i focolai di tensione."

106. Bonfiglioli, "La tragedia del Medio Oriente."

107. Chamberlin, *Global Offensive*, 24–25.

108. Unione Generale degli Studenti Palestinesi in Italia, *15 maggio 1948–15 maggio 1967 19 anni di vergogna*, in Central Archive of the State (Rome), Interior Ministry, Cabinet, 1967–70, folder 327, file 15583/41, Studenti palestinesi in Italia.

109. *Lotta continua*, "Israele avamposto fascista dell'imperialismo."

110. D'Annibale, De Sanctis, and Donati, *Il filoarabismo nero*.

111. Rossi, *La destra e gli ebrei*, 110.

112. Mussolini, "Gerusalemme ieri e oggi."

113. Falciola, "Wearing a Keffiyeh," 23.

114. From the Padova Chief of Police to the Italian Ministry of the Interior (Padova: 23-04-1968) in Central Archive of the State (Rome), Interior Ministry, Cabinet, 1967–70, folder 327.

115. Telegrams from the Prefect of Perugia to the Italian Ministry of the Interior, Perugia June 22, 23, 24, and 25, 1971, in Central Archive of the State (Rome), Interior Ministry, Cabinet, 1971–75, folder 32; file 110158, Perugia ordine pubblico e incidenti.

116. Santoni, *Il PCI e i giorni del Cile*, 115.

117. Pons, *Berlinguer e la fine del comunismo*, chap. 1, "Il tempo della distensione e l'invenzione dell'eurocomunismo."

118. Quirico and Lomellini, "Italy: The 'Chilean Lesson'"; Mignini, "Dalla Moneda a Modena."

119. Bobbio, *Lotta continua*, 127.

120. From Torino Chief of Police to the Italian Ministry of the Interior, Turin, November 18, 1973) in Central Archive of the State (Rome), Interior Ministry, Cabinet, 1971–75, folder 72, file 11021, Cile avvenimenti vari; *Lotta continua*, "La manifestazione di oggi a Torino."

121. *La stampa sera*, "Manifestano in 60 mila."

122. Lotta Continua–Pistoia, *Armi al MIR!*, in Central Archive of the State (Rome), Interior Ministry, Cabinet, 1971–75, folder 72, file 11021, Cile avvenimenti vari; *Lotta continua*, "Armi al MIR!"

123. Panvini, *Ordine nero, guerriglia rossa*, 187 and 273.

124. Tripodi, "Impareranno la lezione."

125. Naccarato, *Difendere la democrazia*. Focardi, *La guerra della memoria*, 54–55.

126. Galfré, *La guerra è finita*.

127. Della Porta, *Movimenti collettivi*, 178

128. Associazione di amicizia e solidarietà Italia Nicaragua, *Que linda Nicaragua!*

129. De Bernardi, *Fascismo e anti-fascismo*, chap. 7, "Oltre il novecento."

130. Valli, "Bella Ciao per cinquemila."

131. Ufficio di Informazione del Kurdistan in Italia, "Per le resistenze."

132. Komun Academy, "La lotta per la libertà dei curdi."

References

Agosti, Aldo. *Il partito provvisorio: Storia del PSIUP nel lungo Sessantotto italiano*. Rome: Laterza, 2013.

Alcalde, Ángel, and Xosé M. Núñez Seixas, eds. *War Veterans and the World after 1945: Cold War Politics, Decolonization, Memory*. New York: Routledge/Taylor and Francis Group, 2018.

Anderson, Perry. "Internationalism: A Breviary." *New Left Review* 2, no. 14 (2002): 5–25.

Associazione di amicizia e solidarietà Italia Nicaragua. *Que linda Nicaragua!* Genova: Fratelli Frilli, 2005.

Avanguardia operaia. "La guerra di popolo in Indocina prepara il crollo dell'imperialismo." No. 14–15 (April 3, 1971): 1–4.

Balampanadis, Ioannis. *Eurocommunism: From the Communist to the Radical European Left.* Abingdon, Oxon: Routledge, 2019.

Barbagallo, Francesco. "La formazione dell'Italia democratica." In *Storia dell'Italia repubblicana*, edited by Francesco Barbagallo, 5–128. Turin: Einaudi, 1994.

Bauerkämper, Arnd. "Marxist Historical Cultures, 'Anti-fascism,' and the Legacy of the Past: Western Europe, 1945–1990." In *Marxist Historical Cultures and Social Movements during the Cold War: Case Studies from Germany, Italy, and Other Western European States*, edited by Stefan Berger and Christoph Cornelissen, 33–64. New York: Palgrave Macmillan, 2019.

Bobbio, Luigi. *Lotta continua: Storia di una organizzazione rivoluzionaria.* Rome: Savelli, 1979.

Bologna, Sergio. "Fascismo in Europa." *Compagni*, no. 2–3 (June 5, 1970).

Bonfiglioli, Roberto. "La tragedia del Medio Oriente." *Patria indipendente*, no. 11 (June 27, 1982).

Bracke, Maud. *Which Socialism? Whose Détente? West European Communism and the Czechoslovak Crisis, 1968.* New York: Central European University Press, 2007.

Brigham, Robert K. *Guerrilla Diplomacy: The NLF's Foreign Relations and the Viet Nam War.* Ithaca, NY: Cornell University Press, 1999.

Casini, Valentina. "La sinistra extraparlamentare nel dibattito interno al Partito comunista italiano: Il Seminario sull'estremismo del gennaio 1975." *Ricerche di Storia Politica* 20, no. 1 (2017): 23–42.

Cecchini, Lucio. *Per la libertà d'Italia, per l'Italia delle libertà: Profilo storico dell'Associazione nazionale partigiani d'Italia.* Rome: Jasilio, 1998.

Césaire, Aimé. *Discours sur le colonialisme: Suivi du, Discours sur la négritude.* Paris: Présence africaine, 2004.

Chamberlin, Paul Thomas. *The Global Offensive: The United States, the Palestine Liberation Organization, and the Making of the Post–Cold War Order.* Oxford: Oxford University Press, 2012.

Chandler, David. "Legacies of World War II in Indochina." In *Legacies of World War II in South and East Asia*, edited by David Koh Wee Hock, 23–35. Singapore: ISEAS–Yusof Ishak Institute, 2007.

Chiarotto Francesca, ed. *Aspettando il Sessantotto: Continuità e fratture nelle culture politiche italiane dal 1956 al 1968.* Turin: Accademia University Press, 2017.

Christiaens, Kim. "Europe at the Crossroads of Three Worlds: Alternative Histories and Connections of European Solidarity with the Third World, 1950s–80s." *European Review of History: Revue européenne d'histoire* 24, no. 6 (2017): 932–54.

Colajanni, Pompeo. "Vo Nguyen Giap il leggendario comandante." *Vie nuove*, no. 21 (May 27, 1965).

Conti, Davide. *L'anima nera della Repubblica: Storia del MSI.* Rome: Laterza, 2013.

Cooke, Philip. *The Legacy of the Italian Resistance.* New York: Palgrave Macmillan, 2011.

Cooke, Philip. *Luglio 1960: Tambroni e la repressione fallita.* Milan: Teti, 2000.

Corriere della sera. "Tafferugli tra estremisti all'Università di Bologna." December 7, 1960.

Crainz, Guido. *Il paese mancato: Dal miracolo economico agli anni ottanta*. Rome: Donzelli, 2003.

Crainz, Guido. *Storia del miracolo italiano: Culture, identità, trasformazioni fra anni cinquanta e sessanta*. Rome: Donzelli, 1996.

D'Annibale, Elisa, Veronica De Sanctis, and Beatrice Donati. *Il filoarabismo nero: Note su neofascismo italiano e mondo arabo*. Rome: Nuova Cultura, 2019.

Davey, Eleanor. *Idealism beyond Borders: The French Revolutionary Left and the Rise of Humanitarianism, 1954–1988*. Cambridge: Cambridge University Press, 2015.

De Bernardi, Alberto. *Fascismo e anti-fascismo: Storia, memoria e culture politiche*. Rome: Donzelli, 2018.

De Bernardi, Alberto, and Paolo Ferrari, eds. *Anti-fascismo e identità europea*. Rome: Carocci, 2004.

Della Porta, Donatella. *Movimenti collettivi e sistema politico in Italia: 1960–1995*. Rome: Laterza, 1996.

Di Figlia, Matteo. *Israele e la sinistra: Gli ebrei nel dibattito pubblico italiano dal 1945 a oggi*. Rome: Donzelli, 2012.

Dimitrov, Georgi. "The Fascist Offensive and the Tasks of the Communist International in the Struggle of the Working Class against Fascism," August 2, 1935. www.marxists.org /reference/archive/dimitrov/works/1935/08_02.htm.

Dogliani, Patrizia. "The Fate of Socialist Internationalism." In *Internationalisms: A Twentieth-Century History*, edited by Glenda Sluga, Patricia Clavin, and Sunil Amrith, 38–60. Cambridge: Cambridge University Press, 2016.

Engerman, David C. "Ideology and the Origins of the Cold War, 1917–1962." In *The Cambridge History of the Cold War*, edited by Melvyn P. Leffler and Odd Arne Westad, 20–43. Cambridge: Cambridge University Press, 2010.

Erll, Astrid. "Travelling Memory." *Parallax* 17, no. 4 (2011): 4–18.

Falciola, Luca. "Wearing a Keffiyeh in Rome: The Transnational Relationships between the Italian Revolutionary Left and the Palestinian Resistance." Draft paper—SISP Conference, Milan, September 2016.

Focardi, Filippo. *La guerra della memoria: La Resistenza nel dibattito politico italiano dal 1945 a oggi*. Rome: Laterza, 2005.

Foot, John. *The Archipelago: Italy since 1945*. London: Bloomsbury, 2018.

Galeazzi, Marco. *Il PCI e il movimento dei paesi non allineati: 1955–1975*. Milan: FrancoAngeli, 2011.

Galfré, Monica. *La guerra è finita: L'Italia e l'uscita dal terrorismo, 1980–1987*. Rome: Laterza, 2014.

Galissot, René. "Internationalisme." In *Dictionnaire critique du marxisme*, edited by Gérard Bensussan and Georges Labica, 615–19. Paris: Presses Universitaires de France, 1982.

Galletti, Mario. "Algeria Eroica." *Il pioniere*, no. 24 (June 12, 1960).

García, Hugo. "Transnational History: A New Paradigm for Anti-fascist Studies?" *Contemporary European History* 25, no. 4 (2016): 563–72.

Giachetti, Diego. *Oltre il Sessantotto: Prima, durante e dopo il movimento*. Pisa: BFS, 1998.

Giannuli, Aldo. *La strategia della tensione: Servizi segreti, partiti, golpe falliti, terrore fascista, politica internazionale: un bilancio definitive*. Milan: Ponte alle Grazie, 2018.

Ginsborg, Paul. *A History of Contemporary Italy: Society and Politics, 1943–1988*. New York: Penguin Books, 1990.

Groppo, Bruno. "Fascismes, anti-fascismes et communismes." In *Le siècle des communismes*, edited by Michel Dreyfus et al., 499–511. Paris: L'Atelier, 2000.

Guiso, Andrea. *La colomba e la spada: "Lotta per la pace" e antiamericanismo nella politica del Partito comunista italiano (1949–1954)*. Soveria Mannelli: Rubbettino, 2006.

Iriye, Akira. *Cultural Internationalism and World Order*. Baltimore, MD: Johns Hopkins University Press, 1997.

ISTAT. *Annuario statistico dell'istruzione italiana 1968*.

ISTAT. *Annuario statistico dell'istruzione italiana 1976*.

Jacoviello, Alberto. "Dal Vietnam alla Grecia." *L'Unità*, April 22, 1967.

Kalter, Christoph. *The Discovery of the Third World: Decolonization and the Rise of the New Left in France, c. 1950–1976*. Cambridge: Cambridge University Press, 2016.

Komun Academy. "La lotta per la libertà dei curdi e l'(anti) imperialismo nel XXI secolo," February 5, 2019. www.uikionlus.com/la-lotta-per-la-liberta-dei-curdi-e-lanti-imperialismo -nel-xxi-secolo.

Kornetis, Kostis. "'Everything Links'? Temporality, Territoriality, and Cultural Transfer in the '68 Protest Movements." *Historein* 9 (2010): 34–45.

Kornetis, Kostis. "Una diaspora adriatica: La migrazione degli studenti universitari greci in Italia." In *Immaginare l'Adriatico: Contributi alla riscoperta sociale di uno spazio di frontiera*, edited by Emilio Cocco and Everardo Minardi, 151–68. Milan: FrancoAngeli, 2007.

La Mangusta. "Pajetta: Mille bugie, una verità (cattiva)." *Secolo d'Italia*, May 20, 1965.

La stampa sera. "Manifestano in 60 mila la solidarietà per il Cile." November 19, 1973.

La stampa sera. "Scontri fra studenti dopo un convegno a Milano." December 12, 1960.

Lenin, V. I. *Imperialism, the Highest Stage of Capitalism*. Lenin Internet Archive, 2005. www .marxists.org/archive/lenin/works/1916/imp-hsc/index.htm#ch07.

Lindekilde, Lasse. "Discourse and Frame Analysis: In-Depth Analysis of Qualitative Data in Social Movement Research." In *Methodological Practices in Social Movement Research*, edited by Donatella Della Porta, 195–227. Oxford: Oxford University Press, 2014.

Lomellini, Valentine. "Prove di pacifismo all'italiana: La critica alla guerra del Vietnam e la genesi dell'altra America: Un punto di incontro tra Pci e Dc?" *Ricerche di storia politica* 22, no. 1 (2019): 37–47.

Lotta continua. "Armi al MIR!" December 1, 1973.

Lotta continua. "Hitler vive a Washington." April 23, 1971.

Lotta continua. "Israele avamposto fascista dell'imperialismo." June 3, 1972.

Lotta continua. "La manifestazione di oggi a Torino: Un punto di arrivo, un punto di partenza." November 18, 1973.

Lovell, Julia. *Maoism: A Global History*. London: The Bodley Head, 2019.

"L'ultimo saluto dei Partigiani a Lorenzo Orsetti - Firenze, 23.06.2019." YouTube video, 1:41, June 24, 2019. www.youtube.com/watch?v=5DwxcFeVeb8.

L'Unità. "Calorosa manifestazione unitaria della gioventù italiana in appoggio all'eroica lotta che l'Algeria conduce da 6 anni." November 11, 1960.

L'Unità. "Con lo sciopero anti-fascista Genova risponde all'attentato." March 8, 1969.

L'Unità. "Crimini di guerra: Ieri e oggi (risponde Aldo de Jaco)." May 20, 1966.

L'Unità. "Imponente la marcia della pace a Milano." March 14, 1965.

L'Unità. "I partigiani si batteranno alla testa del popolo per la pace." March 22, 1949.

L'Unità. "I sopravvissuti di Marzabotto chiamano alla difesa della pace." March 3, 1951.

L'Unità. "Migliaia di cittadini hanno manifestato contro l'assassinio di Patrice Lumumba." January 20, 1961.

Magni, Beatrice. "La strage di Marzabotto nel cinquantennio repubblicano." *Storia e problemi contemporanei* 11, no. 21 (1998): 175–82.

Malvezzi, Pietro, and Giovanni Pirelli, eds. *Lettere di condannati a morte della Resistenza italiana.* Turin: Einaudi, 1952.

Mammone, Andrea. *Transnational Neofascism in France and Italy.* New York: Cambridge University Press, 2015.

Marano, Sara. "La cultura politica dell'anti-fascismo e della resistenza nelle riviste della nuova sinistra (1960–67)." *Asti contemporanea,* no. 15 (2016): 99–127.

Mariuzzo, Andrea. "Stalin and the Dove: Left Pacifist Language and Choices of Expression between the Popular Front and the Korean War (1948–1953)." *Modern Italy* 15, no. 1 (2010): 21–35.

Mark, James, Nigel Townson, and Polymeris Voglis. "Inspirations." In *Europe's 1968,* edited by Robert Gildea, James Mark, and Anette Warring, 72–103. Oxford: Oxford University Press, 2013.

Martellini, Amoreno. *All'ombra delle altrui rivoluzioni: Parole e icone del Sessantotto.* Milan: Mondadori, 2012.

Marzano, Arturo. "Il mito della Palestina nell'immaginario della sinistra extraparlamentare italiana egli Anni Settanta." *Italia contemporanea,* no. 280 (May 2016): 15–39.

Marzano, Arturo, and Guri Schwarz. *Attentato alla Sinagoga: Roma, 9 ottobre 1982 : Il conflitto israelo-palestinese e l'Italia.* Rome: Viella, 2013.

Marzullo, Kino. "Papà Cervi." *L'Unità,* May 6, 1965.

Mausbach, Wilfried. "Auschwitz and Vietnam: West German Protest against America's War during the 1960s." In *America, the Vietnam War, and the World: Comparative and International Perspectives,* edited by Andreas W. Daum, Lloyd C. Gardner, and Wilfried Mausbach, 279–98. Washington, DC: German Historical Institute; New York: Cambridge University Press, 2003.

Mazower, Mark. *Governing the World: The Rise and Fall of an Idea.* London: Allen Lane, 2012.

Mercer, Ben. "Specters of Fascism: The Rhetoric of Historical Analogy in 1968." *Journal of Modern History* 88, no. 1 (2016): 96–129.

Mignini, Alfredo. "Dalla Moneda a Modena: Per una storia orale dell'esilio cileno e dell'accoglienza in Emilia Romagna." *E-Review: Rivista degli Istituti Storici dell'Emilia-Romagna in Rete* 6 (2018). e-review.it/mignini-esilio-cileno.

Molden, Berthold. "Vietnam, the New Left, and the Holocaust: How the Cold War Changed Discourse on Genocide." In *Memory in a Global Age: Discourses, Practices, and Trajectories,* edited by Aleida Assmann and Sebastian Conrad, 79–96. London: Palgrave Macmillan, 2010.

Molinari, Maurizio. *La sinistra e gli ebrei in Italia, 1967–1993.* Milan: Corbaccio, 1995.

Montessoro, Francesco. "Il mito del Vietnam nell'Italia degli anni Sessanta." *Trimestre* 37, no. 13–14 (2004): 273–97.

Mussolini, Vittorio. "Gerusalemme ieri e oggi." *Secolo d'Italia,* June 25, 1967.

Naccarato, Alessandro. *Difendere la democrazia: Il PCI contro la lotta armata.* Rome: Carocci, 2015.

Nencioni, Tommaso. "Tra neutralismo e atlantismo: La politica internazionale del Partito socialista italiano 1956–1966." *Italia contemporanea,* no. 3 (2010): 1000–1033.

Niccolai, Roberto. *Quando la Cina era vicina: La rivoluzione culturale e la sinistra extraparlamentare italiana negli anni '60 e '70*. Pisa: BFS; Pistoia: Associazione centro di documentazione di Pistoia, 1998.

Occhetto, Achille. "Ho ci Minh ci grida 'tornate interi.'" *Vie nuove*, May 27, 1965.

Ottaviano, Franco. *La rivoluzione nel labirinto*. Soveria Mannelli: Rubbettino, 1993.

Pajetta, Gian Carlo. "Il coraggio di dire di no." *Rinascita*, no. 13 (March 27, 1965).

Pajetta, Gian Carlo. "La contro-rivoluzione non si Esporta." *Rinascita*, no. 7 (February 13, 1965).

Panvini, Guido. *Ordine nero, guerriglia rossa: La violenza politica nell'Italia degli anni Sessanta e Settanta (1966–1975)*. Turin: Einaudi, 2009.

Panvini, Guido. "Third Worldism in Italy." In *Marxist Historical Cultures and Social Movements during the Cold War: Case Studies from Germany, Italy, and Other Western European States*, edited by Stefan Berger and Christoph Cornelissen, 289–308. New York: Palgrave Macmillan, 2019.

Pappagallo, Onofrio. *Verso il nuovo mondo: Il PCI e l'America Latina (1945–1973)*. Milan: FrancoAngeli, 2017.

Paputsis, Costantinos. *Il grande sì: Il caso Kostas Georgakis*. Genova: Erga, 2000.

Pavone, Claudio. *Una guerra civile: Saggio storico sulla moralità nella Resistenza*. Turin: Bollati Boringhieri, 1991.

Pons, Silvio. *Berlinguer e la fine del comunismo*. Turin: Einaudi, 2006.

Pons, Silvio. *The Global Revolution: A History of International Communism, 1917–1991*. Oxford: Oxford University Press, 2014.

Quirico, Monica, and Valentine Lomellini. "Italy: The 'Chilean Lesson' between the Legacy of the Struggle against Fascism and the Threat of New Authoritarian Shift." In *European Solidarity with Chile 1970s–1980s*, edited by Kim Christiaens, Idesbald Goddeeris, and Magaly Rodriguez Garcia, 239–56. Frankfurt: Peter Lang, 2014.

Raftopoulos, Rigas. "La dittatura dei colonnelli in Grecia (1967–1974): Tra Grecia e Italia: resistenza, dittatura e la guerra fredda che si scongela." PhD diss., University of Teramo, 2010.

Rapini, Andrea. *Anti-fascismo e cittadinanza: Giovani, identità e memorie nell'Italia repubblicana*. Bologna: Bononia University Press, 2005.

Riccardi, Luca. *Il problema Israele: Diplomazia italiana e PCI di fronte allo stato ebraico (1948–1973)*. Milan: Guerini Studio, 2006.

Riccardi, Luca. *L'internazionalismo difficile: La diplomazia del PCI e il Medio Oriente dalla crisi petrolifera alla caduta del muro di Berlino (1973–1989)*. Soveria Mannelli: Rubbettino, 2013.

Ridolfi, Maurizio. "Rituali della memoria e linguaggi dell'anti-fascismo." In *Anti-fascismo e identità europea*, edited by Alberto De Bernardi and Paolo Ferrari, 35–51. Rome: Carocci, 2004.

Rossi, Gianni. *La destra e gli ebrei: Una storia italiana*. Soveria Mannelli: Rubbettino, 2003.

Rothberg, Michael. *Multidirectional Memory: Remembering the Holocaust in the Age of Decolonization*. Stanford, CA: Stanford University Press, 2006.

Santoni, Alessandro. *Il PCI e i giorni del Cile: Alle origini di un mito politico*. Rome: Carocci, 2008.

Schwarzmantel, J. J. *Socialism and the Idea of the Nation*. New York: Harvester Wheatsheaf, 1991.

Scotti, Mariamargherita. *Vita di Giovanni Pirelli: Tra cultura e impegno militante*. Saggi. Storia e Scienze Sociali. Rome: Donzelli Editore, 2018.

Secolo d'Italia. "Estremo rimedio." April 23, 1967.

Slobodian, Quinn. *Foreign Front: Third World Politics in Sixties West Germany.* Durham, NC: Duke University Press, 2012.

Soave, Paolo. *La democrazia allo specchio: L'Italia e il regime militare ellenico (1967–1974).* Bologna: Rubettino, 2014.

Sorgonà, Gregorio. *La scoperta della destra: Il Movimento sociale italiano e gli Stati Uniti.* Rome: Viella, 2019.

Srivastava, Neelam. *Italian Colonialism and Resistances to Empire, 1930–1970.* London: Palgrave Macmillan, 2018.

Tartaro, Gianni. "Troppi i focolai di tensione in un mondo che ha bisogno di pace." *Patria indipendente,* no. 19 (November 11, 1977).

Taviani, Ermanno. "L'anti-americanismo nella sinistra italiana al tempo del Vietnam." *Annali della facoltà di Scienze della formazione Università degli studi di Catania* 6 (2011): 165–85.

Taviani, Ermanno. "PCI, estremismo di sinistra e terrorismo." In *L'Italia repubblicana nella crisi degli anni settanta. Sistema politico e istituzioni,* vol. 4, edited by Gabriele De Rosa and Giancarlo Monina, 235–75. Soveria Mannelli: Rubettino.

Tolomelli, Marica. *L'Italia dei movimenti: Politica e società nella Prima repubblica.* Rome: Carocci, 2015.

Tripodi, Nino. "Impareranno la lezione." *Secolo d'Italia,* September 21, 1973.

Ufficio di Informazione del Kurdistan in Italia. "UIKI: Per le resistenze di ieri e di oggi, celebriamo il 25 aprile!" April 22, 2016. www.uikionlus.com/uiki-per-le-resistenze-di-ieri-e -di-oggi-celebriamo-il-25-aprile.

Valli, Wanda. "Bella Ciao per cinquemila: Scalfaro attacca Berlusconi." *La repubblica,* April 26, 2002.

Ventrone, Angelo. *Vogliamo tutto: Perché due generazioni hanno creduto nella rivoluzione, 1960–1988.* Rome: Laterza, 2012.

Vie nuove. "Se questo è l'uomo." November 12, 1964.

Wu, Judy Tzu-Chun. *Radicals on the Road: Internationalism, Orientalism, and Feminism during the Vietnam Era.* Ithaca, NY: Cornell University Press, 2013.

"Zhdanov and the Cominform on the Imperialist and Anti-imperialist Camps, 1947." In *The Cold War through Documents: A Global History,* edited by Edward H. Judge and John W. Langdon, 50–51. Lanham, MD: Rowman and Littlefield, 2017.

"America's Scapegoats"

Ideas of Fascism in the Construction of the US Latina/o/x Left, 1973–83

Michael Staudenmaier

In 1980, speaking to the United Nations Special Committee on Decolonization, the Chicago-based Puerto Rican independence activist José E. López railed against the specter of fascism in the United States. He argued strenuously that the Caribbean commonwealth of his birth—formally known as a "Freely Associated State" and in legal terms an unincorporated territory of the United States—was in fact a colony, and thus should fall under the purview of the UN Committee. López drew on the exemplary case of Nazi Germany to connect the problem of colonialism on a global stage with the threat of fascism: "One has only to look at Hitler addressing one million applauding German workers to understand that his ability to do this was at the expense of millions of lives of Jews, Poles, and other Slavs, whom he sacrificed as scapegoats. One does not have to be a wise man to decipher who are to be America's scapegoats. They most certainly will be found," he concluded, "in this country's internal colonies—the Blacks, the Chicano-Mexicanos, the Puerto Ricans and the Native Americans."[1]

By 1980, López was an experienced community organizer and a leading member of a small US-based revolutionary group named the Movimiento de Liberación Nacional (National Liberation Movement, or MLN). The MLN was one tiny part of a wave of radicalism to emerge in the United States in the aftermath of the upheaval of the late 1960s. While the decade of the 1960s has remained fixed in

Radical History Review

Issue 138 (October 2020)   DOI 10.1215/01636545-8359247

© 2020 by MARHO: The Radical Historians' Organization, Inc.

popular memory for its radicalism, the 1970s featured its own dizzying array of community organizing projects, cultural centers, study groups, and self-declared revolutionary parties, most of which were motivated by various combinations of Marxism, nationalism, feminism, and other ideological frameworks.[2] What made the
MLN unique in this broad milieu was its binational character as a group that brought
together two specific sets of revolutionaries under one organizational umbrella: its
members included both Puerto Rican nationalists and Chicana/o/x militants, who
routinely labeled themselves "Mexicanos" because they rejected the post-1848 border separating the United States from Mexico.[3] Its activism principally focused on
resisting its own repression by the federal government, and López perhaps predictably held that the danger of fascism, whether in the United States or elsewhere in
the Americas, was directly linked to the power of the state to stifle dissent in racially
charged ways.

López's UN speech, and indeed the overall body of work of the MLN, exem-
plified one crucial vector of a broader trend among radicals of color in the 1970s and
1980s that linked state repression, colonialism, and fascism, frequently with unexpected repercussions for broader issues of race and ethnicity. In this particular case,
a relative handful of committed militants helped develop and promote a notion of
US Latina/o/x panethnicity. They did so because they believed this was a necessary
precondition for, among other tasks, defeating the threat fascism presented to
Puerto Ricans, Chicana/o/xs, and other distinct national groupings. While the
1970s are frequently identified as a pivotal decade for the construction, whether
from above or below, of what today is sometimes referred to as "Latinidad" (a common, if complicated, identity based on shared experiences among US residents of
Latin American birth or heritage), the role of political radicals in this development
has largely been ignored.[4] Nonetheless, for organized Left forces in diverse Latina/
o/x communities during the post-1960s era, fascism provided a coherent frame for
understanding a common threat. It also offered a clear impetus to collective action,
which in turn further advanced the development of panethnic connections within
and beyond radical sectors. In the event, Chicana/o/x and Puerto Rican revolutionaries built deliberate political alliances with each other as a way to respond both to
rising attacks on their communities and to the defeats suffered by inspirational Left
forces abroad.

The idea of fascism helped Puerto Rican and Chicana/o/x radicals theorize
not only their own oppression as internally colonized peoples in continental North
America but also their relationships with a rapidly transforming Latin America.
During the decade after the US-sponsored right-wing coup in Chile removed Salvador Allende from power in 1973, the MLN and other participants in the US Lat-
ina/o/x Left denounced as fascist Latin American leaders as disparate as Chilean dictator Augusto Pinochet, Mexican president Luis Echeverría, and Puerto Rican

governor Carlos Romero Barceló. While the precise utility of the term *fascism* as a descriptor for these figures and others was (and remains) subject to challenge, the rise of the New Right and ultraconservative forces certainly represents a major theme in the transnational political historiography of the Western Hemisphere in the 1970s and 1980s, from Pinochet and Ronald Reagan to Central American death squads and a resurgent Ku Klux Klan.[5] Dealing with issues ranging from police brutality to border enforcement, US Latina/o/x activists found themselves and their allies repeatedly on the defensive and, in response, they accelerated the process of developing a shared identity through common struggles on both a regional and transnational scale. It is clear—and on some level deeply ironic— that the rise of ultraconservative and/or fascist tendencies in the United States and on the hemispheric stage helped lay the groundwork for contemporary ideas of Latina/o/x identity, against which so much twenty-first-century white nationalism in the United States has in turn been deployed.

This article situates the MLN as a case study of this two-part process, both reactive and proactive. Responding to intense state repression, the MLN developed a theory of fascism that, despite analytical limits, helped mobilize a broader radical response to the threat of right-wing governments both in the United States and across Latin America. This defensive maneuver contributed directly to an ambitious and forward-looking attempt to organize Latina/o/xs across lines of national identity. The MLN's binational life span was brief; by 1983 the group split amicably into two separate organizations, one Puerto Rican and the other Mexicana/o/x.[6] Nonetheless, this tiny grouping, in its relatively short window of organizational unity, had an outsized impact on the construction of Latinidad, helping set in motion the emergence of US Latina/o/x identity as it exists in the twenty-first century.

The Emergence of the MLN: State Repression and Pan-Latina/o/x Radicalism

The logic of scapegoating that López described in 1980 was built on an analysis of decades of direct government attacks on Puerto Rican radicals, both in Puerto Rico and stateside. Many facets of the infamous COINTELPRO program—in which the FBI attempted to surveil and disrupt potentially "subversive" political activity that in theory should have been constitutionally protected under the First Amendment— were pioneered in Puerto Rico before being implemented in the United States proper, with independence activists being the primary targets.[7] By the mid-1970s, repression against the Puerto Rican independence movement had reached new heights. The emergence of a highly visible armed clandestine wing of the movement, most prominently in the form of the Fuerzas Armadas de Liberación Nacional (Armed Forces of National Liberation, or FALN) active after 1974 in New York, Chicago, and other diasporic centers, generated a polarizing debate about revolutionary strategy among both Puerto Rican and Chicana/o/x radicals, but it also precipitated a predictably aggressive response from the federal government. The FBI actively investigated anyone with even a tangential connection to the diasporic independence movement, and by 1976 multiple federal grand juries had begun targeting both Puerto Rican and Chicana/o/x activists. Those called as witnesses had little choice beyond either testifying against comrades or accepting jail time as a punishment for the refusal to do so.[8]

In June 1977, Puerto Ricans based in New York and Chicago, as well as Chicana/o/xs active in Chicago, Colorado, New Mexico, and elsewhere, founded the Movimiento de Liberación Nacional. The MLN conceived of itself as a vehicle for "the strategic unity of Chicanos-Mexicanos and Puerto Ricans within the framework of one organization."[9] Much of the impetus to create the MLN's innovative panethnic organization was reactive, since in some ways the central common experience of Chicana/o/x and Puerto Rican militants in the 1970s was repression and attacks by the US government. Almost every member of the founding leadership of the organization had already been subpoenaed to one or more of the grand juries. As José López recalled decades later, Puerto Rican and Mexicana/o/x radicals had by 1977 reached the point where "we understood that we could no longer do this work as separate entities. We needed a unified world view for the people facing grand jury repression. Mexican people were going to prison and at that time we saw the importance of unifying what few resources we had as Puerto Ricans and Mexicans."[10] The binational structure of the MLN was highly unorthodox, but the notion of multiethnic alliances, especially those connecting black organizers with either Puerto Rican or Chicana/o/x activists, had been popularized over the previous decade by efforts like Martin Luther King Jr.'s Poor People's Campaign and the original Rainbow Coalition in Chicago, led by the local chapter of the Black Panther Party for Self Defense.[11] While acknowledging the need for all colonized racial groups to collaborate in an anti-imperialist framework, the MLN's very existence suggested that the links connecting its two constituent nationalities were stronger than those that tied them to black and indigenous allies, or to radicals in the nominally sovereign nations of Latin America itself, from Mexico to Chile.

The militants who founded the MLN had come of age in the midst of the initial high period of the Chicana/o/x and Puerto Rican movements of the late 1960s and early 1970s, and many had experience in older organizations like the Young Lords and Puerto Rican Socialist Party in Chicago and New York City, and the Crusade for Justice in Denver. While profoundly nationalist in their outlook, they increasingly came to see their own experiences of oppression and resistance as intimately linked to those of others, living inside the borders of the United States, who shared Latin American heritage. Like prior generations, their Marxist commitment to internationalism led them to advocate a transnational approach to revolutionary politics that attempted to link struggles in Chile and Mexico (among other Latin American countries) with US urban centers and rural regions containing large Spanish-speaking populations.[12]

The Chilean case proved particularly influential on the MLN's founders. The 1973 coup and its aftermath had coincided with their own political coming-of-age, and it presented a case study in the twin dangers of state repression and fascism. The example resonated even more intensely once several leading members of the newly established MLN found themselves sitting in federal prison, held in contempt of court for refusal to testify in front of the grand juries. In September 1977, just three months after the founding of the MLN and on the fourth anniversary of Pinochet's coup, they issued a communiqué from jail that highlighted the transnational impact of the Chilean tragedy while signaling the comparable dangers throughout the Southern Cone and as far north as the Caribbean and the United States. The communiqué argued, in part, that "the fall of the Salvador Allende government in Chile, as well as the emergence of fascism in Uruguay, Bolivia, and Argentina, have had a profound impact on the Puerto Rican people and its independence movement."[13] Framed as an open letter to the Chilean revolutionary group Movimiento de Izquierda Revolucionaria (Revolutionary Left Movement, or MIR), the document built an analogy from the Chilean experience to the situation of the US Latina/o/x populations, with the dangers of a totalitarian state as the unifying thread.

The need for a theory of fascism formed the core lesson the MLN prisoners took from the Chilean experience. And the importance of Chile to the state of hemispheric politics in the 1970s highlighted the shared Latin American cultural heritage that brought Puerto Rican and Chicana/o/x radicals together in and around the MLN. But conditions were not the same in every locale, and the imperatives of internationalist anti-fascism looked different inside the imperial stronghold of the United States. Here, the particular contours of internal colonialism brought together Puerto Ricans and Mexicans specifically and prompted them to collective action. For many early members and supporters of the MLN, FBI counterintelligence efforts and the use of federal grand juries as a political weapon appeared to be first steps toward a fascist turn inside the United States that had already proven horrifically disastrous in Chile. This analysis proved wrong in the event, but for the Puerto Rican and Chicana/o/x radicals who participated in or supported the MLN during the 1970s and 1980s, it did much to promote an embryonic sense of panethnicity, and even more to sensitize them to the threat of fascism, however that fraught term was defined.

Defining Fascism: Mexico and Puerto Rico

Pinochet's brutality, as well as the lasting influence of the Black Panther Party (in particular, their high-profile 1969 conference promoting a "United Front Against Fascism"), led many radicals to utilize *fascist* as a broadly applicable and frequently deployed epithet.[14] But the term did not go untheorized in Puerto Rican and Chicana/o/x movement circles. For the MLN and many other US Latina/o/x radicals of the late 1970s, fascism was first and foremost an extreme variant of state repression under capitalism. Much of the US Leninist Left during this period, regardless of national origin, drew on the classic phrasing that originated in theses approved by the Thirteenth Plenum of the Executive Committee of the Soviet-led Communist International (the so-called Third International or Comintern) in 1933: "Fascism is the open terroristic dictatorship of the most reactionary, most chauvinistic and most imperialist elements of finance capital."[15] The context for this declaration, which has largely been associated with Giorgi Dimitrov, a Bulgarian Communist who popularized the formulation as head of the Comintern beginning in 1934, was the sharp rightward turn in Europe in the context of the Great Depression, and especially Adolf Hitler's rise to power in Germany months before the Thirteenth Plenum. The logic and usefulness of Dimitrov's definition has been skillfully and appropriately challenged in various ways by generations of anti-fascist activists and scholars, who have instead highlighted the autonomous and insurgent character of fascism as a social movement frequently subject to forms of state repression that mirror those applied to Left insurgencies.[16]

Whatever the flaws in such an understanding, the MLN put significant effort into applying it to then-contemporary conditions in the United States and across the Western Hemisphere. It saw echoes of the Depression in the global economic downturn of the 1970s, and of Nazi Germany in the government attacks political radicals were facing during the second half of the 1970s. This latter category included not only the grand juries in the United States and the generalized repression in Chile, but also military and police violence in Mexico, Puerto Rico, and elsewhere. In a historical and theoretical analysis of new trends in international capitalism, published in 1979, the MLN maintained that "the choice of fascism was thus a new political option open to capitalism for internal dominance. Fascism is an intensely ideological form of capitalist thought, tending to the mobilization of an entire society for the implementation of imperialist policies."[17] The link to López's speech to the UN the next year was clear: fascism, whether in Depression-era Europe or the stagflation-plagued 1970s, built collective unity in a crisis-ridden society by targeting—"scapegoating"—marginalized peoples.

This analysis clearly echoed the classic 1950 essay "Discourse on Colonialism" by the Martinican writer Aimé Césaire. For Césaire, fascism was the imposition at home of the horrors of imperialism that were previously restricted to the colonies themselves. In his construction, first world liberals—embodied in "the very distinguished, very humanistic, very Christian bourgeois of the twentieth century"—fundamentally misunderstand the nature of fascist criminality: "At bottom, what he cannot forgive Hitler for is not *the crime* itself, *the crime against man*, it is not *the humiliation of man as such*, it is the crime against the white man, and the fact that he applied to Europe colonialist procedures which until then had been reserved exclusively for the Arabs of Algeria, the 'coolies' of India, and the 'niggers' of Africa."[18] In 1966, Césaire's treatise was translated into Spanish and published in Cuba; it took until 1972 for it to be translated into English.[19] Like the various theories of internal colonialism developed in the United States in the late 1960s, Césaire served as a lodestone for both the MLN and other Spanish-speaking radicals across the hemisphere.[20]

Nor were the imprisoned MLN members the first to describe the various South American military dictatorships as fascist. When the US backed military coup overthrew Allende in 1973 and installed General Augusto Pinochet as dictator, many in the Latin American Left were quick to label the outcome. Within weeks, Cuban leader Fidel Castro denounced Pinochet as the head of a "fascist coup" and boldly claimed that "the Chilean people will fight fascism."[21] Student protesters in Mexico City the following June carried signs reading "Muera el fascismo Chileno y sus bufones" (Death to Chilean fascism and its clowns).[22] Seeing fascism as a top-down, right-wing modality of capitalism, rather than an insurgent threat from the far right that challenged capitalist hegemony, it became easier to categorize a wide variety of ruling elites across the globe as fascist.

This theory of fascism also generated specific strategic imperatives. As the state itself became for the MLN and other Latina/o/x radicals the essential element of fascism, it also came to be seen as an illegitimate strategic orientation for anti-fascists. That is to say, the MLN strongly opposed using appeals to government authorities—whether in Puerto Rico or stateside—as a mechanism in the fight against fascism. The MLN's approach deliberately echoed an older formulation, *retraimiento* (literally, "withdrawal"), associated with the mid-century Puerto Rican nationalist leader Pedro Albizu Campos, who argued for total noncollaboration with the colonial regime. More recent notions of "no platform"—the use of direct action rather than appeals to police in order to prevent fascist and far-right activists from appearing in public—have in some ways carried forward the tradition of distancing anti-fascist organizing from the state. As Mark Bray notes regarding twenty-first-century struggles against fascism, "militant anti-fascists oppose harnessing state power to suppress fascism because of their anti-state politics and their belief that any such measures would more often be turned against the left."[23] While the MLN was not anti-statist per se, the latter concern regarding state repression was integral to its own existence, not merely hypothetical.

For the MLN, *retraimiento* served as a guiding principle in defining the limits and possibilities of the battle against fascism and the state. Speaking at an anti-fascist conference in San Francisco in 1981, Steven Guerra, a Chicano-Mexicano member of the MLN from Chicago, challenged the use of state repression against the Klan: "We must recognize that the state is our prime enemy, and no compromise with it is possible. And for this reason, we must never collaborate with the state in any endeavor. To call for grand jury investigations of the Klan or police killings, is to ask for a cancer to cure itself."[24] The alternative, for Guerra and the rest of the MLN, was to build panethnic unity, both among self-identified leftists and within broader, transnational communities. For the binational MLN, this strategic principle extended well beyond the United States. In fact, the sovereign and non-sovereign homelands of the MLN's two component national groups, Mexico and Puerto Rico, became crucial proving grounds for their theory of fascism and their strategy for fighting it.

In the late 1960s and into the 1970s, as Alan Eladio Gómez has detailed, the Chicana/o/x movement in the United States was deeply divided over the question of how to understand the political character of Mexico itself. For the cultural nationalists who made up the largest tendency within the movement, Mexico was, first and foremost, the once and future national homeland and was thus to be praised by contrast with the imperialist United States. Luis Echeverría, president of Mexico from 1970 to 1976, staked out a populist politics that appealed to widespread pride in Mexican identity within and beyond the republic. He also readily granted asylum to political refugees from Chile and other Latin American countries under right-wing military dictatorships, most prominently Allende's widow, Hortensia Bussi. Such actions were lauded by many Chicana/o/x nationalists in the United States, even though, as Fernando Herrera Calderón and Adela Cedillo note, "welcoming political exiles reveal[ed] a number of contradictions within Mexico's foreign and domestic policies. By providing asylum, the PRI [Partido Revolucionario Institucional, or Institutional Revolutionary Party] supported, for 'humanitarian' reasons, guerillas abroad while persecuting in the name of patriotism, anyone who questioned its revolutionary nationalism at home."[25] Indeed, a core of Chicana/o/x leftists of the era denounced Echeverría for his role in the 1968 Tlatelolco Massacre of student militants in Mexico City, for his record of imprisoning leftists, and for collaborating with the Nixon administration to spy on radicals on both sides of the Rio Grande.

Thus, when Echeverría visited San Antonio, Texas, in 1976, leftist Chicana/o/x protesters, led by Mario Cantú, demonstrated against his arrival. In the absence of significant police protection, Cantú was able to confront Echeverría in person, holding a sign that read (in Spanish) "Free Political Prisoners." In Gómez's telling,

> As they came face to face, Echeverría took Cantú's sign, tore it in half, and
> called him a "pequeño joven fascista" (little fascist). Returning the "fascist"
> insult, Cantú then held an impromptu press conference to announce he was
> cancelling the protest for the rest of the week in light of the violence.
> "[Echeverría] demonstrated to the world that he is a fascist," Cantú said. "He
> should be responsive. He has the attitude of a dictator, like in Chile."[26]

This vignette connects several of threads in the tapestry of the MLN and Latina/o/x radical analysis of fascism in the 1970s. Cantú himself had never been directly connected with the MLN, but he been radicalized as a Chicana/o/x nationalist while in prison in the United States. Among those who helped inspire his politicization were several Puerto Rican nationalist prisoners, including Rafael Cancél Miranda, who also had a direct influence on the MLN's political development. Further, Cantú's comparison of Mexico to Chile, as previously noted, was particularly potent in the period after the 1973 coup, when part of Echeverría's credibility came from his willingness to grant asylum to Bussi, the widow of Allende. And, finally, Cantú's quick turnabout of Echeverría's insult reflected the delicate balance between "fascist" as a catchall insult and fascism as a constituent element of the conjuncture against which any revolutionary US Latina/o/x politics must position itself.

Under the regime of Echeverría's successor as president of Mexico, José López Portillo, the MLN, and other Chicana/o/x radicals began to use fascism as a lens to understand the continuous one-party rule of the PRI in Mexico since the 1920s. In 1982, the MLN and other groups organized a protest at the Mexican consulate in Denver, Colorado. Amid a laundry list of demands, protesters aimed "to expose the fascist nature of the repressive PRI government, which is nothing more than a built-in dictatorship, in control for over 60 years."[27] That same year, white radicals in the Prairie Fire Organizing Committee, which publicly declared that it took leadership on US Latina/o/x issues from the MLN, argued that "behind the PRI's carefully constructed 'progressive' mask is the face of fascism," and, commenting specifically on the Central American civil wars that were then heating up, maintained that "when revolution is on its doorstep, threatening the stability of Mexico itself, the façade of internationalism can't be maintained and fascist repression is the response."[28] While this analysis of PRI fascism never gained a wide foothold within the US Latina/o/x Left, it did at least superficially resonate with increasingly common criticisms of Mexico's authoritarian system of one-party rule.

The specifics in Puerto Rico were rather different, but a comparable analysis identified the threat of fascism in power during the same era. Puerto Rico's nominal status as "self-governing" was (and remains) largely based on its free and open elections structured around a political party system that partially resembled that in the United States itself. Of the main political parties, the New Progressive Party (PNP), which advocated for Puerto Rico's admission as the fifty-first state, was widely understood as the archipelago's most conservative political tendency. In 1980, the MLN applied the group's theory of fascism to the situation on the island by targeting the PNP, or at least sections of it, in a discussion paper: "In 1976, an ideologized fascist clique at the head of the PNP, came to power in colonial elections. . . . The colonial fascist[s] under the leadership of [Governor] Carlos Romero Barceló set about the transformation of the balance of forces in our homeland, and the mobilization of the masses of Puerto Ricans to support statehood."[29] Here again, for the MLN and other pro-independence groups, the link between fascism, colonialism, and government repression was clear: becoming a state would permanently cement the colonial subjugation of the Puerto Rican nation by the United States, and the MLN argued that the PNP's "fascist clique" was actively utilizing the power of the (colonial) state to promote statehood and to crack down harshly on dissent from the Left. This was a problematic interpretation, to say the least. The notion that pro-statehood control of the Puerto Rican government amounted to fascism implied a fundamental contradiction within the MLN's overall theoretical frame: if Puerto Rico was indeed a colony controlled by the United States, then self-rule was a myth, in which case the PNP did not actually hold the sort of state power that the MLN and others believed was central to their definition of fascism. Nor would statehood itself produce fascism, since the constraints of the constitutional system necessarily made states subordinate to the federal government.

Nonetheless, whether accurately described as fascist or not, the government of Puerto Rico during the 1970s was undeniably brutal. It was, as the MLN noted, deeply engaged in a wide variety of counterinsurgency measures. Describing a later period of PNP control in the 1990s, Marisol LeBrón has used the term *punitive governance* to describe "the ideological work undertaken by the state to promote an understanding that punishment, justice, and safety are intrinsically linked."[30] The similarities between LeBrón's formulation and José López's notion of "scapegoating" are made clear in any assessment of the PNP's regime in the later 1970s. Romero Barceló's government inherited and actively utilized a long-standing counterintelligence apparatus that kept files on thousands of dissidents in a system of *carpetas* (folders) that resembled and was frequently coordinated with the FBI's COINTELPRO efforts.[31] Dozens of radical activists were targeted for more proactive forms of harassment, including arrests, grand juries, and police violence.

In the most notorious case, undercover police lured two young pro-independence militants to a remote mountaintop and murdered them after they had surrendered without resistance. The incident, universally known by its location, Cerro Maravilla, scandalized Puerto Ricans on all sides of the status question, in part because the entrapment was so egregious and in part because the extrajudicial killings were so brutal.[32] It also led directly to the disclosure of the long-hidden carpetas. If "America's scapegoats" were marginalized racial groups, the PNP targeted both marginalized populations and fringe political organizations, including the most radical sectors of the independence movement. Surveillance, investigations, and targeted violence against pro-independence revolutionaries served a double purpose: to discredit or even to dismember the militant Left, and to convince a majority of Puerto Ricans that backing statehood was the only solution to so-called terrorist subversion.

Like Echeverría, Romero Barceló attempted to fuse political repression with populist rhetoric, which was more than enough for the MLN and other radical US Latina/o/x militants to label him a fascist. For the membership and leadership of the MLN, based neither in Mexico nor in Puerto Rico, the very breadth of the fascist danger, stretching from the Southern Cone to Mesoamerica to the Caribbean, served as an object lesson in the necessity of panethnic identity and binational organization. Inside the continental United States, the stakes were, if anything, even higher.

Surviving Reagan's America(s)

If fascist threats in Latin America presented a cause for concern within the MLN and among other US Latina/o/x militants, not even high-profile acts of state terror at Cerro Maravilla and Tlatelolco could match the urgent challenge of responding to fascism within the United States. For the MLN, fascism in the United States was a double danger, as both governmental and vigilante groups targeted marginalized racial groups for attacks. Under this theory, Puerto Ricans were the primary targets of state attacks, via the grand juries and police harassment, while Chicana/o/xs were the core targets of violence perpetrated by the extragovernmental far right. Thus, while the two communities faced different immediate threats, the MLN interpreted them as two aspects of a singular reality: Latina/o/x people, regardless of national or ethnic distinctions, had become "America's scapegoats"; to fight back successfully, they would need to work together.

For Chicana/o/xs in particular, this marked a dramatic shift that required some rethinking of the theory of fascism that the MLN had developed with reference to Latin America. While right-wing paramilitary groups were endemic to the region as a whole during this period, the strength of the repressive state actually made them atypically scarce in the three places to which Puerto Rican and Chicana/o/x radicals of the era paid the most attention: Chile, Mexico, and Puerto Rico. In the United States, by contrast, the 1970s featured a resurgent Ku Klux Klan and a small but vibrant neo-Nazi movement, both of which began to target Mexican and Mexican-descended people for violence and intimidation.

Two distinct transformations in extragovernmental right-wing domestic politics during the late 1970s ensured that fascist activity specifically targeted Chicana/o/x residents of the southwestern United States, alongside Mexican immigrants to that region. First, as Raquel Minian has demonstrated, the militarization of the US-Mexico border, beginning under Richard Nixon and continuing through the following decades, created an opening for white nationalists of the post–Civil Rights era to reframe their racist sentiments in the more acceptable rhetoric of opposition to immigration, while carefully pretending to do so without explicit reference to race or ethnicity.[33] Second, by the end of the decade, old-line Ku Klux Klan forces had begun a realignment that anti-fascist activist Michael Novick has described as "the Nazification of the KKK."[34] Kathleen Belew suggests that the core principle uniting these previously antagonistic strands of white power was a shared desire "for a war against communists, blacks, and other enemies."[35] US Latina/o/x radicals found themselves a direct target of this evolving new phase of fascist organizing.

One early venue in which these new trends began to emerge was the anti-immigrant "Border Watch," sometimes known as "Klan Border Watch," established by white nationalists in the US Southwest in the mid-1970s. Led in southern California by Tom Metzger and a handful of other KKK organizers, this effort aimed to demonize Mexican immigrants as "illegal alien mixed-bloods" and promoted paramilitary violence against them as a way to establish the white racial purity of the southwestern United States.[36] Metzger, a rising Klan organizer in Southern California and future founder of the White Aryan Resistance (WAR), typified the convergence of neo-Nazi and old-line Klan tendencies, as well as the willingness of far-right activists to advocate for, and secure for themselves if necessary, the militarization of the border.

Some US-based radicals first seriously took note of the surging domestic danger of fascism when it was highlighted with violent severity near the end of 1979 in Greensboro, North Carolina. Over the course of that year, Klan and neo-Nazi forces in the Carolinas had worked diligently to develop a working alliance called the United Racist Front.[37] On November 3, the Front attacked a "Death to the Klan" rally in a public housing project, killing five members of a small Maoist organization, the Communist Workers Party (CWP), in what subsequently became known as the Greensboro massacre. It was not lost on the US Latina/o/x Left, in particular, that one of the five dead was César Vicente Cauce, a twenty-five-year-old Cuban immigrant and CWP organizer. Cauce, who had been radicalized as a student, did not fit the typical profile of the MLN or other wings of the Puerto Rican and Chicana/o/x Left: his father had been a cabinet secretary under Cuban dictator Fulgencio Batista, and his parents had fled to the United States with other wealthy elites after the 1959 revolution that brought Fidel Castro to power.[38] These particulars didn't impress white power militants, who later falsely claimed that Cauce had arrived in the United States as part of the Mariel boatlift, which in fact didn't begin until five months after the massacre in Greensboro. For far-right anti-immigration ideologues, Mariel represented the Caribbean equivalent of Mexicans crossing the southwestern land border. In 1983, one fascist publication posthumously connected Cauce to the "thousands of undesirables" Castro had supposedly sent as an advance guard "for his planned communist overthrow of the U.S. government," rearticulating the anti-immigrant and anti-Latina/o/x racism of Metzger's Klan Border Watch within the now-unified Klan and neo-Nazi nexus.[39]

In the aftermath of the Greensboro massacre, leftists of various stripes began to assess the threat of Klan and fascist violence in a new light. It had suddenly become harder to deny the risks run by the organized Left, as well as the danger to working-class and frequently immigrant-heavy communities of color. Radicals of color sat at the intersection of these two lines of attack. Having been subject to targeted far-right violence for more than a generation, they brought particular historical and theoretical insights to these conversations. In November 1981, commemorating the second anniversary of Greensboro, a national anti-Klan conference was held in San Francisco. Guillermo Suarez, a Chicano-Mexicano from Los Angeles, spoke on behalf of the MLN, highlighting the special threat fascism presented to colonized people living in the United States during the Reagan era.

Speaking to a largely white audience of anti-Klan activists, Suarez offered an extended history lesson in which the annexation of northern Mexico by the United States via the 1848 Treaty of Guadalupe Hidalgo was the crucial pivot point. In this context, Suarez argued, "the Klan today represents but a continuation of that mentality . . . of white supremacy."[40] But while the line was straight, it wasn't necessarily continuous. Although a small number of local Klan factions in the Southwest expressed hostility to Mexican migrant laborers prior to 1924, historian Thomas Pegram notes that "Ku Kluxers in other centers of Mexican American settlement, however, remained silent."[41] Indeed, Suarez next turned to the Johnson-Reed Immigration Act of 1924, which created the United States Border Patrol. He argued that the second-era KKK's endorsement of the patrol marked "the first time that the Klan makes its appearance with respect to Mexicano people."[42] By the 1970s, Metzger's Border Watch efforts had yet again made the Klan a top-tier concern for Chicana/o/x radicals, and Suarez detailed extensive organizing done by the Brown Berets and other militant groups to prevent Metzger from completing a Klan-sponsored car caravan from San Diego to Brownsville, Texas, designed to intimidate immigrants.

Drawing on the MLN's critique of state power, Suarez maintained that "ultimately the question of the Klan must be tied to the question of the state, and without a clear understanding of the state and its repressive role, and without a clear understanding of the strategy to defeat it, we will not be able to eliminate the Klan."[43] Since the MLN demanded the socialist reunification of Mexico on the basis of the pre-1848 border, "the struggle against the Klan has to be tied to the struggle [for] the destruction of the United States, as we currently know it"; alternatively phrased, "the only way they [the KKK] will be defeated is through the destruction of US imperialism."[44] Indeed, this broader project of revolutionary anti-imperialism represented the indispensable strategic core of the MLN's politics, to which Suarez hoped to recruit a broader audience of anti-Klan militants.

Nonetheless, the threat of fascism was not limited to the intersection between the state's repressive apparatus and the self-avowed white power movement. Ronald Reagan's ability to unify a broad swath of right-wing tendencies was particularly notable for its mobilization of conservative Christians. In 1983, the MLN published an essay written by Oscar López Rivera, a political prisoner and José López's older brother. In it, López Rivera examined the rising power of right-wing evangelicals in both the United States and Latin America. "Every Latin American and progressive North American," he argued, "must be conscious of these fundamentalist sects because they are the stronghold of imperialism and the ideological bastion of fascism."[45] He further suggested that they "intend to break the cultural wall and establish the base for fascist ideology in the U.S."[46] Where his brother had focused on identifying "America's scapegoats," López Rivera was more concerned with determining who was planning to do the scapegoating and how. Writing well before the full extent of the Guatemalan genocide of the 1980s was clear, López Rivera maintained that US-based evangelicals helped bring the born-again General Efraín Ríos Montt to power in Guatemala, and suggested they would next turn their attentions toward their own country.[47] A decade after the Chilean coup, the connection between Latin American fascism and US fascism remained clear, at least in the depictions offered by the MLN.

Conclusion

The MLN's unique experiment in cross-national organization ended in 1983 with a declaration that "our organization has reached a level of political growth and maturity, that in actual fact, does not permit us to continue with the same organizational structure that has characterized it since its beginning."[48] To some extent, this reflected the continuing problem of government repression: according to the communiqué, "in the past two years, over fifty members and sympathizers have been arrested or detained by US authorities on unsubstantiated charges," including "four members of our national leadership [who] are presently facing a three year sentence for criminal contempt."[49] One of these was Steven Guerra, who ended up serving slightly less than two years in federal prison due to his refusal to cooperate with yet another federal grand jury investigating the Puerto Rican independence movement. At the height of the Reagan revolution, the MLN thus devolved into two distinct groups, the MLN-PR and the MLN-M, which remained friendly but pursued their respective projects of national liberation independently.

Despite this breakup, the overall project of Latinidad as a panethnic identity in the United States was actually far stronger by the mid-1980s than it had been a dozen or even a half dozen years before. Grassroots activists had successfully forced the United States Census Bureau to add a question to the 1980 census regarding "Hispanic" identity, with the eventual result that, as Cristina Mora puts it, the bureau's "reports and charts insinuated that Hispanics constituted a distinct group that was commensurate with whites and blacks."[50] Of course, this process was a double-edged sword: on the one hand, it generated economies of scale for the US Latina/o/x population in terms of both electioneering and the distribution of governmental resources, resulting in a rapid increase in Puerto Rican and Chicana/o/x officeholders as well as greater visibility for the communities' political demands. But it did little to benefit the organized Latina/o/x Left, of which the MLN was a small but significant part. Further, it legitimated long-standing far-right fears of the racial degeneration of the United States, even as it gave cover to racist attacks on Latina/o/x people as the source of the impurity.

The MLN, never a large or well-known organization, strenuously rejected any and all appeals to the US government as reformist and characteristic of a colonial mentality. Nonetheless, it contributed in an outsized fashion to the slow emergence of US Latina/o/x identity during and after this period. The group combined three elements into a potent mixture: a hemispheric political analysis of allies and enemies; a shared culture of resistance against internal colonialism; and an understanding of a common enemy in the fascist potentials of state power. In doing so, the MLN helped ensure that grassroots activists of widely divergent politics and various ethnonational backgrounds struggled together to defend their communities against the attacks of an emboldened far right. Many of the local organizers who embraced this panethnic logic—educators, public health workers, and others doing the quotidian work the Black Panthers had labeled "survival pending revolution"—did not identify as nationalists, which allowed them to embrace panethnicity all the more thoroughly.[51]

In this context, it is unsurprising that the MLN itself could not survive the transformations of the 1980s. As Mora notes, the success of Latinidad depended precisely on the failure of its advocates to define the limits of membership: "Ambiguity was important because it allowed the stakeholders to bend the definition of Hispanic panethnicity and use the notion instrumentally—as a means to an end."[52] While the MLN certainly mobilized its binational identity in an instrumental fashion, it hesitated to accept the implications of this strategy for the constituent national communities it hoped to organize. Instead, the group held tightly to its precisely detailed definitions of national identity and to the fundamental and presumably unambiguous distinction between Puerto Ricans and Chicana/o/xs. In the end, then, the MLN could not accommodate the lack of clarity on which the overall project of developing US Latina/o/x identity depended. As other, less ideologically rigid groupings increasingly embraced Latinidad as an organizing principle, the MLN devolved into parallel, nationally bounded organizations. By the turn of the millennium, the Puerto Rican MLN had ceased to exist, while the Mexicana/o/x MLN had faded to a shadow of its former self. Still, in retrospect, the group represented a set of possibilities, even if these were never actually realized in the moment.

In the twenty-first century, many of the same dynamics that drove the transformations of the 1970s and 1980s have resurfaced with a vengeance. Latina/o/x people in the United States remain, in López's prescient words, "America's scapegoats." Immigration is perhaps the hot-button political issue of the current moment, and Donald Trump has successfully weaponized the false equation between immigrants and Latina/o/x people that Metzger and others had developed in the 1970s. The direct inheritors of the Klan and neo-Nazi fusion that Metzger helped pioneer have gained greater strength than at any time since the 1980s, surging to prominence before and after the deadly "Unite the Right" rally in Charlottesville, Virginia, in August 2017.[53] Meanwhile, Democratic Party candidates for elective office frequently scramble to appeal to an undifferentiated Latina/o/x constituency and sometimes seem incredulous at Republican successes in targeting specific subsets of voters. Recent judicial skirmishes over the 2020 US census, regarding the possibility of asking respondents whether or not they are US citizens, are widely understood to be a proxy battle over the suppression (or not) of US Latina/o/x participation in the political process itself.[54]

In terms of more explicitly left forces, the MLN is long gone, but the radical student group MEChA, one of the few still remaining from the peak period of revolutionary nationalism in the 1970s, initiated a process in 2019 to drop the specifically Mexican-centered words *Chicanx* and *Aztlan* from its name in order to connect with a broader US Latina/o/x constituency and to better acknowledge Afro-descended and indigenous identities under the larger umbrella.[55] In this context, the little-known history of how Puerto Rican and Chicana/o/x radicals developed a shared (if flawed) understanding of the threat of fascism, in the United States and beyond, can help shape future struggles on behalf of all those threatened by contemporary manifestations of fascism.

Michael Staudenmaier (mjstaudenmaier@manchester.edu) is assistant professor of history at Manchester University in North Manchester, Indiana. He teaches and writes about Chicago's Puerto Rican community, Latina/o/x social movements in the second half of the twentieth century, and the role of race, racism, and antiracism in United States history.

Notes

1. López, "Statement," 14.
2. The literature on the 1970s Left is now quite extensive. See, among others, Berger, *Hidden 1970s*; Elbaum, *Revolution in the Air*; Pulido, *Black, Brown, Yellow, and Left*; and Blackwell, *¡Chicana Power!*
3. I use the suffix *a/o/x* to refer to people of Latin American birth or ancestry living in the United States ("Latina/o/x"), including specifically people of Mexican ("Chicana/o/x" or "Mexicana/o/x") birth or ancestry. The rise of gender-inclusive terminology—including *a/o* to note both feminine and masculine genders in Spanish, as well as the use of *x* as a marker of gender nonbinary identity—is an important, ongoing, and contested development in Latina/o/x studies. See Trujillo-Pagán, "Crossed Out by LatinX," and Vidal-Ortiz and Martínez, "Latinx Thoughts" for especially thoughtful reflections on the terminological and political questions raised by "the *x*."
4. The focus on the 1970s can be seen in Padilla, *Latino Ethnic Consciousness*, and Mora, *Making Hispanics*. While both sources address the role of grassroots activists, self-described radicals are largely absent.
5. On the rightward turn in the United States, see McGirr, *Suburban Warriors*; Self, *All in the Family*; and Belew, *Bring the War Home*. On comparable processes in Latin America, with a stronger emphasis on state power, see Finchelstein, *Ideological Origins*; Power, *Right-Wing Women*; and Lindo-Fuentes and Ching, *Modernizing Minds*.
6. Movimiento de Liberación Nacional, "On the Separation within the M.L.N."
7. Churchill and Vander Wall, *COINTELPRO Papers*, 63–90. On COINTELPRO more broadly, see Cunningham, *There's Something Happening Here*.
8. For more on the grand jury resistance efforts surrounding the FALN investigations, see Deutsch, "Improper Use of the Federal Grand Jury."

9. Movimiento de Liberación Nacional, *Struggle of Vieques*, 2. For more on the origin and ideology of the MLN and the context of the stateside Puerto Rican Left of the 1970s in which it emerged, see Torres, "Introduction," 5–15, and Starr, "'Hit Them Harder.'"
10. López, "Making the Impossible Happen," 12.
11. On the multiracial character of the Poor People's Campaign both before and after King's assassination, see Mantler, *Power to the Poor*. On the original Rainbow Coalition, see Williams, *From the Bullet to the Ballot*. Other black-brown alliances are described in Araiza, *To March for Others*, and Lee, *Building a Latino Civil Rights Movement*.
12. On stateside Puerto Rican internationalism before the 1970s, see Sánchez-Korrol, *From Colonia to Community*, and Thomas, *Puerto Rican Citizen*. On pre-1970s internationalism among Mexican Americans, see Flores, *Mexican Revolution in Chicago*, and Akers Chacón, *Radicals in the Barrio*.
13. Movimiento de Liberación Nacional, *The Time Is Now*, 48.
14. On the high-profile if idiosyncratic use of the term *fascism* by the Black Panther Party, see Bloom and Martin, *Black against Empire*, 299–302.
15. *Communist International*, 3:293.
16. For a brief recent academic gloss on this criticism, see Griffin, *Fascism*, 15–17.
17. Political Studies Commission, *Trilateral Commission*, 23. There is a long history of both left- and right-wing criticism of the Trilateral Commission, including some fascist conspiracy theories. On the Left, see Sklar, *Trilateralism*. For a brief summary of right-wing criticisms, see Gill, *American Hegemony*, 167–69.
18. Césaire, *Discourse on Colonialism*, 36.
19. Oliva, "La figura de Aimé Césaire," 15n5.
20. For more on theories of internal colonialism, see Gutiérrez, "Internal Colonialism."
21. Castro, "On the Coup in Chile," 76, 78.
22. Martínez, "Transnational Connections," 159.
23. Bray, *Antifa*, 151. Thank you to an anonymous reader of an early draft of this manuscript for highlighting the connection here to contemporary ideas.
24. Guerra, "Speech to the Statewide Anti-Klan Conference," 3.
25. Herrera Calderón and Cedillo, "Introduction," 5.
26. Gómez, *Revolutionary Imaginations*, 164.
27. *Conciencia Mexicana*, "16 de Septiembre in Denver," 5.
28. *Breakthrough*, "Mexico and Revolution," 28.
29. Movimiento de Liberación Nacional, *Struggle of Vieques*, 15.
30. LeBrón, *Policing Life and Death*, 3.
31. Blanco-Rivera, "Forbidden Files."
32. Suarez, *Two Lynchings on Cerro Maravilla*.
33. Minian, *Undocumented Lives*.
34. Novick, *White Lies, White Power*, 51.
35. Belew, *Bring the War Home*, 60.
36. Langer, *Hundred Little Hitlers*, 129. The quote is from a leaflet distributed on December 8, 1974, at the San Ysidro–Tijuana border crossing by Metzger and others.
37. Belew, *Bring the War Home*, 60–63.
38. Bermanzohn, *Through Survivors' Eyes*, 161.
39. Quoted in Belew, *Bring the War Home*, 68.
40. Suarez, "Speech to the Statewide Anti-Klan Conference," 3.
41. Pegram, *One Hundred Percent American*, 58.

42. Suarez, "Speech to the Statewide Anti-Klan Conference," 4.
43. Suarez, "Speech to the Statewide Anti-Klan Conference," 1.
44. Suarez, "Speech to the Statewide Anti-Klan Conference," 8.
45. López-Rivera, "Phenomenon of the 'Moral Majority,'" 6.
46. López-Rivera, "Phenomenon of the 'Moral Majority,'" 6.
47. For historical context on Ríos Montt's regime, see Garrard-Burnett, *Terror in the Land of the Holy Spirit*.
48. Movimiento de Liberación Nacional, "On the Separation within the M.L.N.," 12.
49. Movimiento de Liberación Nacional, "On the Separation within the M.L.N.," 11.
50. Mora, *Making Hispanics*, 115.
51. Bloom and Martin, *Black against Empire*, 474n4. While the phrase is often attributed to Huey Newton, its first use in print came in an article by Gwen V. Hodges.
52. Mora, *Making Hispanics*, 5.
53. Lyons, *Insurgent Supremacists*.
54. For a brief summation of the census issue as it stood in late June 2019, see Williams, "What You Need to Know."
55. On the MEChA name change, see *Remezcla*, "Message."

References

Akers Chacón, Justin. *Radicals in the Barrio: Magonistas, Socialists, Wobblies, and Communists in the Mexican American Working Class*. Chicago, IL: Haymarket Press, 2018.

Araiza, Lauren. *To March for Others: The Black Freedom Struggle and the United Farm Workers*. Philadelphia: University of Pennsylvania Press, 2014.

Belew, Kathleen. *Bring the War Home: The White Power Movement and Paramilitary America*. Cambridge, MA: Harvard University Press, 2018.

Berger, Dan, ed. *The Hidden 1970s: Histories of Radicalism*. New Brunswick, NJ: Rutgers University Press, 2010.

Bermanzohn, Sally Avery. *Through Survivors' Eyes: From the Sixties to the Greensboro Massacre*. Nashville, TN: Vanderbilt University Press, 2003.

Blackwell, Maylei. *¡Chicana Power! Contested Histories of Feminism in the Chicano Movement*. Austin: University of Texas Press, 2011.

Blanco-Rivera, Joel A. "The Forbidden Files: Creation and Use of Surveillance Files against the Independence Movement in Puerto Rico." *American Archivist* 68 (2005): 297–311.

Bloom, Joshua, and Waldo E. Martin Jr. *Black against Empire: The History and Politics of the Black Panther Party*. Berkeley: University of California Press, 2016.

Bray, Mark. *Antifa: The Anti-fascist Handbook*. Brooklyn, NY: Melville House, 2017.

Breakthrough. "Mexico and Revolution in the Americas." Spring 1982, 26–30. Breakthrough Collection, Freedom Archives, San Francisco, CA.

Castro, Fidel. "On the Coup in Chile." In *Chile: The Other September 11: An Anthology of Reflections on the 1973 Coup*, edited by Pilar Aguilera and Ricardo Fredes, 68–85. New York: Ocean Press, 2006.

Césaire, Aimé. *Discourse on Colonialism*, translated by Joan Pinkham. New York: Monthly Review Press, 2000.

Churchill, Ward, and Jim Vander Wall. *The COINTELPRO Papers: Documents from the FBI's Secret Wars against Dissent in the United States*. Boston, MA: South End Press, 1990.

The Communist International, 1919–1943: Documents. Selected and edited by Jane DeGras. 3 vols. New York: Oxford University Press, 1956.

Conciencia Mexicana. "16 de Septiembre in Denver." December 1982, p. 5. Movimiento de Liberación Nacional (MLN) Collection, Freedom Archives, San Francisco, CA.

Cunningham, David. *There's Something Happening Here: The New Left, the Klan, and FBI Counterintelligence*. Berkeley: University of California Press, 2004.

Deutsch, Michael E. "The Improper Use of the Federal Grand Jury: An Instrument for the Internment of Political Activists. *Journal of Criminal Law and Criminology* 74, no. 4 (1984): 1159–96.

Elbaum, Max. *Revolution in the Air: Sixties Radicals Turn to Lenin, Mao, and Che*. New York: Verso, 2002.

Finchelstein, Federico. *The Ideological Origins of the Dirty War: Fascism, Populism, and Dictatorship in Twentieth Century Argentina*. New York: Oxford University Press, 2014.

Flores, John H. *The Mexican Revolution in Chicago: Immigration Politics from the Early Twentieth Century to the Cold War*. Urbana: University of Illinois Press, 2018.

Garrard-Burnett, Virginia. *Terror in the Land of the Holy Spirit: Guatemala under General Efraín Ríos Montt, 1982–1983*. New York: Oxford University Press, 2011.

Gill, Stephen. *American Hegemony and the Trilateral Commission*. New York: Cambridge University Press, 1990.

Gómez, Alan Eladio. *The Revolutionary Imaginations of Greater Mexico: Chicana/o Radicalism, Solidarity Politics, and Latin American Social Movements*. Austin: University of Texas Press, 2016.

Griffin, Roger. *Fascism*. Medford, MA: Polity, 2018.

Guerra, Steven. "Speech to the Statewide Anti-Klan Conference, San Francisco, CA." November 14, 1981. MLN Collection, Freedom Archives, San Francisco, CA.

Gutiérrez, Ramón A. "Internal Colonialism: An American Theory of Race." *Du Bois Review: Social Science Research on Race* 1, no. 2 (2004): 281–95.

Herrera Calderón, Fernando, and Adela Cedillo. "Introduction: The Unknown Mexican Dirty War." In *Challenging Authoritarianism in Mexico: Revolutionary Struggles and the Dirty War, 1964–1982*, edited by Fernando Herrera Calderón and Adela Cedillo, 1–18. New York: Routledge, 2012.

Langer, Elinor. *A Hundred Little Hitlers: The Death of a Black Man, the Trial of a White Racist, and the Rise of the Neo-Nazi Movement in America*. New York: Metropolitan Books, 2003.

LeBrón, Marisol. *Policing Life and Death: Race, Violence, and Resistance in Puerto Rico*. Berkeley: University of California Press, 2019.

Lee, Sonia Song-ha. *Building a Latino Civil Rights Movement: Puerto Ricans, African Americans, and the Pursuit of Racial Justice in New York City*. Chapel Hill: University of North Carolina Press, 2014.

Lindo-Fuentes, Héctor, and Erik Ching. *Modernizing Minds in El Salvador: Education Reform and the Cold War, 1960–1980*. Albuquerque: University of New Mexico Press, 2012.

López, José. "Making the Impossible Happen: An Introduction to the Life of José López in His Own Words." In *Tribute to José López*, October 31, 1999, Chicago, IL. Free Puerto Rican POWs and Political Prisoners Collection, Freedom Archives, San Francisco, CA.

López, José. "Statement before the Committee on Decolonization of the United Nations on the Colonial Case of Puerto Rico and Puerto Ricans in the United States on Behalf of the Movimiento de Liberación Nacional." *De pie y en lucha*, Fall 1980, 12–15, 19. In the author's possession.

López-Rivera, Oscar. "The Phenomenon of the 'Moral Majority' and the Development of Fascism in the U.S." *De pie y en lucha*, Summer/Fall, 1983, 3–6. MLN Collection, Freedom Archives, San Francisco, CA.

Lyons, Matthew N. *Insurgent Supremacists: The US Far Right's Challenge to State and Empire*. Montreal: Kersplebedeb, 2018.

Mantler, Gordon K. *Power to the Poor: Black-Brown Coalition and the Fight for Economic Justice, 1960–1974*. Chapel Hill: University of North Carolina Press, 2013.

Martínez, Nydia A. "Transnational Connections of the Mexican Left with the Chicano Movement, 1960s–1970s." PhD diss., University of New Mexico, 2015.

McGirr, Lisa. *Suburban Warriors: The Origins of the New American Right*. Princeton, NJ: Princeton University Press, 2001.

Minian, Ana Raquel. *Undocumented Lives: The Untold Story of Mexican Migration*. Cambridge, MA: Harvard University Press, 2018.

Mora, G. Cristina. *Making Hispanics: How Activists, Bureaucrats, and Media Constructed a New American*. Chicago: University of Chicago Press, 2014.

Movimiento de Liberación Nacional. *The MLN and the Struggle of Vieques: Discussion Document No. 7*. Chicago: Rebeldia Publications, 1980. MLN Collection, Freedom Archives, San Francisco, CA.

Movimiento de Liberación Nacional. "On the Separation within the M.L.N." *De pie y en lucha* Summer/Fall, 1983, 10–12. MLN Collection, Freedom Archives, San Francisco, CA.

Movimiento de Liberación Nacional. *The Time Is Now: A Discussion Paper*. Chicago, n.d. MLN Collection, Freedom Archives, San Francisco, CA.

Novick, Michael. *White Lies, White Power: The Fight against White Supremacy and Reactionary Violence*. Monroe, ME: Common Courage Press, 1995.

Oliva, Elena. "La figura de Aimé Césaire: Trayectoria y pensamiento anticolonial en el poeta de la negritud." In *Aimé Césaire desde América Latina: Diálogos con el poeta de la negritud*, edited by Elena Oliva, Lucía Stecher, and Claudia Zapata, 10–20. Santiago de Chile: Facultad de Filosofía y Humanidades, Universidad de Chile, 2011.

Padilla, Felix. *Latino Ethnic Consciousness*. Notre Dame, IN: University of Notre Dame Press, 1985.

Pegram, Thomas R. *One Hundred Percent American: The Rebirth and Decline of the Ku Klux Klan in the 1920s*. Chicago, IL: Ivan R. Dee, 2011.

Political Studies Commission of the Movimiento de Liberación Nacional. *Trilateral Commission: The New US Imperialist World Strategy*. Chicago: Rebeldia, 1979. MLN Collection, Freedom Archives, San Francisco, CA.

Power, Margaret. *Right-Wing Women in Chile: Feminine Power and the Struggle against Allende, 1964–1973*. University Park: Pennsylvania State University Press, 2002.

Pulido, Laura. *Black, Brown, Yellow, and Left: Radical Activism in Los Angeles*. Berkeley: University of California Press, 2006.

Remezcla. "A Message from ME(ChA)'s National Board: Why We Decided to Change the Name of our Movimiento." April 5, 2019. remezcla.com/features/culture/mecha-national-board -statement-on-name-change.

Sánchez-Korrol, Virginia. *From Colonia to Community: The History of Puerto Ricans in New York City, 1917–1948*. Berkeley: University of California Press, 1994.

Self, Robert O. *All in the Family: The Realignment of American Democracy since the 1960s*. New York: Hill and Wang, 2013.

Sklar, Holly, ed. *Trilateralism: The Trilateral Commission and Elite Planning for World Management*. Boston, MA: South End Press, 1980.

Starr, Meg. "'Hit Them Harder': Leadership, Solidarity, and the Puerto Rican Independence Movement." In *The Hidden 1970s: Histories of Radicalism*, edited by Dan Berger, 135–54. New Brunswick, NJ: Rutgers University Press, 2010.

Suarez, Guillermo. "Speech to the Statewide Anti-Klan Conference, San Francisco, CA." November 15, 1981. MLN Collection, Freedom Archives, San Francisco, CA.

Suarez, Manuel. *Two Lynchings on Cerro Maravilla: The Police Murders in Puerto Rico and the Federal Government Cover Up*. San Juan, PR: Editorial del Instituto de Cultura Puertorriqueña, 2003.

Thomas, Lorrin. *Puerto Rican Citizen: History and Political Identity in Twentieth-Century New York City*. Chicago: University of Chicago Press, 2010.

Torres, Andrés. "Introduction: Political Radicalism in the Diaspora—the Puerto Rican Experience." In *The Puerto Rican Movement: Voices from the Diaspora*, edited by Andrés Torres and José E. Velázquez, 1–22. Philadelphia: Temple University Press, 1998.

Trujillo-Pagán, Nicole. "Crossed Out by LatinX: Gender Neutrality and Genderblind Sexism." *Latino Studies* 16, no. 3 (2018): 396–406.

Vidal-Ortiz, Salvador, and Juliana Martínez. "Latinx Thoughts: Latinidad with an X." *Latino Studies* 16, no. 3 (2018): 384–95.

Williams, Jakobi. *From the Bullet to the Ballot: The Illinois Chapter of the Black Panther Party and Racial Coalition Politics in Chicago*. Chapel Hill: University of North Carolina Press, 2013.

Williams, Timothy. "What You Need to Know about the Census Citizenship Question." *New York Times*, June 27, 2019. www.nytimes.com/2019/06/27/us/citizenship-question-census .html.

The Very Quintessence of Persecution

Queer Anti-fascism in 1970s Western Europe

Rosa Hamilton

Queer[1] activists have played a vital role in the renewed anti-fascist movements which have organized since the mid-2010s in response to the sweeping gains made globally by fascist movements. Inspired by these activists and new anti-fascist scholarship, this article asks: What is the history of queer activists' engagement in postwar anti-fascism, and to what extent has there been a uniquely queer anti-fascism different from other mass anti-fascist movements?[2] To answer these questions, this article examines a transnational network of activists operating throughout the 1970s in Britain, Germany, France, Italy, and Spain. Much like the present moment, fascist activity in Europe increased substantially.[3] In addition to a rightward backlash in European politics, several fascist parties either emerged or expanded, including the National Front in Britain, the National Democratic Party of Germany, the Italian Social Movement, and the Front National in France. Meanwhile, fascist Spain entered a late stage of intensified repression of the underground queer community. All of these fascist movements targeted queer people as perceived threats to the family, nation, and race.

Drawing on oral histories, activists' private collections, and against-the-grain archival research, this article argues that a uniquely queer anti-fascism emerged in the early 1970s led by transgender and gender-nonconforming people and cisgender lesbians to counter the rise of postwar fascism in western Europe.[4] Queer anti-fascists recognized the specific danger of fascism while connecting it to their

Radical History Review
Issue 138 (October 2020)   DOI 10.1215/01636545-8359259
© 2020 by MARHO: The Radical Historians' Organization, Inc.

experience in marginalized communities. Ostracized by cisgender-heterosexual (cis-het) society and opposed to assimilationist gay rights politics, these activists devised a robust anti-fascism rooted in revolutionary queerness and an analysis of everyday fascism as inherent to capitalist society and connected to existing oppressive structures of heteropatriarchy and racism. For these activists, queerness was necessarily anti-fascist, revolutionary, and intersectional.[5]

This article is the first transnational historical study of queer anti-fascism and the first to argue that queer anti-fascism offered a unique anti-fascist theory and praxis.[6] This article hopes to intervene in historiographies of anti-fascism and of gender and sexuality: historians in general have overlooked queer anti-fascism.[7] This historiographic gap reflects and partly results from cis-het anti-fascists' historical marginalization of queer anti-fascist voices and their consequent silencing in sources and accounts. Many cis-het anti-fascists saw queer liberation as secondary to the real goal of class revolution. As queer activist and historian Jeffrey Weeks wrote in 1977, the cis-het Left regarded queerness as a "bourgeois deviation and decadence," an apolitical pursuit of superstructural change for the privileged.[8] Others went further, drawing on discourses constructing fascism itself as queer. Citing Gregory Wood's thesis of the "myth of fascistic homosexuality," Christopher Vials argues that "as early as the 1930s gays and lesbians faced a persistent notion, manifested across the political spectrum in Europe and North America, that Nazism was somehow innately homosexual."[9] Marxist psychoanalyst Wilhelm Reich was the first to give this discourse intellectual credibility, writing that homosexuals' supposed incomplete psychosexual development made them more likely to be fascist.[10] Reich's work influenced a generation of medical experts, while historians simultaneously popularized narratives of fascist homosexuality, as in William Shirer's massively popular *The Rise and Fall of the Third Reich*.[11] Fascism-as-queer discourses also found fertile ground amidst postwar economic rebuilding and expansion projects heavily reliant on heteropatriarchal re-entrenchment and conservative sexual politics.[12]

Whether drawing on class-first leftism or fascism-as-queer discourses, cis-het anti-fascists marginalized queer anti-fascists who found it difficult to organize as a result. Nonetheless, queer activists responded with a unique theory and praxis of revolutionary anti-fascist politics that insistently argued that queerness was necessarily anti-fascist. Queer anti-fascists recognized the revolutionary potential of queer identity and centered their lived experience of oppression in their activism. This led them to adopt a structural interpretation of fascism, which anti-fascists had to confront with both direct action against explicit fascists and everyday anti-fascism against white supremacy, heteropatriarchy, and capitalism: anti-fascism as social revolution. While mass cis-het anti-fascist movements developed in the mid to late 1970s, queer anti-fascists organized in the early 1970s and worked across borders, recognizing the transnational nature of oppressive structures. Drawing from shared influences in Black Power and women's liberation movements and Marxism, queer anti-fascists across Britain, France, Germany, Italy, and Spain adopted an intersectional theory and praxis centering queerphobia as constitutive of fascist ideology and conceptions of self, race, and nation. For a time in the 1970s, queers drew revolutionary potential from their social location and pointed to what a truly radical and inclusive anti-fascism should look like.

"Gay, Gay Power to the Gay, Gay People!": Transatlantic Origins of Gay Liberation
European queer anti-fascism grew out of the radical gay liberation movements founded by trans and queer people of color in the United States beginning with the Stonewall uprising in June 1969.[13] Before founding the first European gay liberation movement in October 1970, the founders of the London Gay Liberation Front (GLF), queer socialists Aubrey Walter and Bob Mellors, met in New York City, protesting outside the Women's House of Detention with the New York City GLF against the imprisonment of Black Panther Party members Angela Davis and Joan Bird. Both Walter and Mellors were living in the United States at the time and were involved in the Black Power and women's liberation movements.[14]

The Black Panther Party in particular provided a model which radical queers took up. In September 1970, Walter and Mellors traveled with NYC GLF founders Sylvia Rivera and Martha Shelley to the Revolutionary People's Constitutional Convention organized by the Black Panthers in Philadelphia.[15] Only a few weeks before the conference, Huey Newton released "A Letter from Huey to the Revolutionary Brothers and Sisters about the Women's Liberation and Gay Liberation Movements," in which he said, "we should try to unite with them in a revolutionary fashion. . . . Homosexuals are not given freedom and liberty by anyone in the society. They might be the most oppressed people in the society."[16] For radical queers, Newton's letter was inspirational. The convention itself further emphasized coalition building between different oppressed groups, providing a model for queer anti-fascists.[17] Inspired by the Panthers' intersectional militancy and the examples set by Shelley, Rivera, and Marsha P. Johnson, Walter and Mellors returned to London three weeks later to found the London Gay Liberation Front, the first European GLF.

Drawing on their combined influences from Black Power and women's liberation movements and Marxism, the London Gay Liberation Front announced itself in its founding documents as "part of the wider movement aiming to abolish all forms of oppression" under capitalism: "We believe no one can be free until everyone is free. We support the struggles of all oppressed peoples."[18] In another widely disseminated pamphlet titled "The Principles of the Gay Liberation Front," the GLF emphasized the need for organizational independence while framing its activism as a militant socialist struggle in coalitional alliance with feminists, antiracists, and anti-colonial revolutionaries around the world.[19] As Walter explained: "The spirit to fight back came from the Vietnam struggle and the cultural revolution in

China, the idea that it was right to make a revolution. Other people's struggles, black people, women, had shown the intelligentsia that you should fight from where you were oppressed yourself."[20]

The London GLF put its intersectional theory into practice working closely with British Black Power activists.[21] One GLF member, John Chesterman, joined the British Black Panther Party soon after its founding, before leaving to found London's White Panther Party, a Panther offshoot for white allies.[22] The GLF organized with Black activists against police brutality, especially in Notting Hill, where the police systematically harassed communities of color. One common police tactic involved repeatedly raiding Black businesses, homes, and events under the pretext of looking for drugs in order to provoke a reaction leading to arrests. A well-known instance of this occurred with the Mangrove Nine, a group of Notting Hill Black activists whom police arrested in July 1970 after repeatedly raiding their meetings.[23] Their arrest set off waves of protest in which Chesterman and other GLF members took an active part. A year later, in 1971, GLF even moved to Notting Hill, expanding these efforts into a full campaign and continuing to support the Black liberation movement in London. And while even the radical sections of GLF remained largely white, most members with experience in contemporary social movements, such as Carla Toney, noted that GLF's membership was relatively more racially and class diverse, especially in comparison to the women's movement.[24]

Developing Queer Anti-fascism: Reclaiming History and Defending Community

Trans and cis lesbian feminists were the first in the movement to point toward how the fascism inherent to capitalist society directly targeted queer people. Just a few months after GLF's founding, British sociologist and lesbian feminist Mary McIntosh attempted to put the following motion up for a vote at a GLF meeting: "Every historic example shows that repression of the working-class, racism and attacks on gay people go together. They are all components of authoritarian capitalism or fascism (e.g. Nazi Germany, Spain, Brazil, Greece, etc.)."[25] However, the cisgender gay men voted the motion down. This reflected a division in the GLF between a radical wing—generally made up of working-class queers, trans and gender-nonconforming people, and cis lesbians—and a reformist wing of cisgender gay men and middle-class activists. Jeffrey Weeks later recalled that a "divide was there right from the beginning, between extreme libertarianism and a sort of liberationism which stressed solidarity and community and involvement with others."[26] This division hampered the movement and was partly responsible for London GLF's breakup in 1973–74. While societal oppression led queers to a deeper critique of social structures, the LGBT+ community was not monolithic, and some preferred reform or free love, especially if their race, class, or gender privileged them in other ways.

When able to work independently within the movement, queer anti-fascists developed their ideas further. Fed up with men asserting control within the movement, GLF women in January 1972 published a scathing zine entitled *Lesbians Come Together*, an intersectional, trans-inclusive, and revolutionary statement of women's anger at both society at large and GLF men. Calling on queer women to come out and lead, the opening article decries that "for too long the Sisters, whilst they have rejected heterosexual men and their values still feel it is safe to lean on the gay brothers, instead of realising that WE have much to teach THEM."[27] Their conception of political womanhood was inclusive and intersectional: trans women contributed significantly, including a major article challenging transphobia in the women's and gay movements, and antiracists promoted ongoing campaigns such as solidarity protests during Angela Davis's trial.[28]

    Lesbians Come Together also includes one of the first discussions of the relationship of fascism and queerness from a European gay liberation group. The zine's first article, entitled "Fascism Is Alive and Well," reclaims the history of the persecution of queer people in the Nazi concentration camps. In the postwar period, there had been no remembrances or reparations to the queer victims of the Nazis. The authors describe this as a "conspiracy of silence," a societal desire to inflict further violence through historical erasure.[29] Recovering this buried history was in itself an act of resistance against fascist attempts to silence and murder queer voices and people. This was not a full-fledged theory of fascism, but it was an early attempt to push back on established narratives: historical reclamation and revision as queer anti-fascist praxis.

    Despite resistance within the movement to early queer anti-fascists such as McIntosh, queer anti-fascism did gain a wider appeal in the LGBT+ community because it provided a response to increased fascist attacks on queer people in the early 1970s. At the time, the National Front consistently made calls for a genocidal extermination of LGBT+ people publicly and in its magazine, *Spearhead*.[30] The National Front also went beyond rhetoric by attacking queer people and venues, especially gay pubs, in London and elsewhere. After a series of particularly brutal attacks in Leeds and London on gay bookstores in 1973, the Manchester Gay Liberation Front mass-distributed a pamphlet entitled "A Few Little Known Facts about Fascism," which begins by connecting the history of the Nazi persecution of queer people with contemporary attacks by the National Front. Calling on GLF's structural analysis, the pamphlet directly connects Nazism and these attacks to anti-abortionists and everyday misogyny.[31]

    The theoretical underpinning of this connection was heteropatriarchy as a main source of fascism and as an ideological prop for the status quo. For queer anti-fascists, fascism was a coherent ideology insofar as it directs popular resentments away from real structural inequalities and toward defined out-groups, whom fascists label as the malign sources keeping the nation and race decadent and degenerate. Fascists prey on anxieties over gender, race, and sexuality to manipulate populations, gain political control, and protect capital. Fascism—by which queer anti-fascists meant an organized politics of hate directed at immigrants, women, queer people, disabled people, Jews, and people of color for the ultimate maintenance of capitalist hegemony—could not be destroyed without a change in class relations and the rooting out of the heteronormativity, sexism, and racism propping up capitalist society. This analysis was straight out of the GLF handbook; it was a queer analysis of fascism. As the pamphlet concludes, queer people's social location made them uniquely suited to understand and thereby challenge fascism and these wider structures. It states that "the Women's and Gay Movements exist to challenge all these male values: Fascism, in its rise, must strengthen them. That's why we are here today." These activists were envisioning a new queer subject whose experience of persecution provided the revolutionary potential to challenge fascism and overthrow heteropatriarchal capitalism.

As a result of their revolutionary and anti-fascist conception of queerness, many queer anti-fascists insisted on organizational independence from cis-het anti-fascists. One such group was the Manchester Gay Libertarians (MGL), an anarchist offshoot of the Manchester Gay Liberation Front. MGL's pamphlet literature provides a succinct example of how queer anti-fascists differentiated themselves from cis-het anti-fascists. In 1974, the MGL distributed one such pamphlet on the anti-fascist tactics of the two largest cis-het anti-fascist organizations in Britain at the time: the Socialist Workers Party and the International Marxist Group.[32] MGL's main criticism was that cis-het anti-fascists focused solely on confronting fascists in the streets while ignoring structural violence. Cis-het anti-fascists' limited praxis resulted from a class-first politics blind to structural oppression under capitalism beyond class and dismissive of queer liberation as a necessary goal for combating fascism and capitalism. Instead, the MGL called for both direct action and the creation of local, nonhierarchical communes that could organize against everyday fascism in their communities and bring about a broader social revolution. A broad, interconnected coalition of decentralized, democratic, and independent liberation movements was necessary to dismantle the structures that gave rise to fascism.

Queer Anti-fascism Moves to the Continent

Queer anti-fascism was not developed by British queers alone: it was a transnational phenomenon. London GLF provided a home for radical queers who founded their own organizations across Europe and continued a commitment to anti-fascist theory and praxis. This was noted by GLF member and anti-fascist Peter Tatchell, who later said that "London GLF was a training ground for many people who went on to start gay movements in other countries. Mario Mieli from Italy, lots of Latin Americans, and the people who set up FHAR [Front Homosexuel d'Action Révolutionnaire] in France."[33] Jonathan Marcus and Mark Bray have shown how postwar mass anti-fascism emerged in early 1980s France in reaction to the growth of fascist skinhead culture and the solidification of the far right under the Front National.[34]

Interestingly, however, FHAR was anti-fascist in its theory and praxis from its inception in February 1971. In its founding publication, *Rapport contre la normalité* (*Report against Normality*), FHAR announced its vision for a radical politics rooted in queerness against structural oppression and for the liberation of all people: "We reclaim our status as a social scourge for the complete destruction of all imperialism. Down with the money society of hetero-cops! Down with the reduced sexuality of the procreative family! . . . [We are] for self-defense groups who will oppose by force the sexist racism of hetero-cops. For a homosexual front that assaults and destroys 'fascist sexual normality.'"[35] This wide-ranging critique tied fascism to the structural repression of gender and sexual minorities. As a "social scourge," queers occupied a unique position to challenge capitalism and the "hetero-cops," an evocative term for all who supported the existing system of racial, heteropatriarchal capitalism.

In its two main newspapers, *Fléau social* and *Antinorm*, FHAR promoted its queer anti-fascist analysis of fascism as structural and not limited to parties alone. Fascism was not just a historical movement; it also encapsulated a set of authoritarian social practices rooted in heteropatriarchy. In 1973, the editors of *Fléau social* developed this critique into its conception of *le fascisme kotidien* (everyday fascism), which broadened the analytical focus of fascism to include not just historical movements but also anti-abortion campaigning, sexual repression, and ableist mental health norms.[36] In the same year, *Antinorm* developed these ideas further while centering discussions of gender. As both a historical movement and political phenomenon, fascism relied on restrictive gender roles, female submission, and the valorization of cis-het male dominance and superiority.[37] On the level of subjectivities, fascism recognized men as subjects with agency while reducing women to passive objects. Their agency denied to them, women under fascism could exist only if they submitted to men, otherwise they could be discarded. Crucially though, this differed from the existing liberal capitalist system only in fascists' greater use of violent coercion in the subjugation of women and queers. Drawing the connections between fascism, capitalism, and heteropatriarchy, *Fléau social* and *Antinorm* encouraged queers to recognize fascism as a living system tied to their experience of oppression.

FUORI! and Gay Communism in Italy

Tatchell's reference to Mario Mieli, a queer, gender-nonconforming Marxist and early attendee of London GLF meetings, reflected Mieli's enormous influence on Italian queer activism.[38] Inspired by GLF, Mieli returned to Milan in 1972 to found Italy's first queer activist group, the Fronte Unitario Omosessuale Rivoluzionario (styled as FUORI!, Italian for "come out!"), but he remained in touch with the London GLF and FHAR for the rest of the decade. Mieli theorized that capitalism was based on heteropatriarchy; queers challenged heteropatriarchy with their very existence and were therefore the revolutionary class most capable of overthrowing capitalism and instituting communism. As his major work, *Towards a Gay Communism*, states, "Today, the real revolutionary movement includes, above all, the movement of women and homosexuals who struggle against the system and against the heterosexual phallocentrism that sustains it."[39] The cis-het Left could never be revolutionary because its class-first analysis overlooked the heteropatriarchal structures upholding capitalism.

Like other queer anti-fascists, Mieli connected these critiques of capitalism and heteropatriarchy to fascism. He argued that fascism's violent antipathy toward queer people was an extension of queerphobia under capitalism, writing that "the extermination of homosexuals under the Third Reich offers the clearest picture, the very quintessence, of the infernal quotidian persecution inflicted on gays by capitalist society."[40] Capitalism requires queerphobia because it relies on cis-het families to reproduce workers; whereas a communist society would socialize childcare in the community, capitalism requires families to do this. This also explains capitalism's reliance on heteropatriarchy: men require and expect women to care for them, the children, and the home. Communism challenges these structures by socializing production and resources, while fascism reinforces them. For Mieli, the crucial difference between liberal capitalism and fascism is degree of enforcement: fascism as a "quintessence of persecution" that violently enforces social norms to an even greater extent through repressive and ideological state apparatuses.

As editor of FUORI!'s eponymous newspaper, Mieli had a platform to promote the importance of anti-fascist activism to the community. Under his editorship, *FUORI!*'s spring 1974 edition featured a special issue on the history of the Nazi persecution of queer people. As in *Lesbians Come Together*, the article showed the radical possibilities of reclaiming silenced history: to remember the dead, and identify and dismantle the systems that supported their murder. To that end, the article challenges how cis-het anti-fascists disingenuously used Nazi SA leader Ernst Röhm's sexuality against queer anti-fascists: if Röhm could be gay, then the Nazis must not have been anti-queer. As the article makes clear, Nazism violently suppressed queer life, and Nazis never accepted or even admitted to knowing about Röhm's homosexuality.[41] The article goes further, questioning whether Goebbels's propaganda machine fabricated Röhm's homosexuality in the wake of the Night of the Long Knives. Once again, historical revision was an essential aspect of queer anti-fascist praxis. Challenging well-established fascism-as-queer discourses, queers sought to reclaim their history of persecution as part of a wider project of promoting the necessarily anti-fascist nature of queerness itself.

Reckoning with the Past: West German Queer Anti-fascists and the Legacies of Nazism

Ronald Van Cleef and other historians generally argue that West German gay liberation had separate origins from American or European organizations.[42] To an extent, West German gay liberation groups regarded themselves as distinct because of the legacies of National Socialism and the Cold War geographic isolation of West Berlin, the most active area in the country for queer organizing. Yet their major influences—Marxism, women's liberation, and Black Power—were the same as seen in the moment historians cite as the origin point of German gay liberation: the airing of Rosa von Praunheim's 1971 television movie, *Nicht der Homosexuelle ist pervers, sondern die Situation, in der er lebt* (*It Is Not the Homosexuale Who Is Perverse, but the Society in Which He Lives*).[43]

Produced in the wake of the decriminalization of same-sex intercourse in 1969, the film shocked West Germany. Heavily influenced by Marxism, women's liberation, and Black Power, it criticized society's sexual repression and the alleged apolitical hedonism of the LGBT+ community. The film is a call to arms for queer people to come out of the closet, as seen in its final lines: "Be proud of your homosexuality. Come out of the [public] toilets, clear out into the streets. Freedom for gays!"[44] Rather than hide away, queers should embrace their revolutionary potential openly. As a way forward, the characters Paul and Achim promote supporting the struggles of socialists and other oppressed groups. One place of unity with the cis-het Left would be the union, as they tell their comrades to "be in solidarity with your colleagues in conflicts with the company and you will also be able to count on their help."[45] Despite historians' attempts to separate German gay liberation from transnational influences, however, the characters call on queers to "fight against the oppression of minorities along with . . . the Black Panthers and the women's movement."[46] This points to early queer organizing as fundamentally transnational: none of the European gay liberation movements emerged independently.

Inspired by these calls to action, gay liberation groups began forming immediately after the film's release. In Frankfurt, RotZSchwul set about translating Huey Newton's letter to the gay and women's movements, once again showing the transnational influence of the Black Panthers on European queers.[47] In West Berlin, Homosexuelle Aktion Westberlin (HAW), the first and subsequently largest queer liberation movement in Germany, formed. In its founding document published in November 1971, HAW echoed sentiments seen in Britain, Italy, and elsewhere: queers shared a common experience of oppression under capitalism, which made them uniquely capable of overthrowing the existing order.[48]

From the beginning of German gay liberation, radical queers centered antifascist struggle due to the legal legacies of National Socialism in West Germany and the revolutionary impulses from trans and cis feminists in the movement. The Nazi regime had used a law known as Paragraph 175 to arrest one hundred thousand queer people and send fifteen thousand to the concentration camps.[49] After the war, this law remained unchanged, and the queer victims of the Nazi regime received no memorialization or reparation. Instead, the Allied Forces kept many in the camps, and the new West German state threatened to rearrest released prisoners if suspected of further homosexual activity.[50] Repealing Paragraph 175 and providing reparations to queer victims were perhaps the most demanded issues in the queer movement. This was vital for the self-conception of the movement as not only a vehicle for queer liberation but also anti-fascism: the Federal Republic was a legal continuation of the Third Reich and therefore fascist itself. This unique legal circumstance made anti-fascism especially relevant for German queers, yet their anti-fascist theory shared much with the rest of the continent: fascism was more than a historical phenomenon, and anti-fascists had to target the institutions of liberal capitalism, including the state.

Trans and cis lesbian feminists were once again key to centering anti-fascism within the movement and connecting the threads of anti-capitalism, anti-fascism, and queer liberation. Already by 1973, lesbians and trans people had formed their own HAW working groups to challenge the moderating policies of privileged cis gay men in the majority. At a major HAW plenum on November 4, 1973, the HAW Feminist Group presented a series of radical proposals centering revolutionary structural change and the fight against heteropatriarchy. Like the rest of the movement, the Feminist Group called for the abolition of Paragraph 175 and the payment of "reparations for the gay prisoners of the camps."[51] They went further, though, by being the first to call for the pink triangle, the symbol worn by LGBT+ prisoners in the concentration camps, as a symbol for the queer movement. The Feminist Group spoke at length about the history and symbolism of the pink triangle, arguing that it was a recognition of the continuation of fascism in the Federal Republic through the oppression of queer people: "[The pink triangle] conveys that there is only a quantitative and not a qualitative difference between the gay oppression in fascism and our own oppression in liberal [West Germany and West Berlin]." Moreover, in their design, the Feminist Group placed the pink triangle on a red background, emphasizing that the queer fight against fascism was also a socialist struggle against capitalism.

Drawing on the symbolism of the pink triangle, the Feminist Group presented a vision of collective struggle for all oppressed peoples. They contrasted this especially with cisgender white male moderates hoping to achieve rights over liberation, writing that "demanding solidarity with one another and with other oppressed peoples (beyond empty rhetoric) is one of the central tasks of the HAW."[52] They then emphasized the need for queers, Jews, women, and Black people to work together. The pink triangle visually embodied the necessarily anti-fascist and intersectional nature of queerness. Once again, trans and cis feminists led the way in constructing and promoting this queer anti-fascism.

Queer Anti-fascist Praxis (I): A Transnational Overview

The following three sections provide an overview of how queer anti-fascists connected theory with various forms of anti-fascist praxis, including monitoring fascists, organizing counterdemonstrations, and working in local communities. In West

Germany, HAW organized numerous protests against the rising neo-Nazi move-ment, but they deliberately connected these protests to systemic injustices and larger critiques of capitalism and the state. For example, on April 26, 1974, HAW organized a counterdemonstration against a neo-Nazi rally and prayer service hon-oring Rudolf Hess. Hess was serving a life sentence in prison for his genocidal crimes, and support for him was a key unifying practice on the German far right. A poster from the HAW counterprotest rightly describes Hess as a mass murderer responsible for the deaths of millions of Jews, queer people, and other minorities.[53] It then emphasizes the utter immorality of a prayer service when "not a single one of the few homosexual survivors ever received reparation for their unhappy suffering." To avenge this suffering and make good on the past, the poster exhorts queers "to fight the Nazis of today!" HAW recognized the significance of direct action but emphasized the need to connect specific protests to larger struggles. The reference to reparations tied neo-Nazism, which West Germany formally opposed, to the Fed-eral Republic itself and therefore the institutions of liberal capitalism.

HAW extended this critique, arguing that fascism never ended for queer peo-ple, as indicated by the title of the poster: "For queer people, the Third Reich is still not over!" West Germany's "apparent liberalization" had papered over the failures of denazification, the continuity of Nazi figures in the West German state and econ-omy, and the underground organizing of neo-Nazi movements. The liberal state could not confront racism and heteropatriarchy because these were at the founda-tions of capitalist society. Even despite the state's best efforts, such as attempts to ban Holocaust denial, West Germany would never be able to attack the roots of fas-cist support. Tying all this back to queerphobia, the poster's conclusion describes the fight against fascism as a fight against not just reaction but also "prejudice and discrimination" against queer people. It then ends with calls to fight fascism by abol-ishing Paragraph 175, making reparation to queer victims of the concentration camps, and protecting free labor organizing in the workplace against capitalist exploitation. Anti-capitalism, anti-fascism, and queer liberation could not be separated.

While the West German context shows how queer anti-fascists connected protesting fascist parties with social justice, the work of French queers demonstrates that queer anti-fascists were monitoring fascist groups across Europe years before antifas took these activities up in the late 1970s.[54] While some historians have emphasized FHAR's confrontational style and rhetoric over substantive change, anti-fascist monitoring points to a practical result of FHAR's revolutionary ener-gies.[55] In 1972, for instance, *Fléau social* published a special report on European Action, a fascist periodical and transnational coordinating network of the largest European fascist parties supporting pan-European white nationalism and a geno-cide of Jews, LGBT+ people, and people of color.[56] Through financial support and media training, European Action worked to prepare fascist movements to take over European governments. The *Fléau social* special report shined a light on these clandestine operations, but despite its importance, the report's impact outside the LGBT+ community is unclear and was likely limited. As Julian Jackson has written, the French Left rejected working with radical queers out of "a belief that homosexuality was a bourgeois vice: revolutionary activists must subordinate their personal lives to the future of the revolution."[57] Facing this consistent marginalization across the continent, queer anti-fascists struggled to convert revolutionary aims, analyses, and actions into mass campaigns.

Queer Anti-fascist Praxis (II): Transnational Support and the Queer Underground in Spain

From 1971 to 1974, a transnational network involving FUORI!, FHAR, London GLF, and Revolt (Sweden) cooperated to support underground queer movements in fascist Spain. Until Francisco Franco's death in 1975, Spain remained a fascist state with the financial and diplomatic backing of the United States and other liberal democracies. Franco's Spain valorized patriarchal families, childbirth, and conformity to rigid gender roles and forced the LGBT+ community to remain underground. In 1970, Franco intensified the persecution of queer people with the Law on Danger and Social Rehabilitation, which explicitly labeled homosexuality and sex work "social hazards." Under Mieli's leadership, FUORI! monitored the situation and produced a special report in 1972 on the incarceration and torture of Spanish queers in asylums.[58] The report emphasized that the persistence of fascist rule in Europe was possible only with the support of capitalist governments and the Catholic Church, underlining the compatibility and close relationship between fascism and mainstream liberal and conservative institutions.

In a fascist state that criminalized and targeted queerness, existence itself was an act of anti-fascist resistance. In response to the 1970 law, Spain's first queer organizations emerged underground. In 1971, Armand de Fluvia founded the Movimiento Español de Liberación Homosexual (MELH), which modeled itself on the London GLF. MELH similarly adopted a radical queer Marxist politics privileging the need for intersectionality and social revolution for all.[59] Based in Barcelona, MELH operated until 1974 with transnational support from FUORI!, FHAR, London GLF, Revolt (Sweden), and the French organization Arcadie. For instance, between January 1972 and November 1973, Arcadie and Revolt helped MELH fund and produce a clandestine newsletter written by mostly Catalan activists for publication throughout Spain.[60] By 1974, the police had identified these activities and shut down the newsletter and MELH. However, these queer activists would be key in Spain's post-1975 transition to democracy.[61] MELH members regrouped after Franco's death in 1975 in the Front d'Alliberament Gai de Catalunya (FAGC), which remains active in Catalonia today. Along with organizations such as the Frente de Liberación Homosexual de Castilla in Madrid, FAGC worked for the decriminalization of homosexuality in 1978.[62] Fascism in Spain had been based on heteropatriarchy and capitalism; by challenging these structures with their very existence, members of MELH and other Spanish activists embodied the connection of queerness and anti-fascism.

Queer Anti-fascist Praxis (III): Punk, Protest, and Coalition Building in Britain

In Britain, queer anti-fascists were heavily involved in protesting against the National Front. One of their earliest engagements occurred in June 1974, when queers in and outside the GLF took part in the Red Lion Square demonstrations. Although Nigel Copsey's authoritative history points to Red Lion Square as one of the starting points of British anti-fascism's 1970s revival, his account leaves out queer anti-fascists.[63] An anti-fascist activist who had been present later estimated that two-thirds of the fifteen hundred anti-fascists who marched against the two hundred fascists were women, and he went on to emphasize the militancy of the "very large women's and gay contingent" that directly confronted the National Front's meeting rather than join a peaceful counterdemonstration nearby.[64] Yet while they successfully disrupted the fascist march, the press reaction sided with the fascists and depicted the anti-fascists as violent. In response, anti-fascist campaigns emerged across the country emphasizing that "The National Front is a Nazi Front."[65]

Queer anti-fascist activity likewise surged. It was at this time that Lucy Toothpaste, a lesbian feminist journalist and punk musician, committed herself to the antifascist cause. From the mid-1970s to the early 1980s, she wrote for numerous leftist publications including the feminist magazine *Spare Rib*, her self-published queer punk zine *Jolt*, and the anti-fascist periodical *Temporary Hoarding*, calling on queer punks to get involved.[66] On April 23, 1977, Toothpaste protested with newly formed queer organizations, including Women Against Racism and Fascism, the All London Gay Groups Against Sexism, Racism, and Fascism (ALGG), and London Gay Socialists, against the largest fascist rally in Britain since the interwar years.[67] Twelve hundred National Front fascists marched through the multicultural, working-class borough of Wood Green in North London looking to intimidate minorities at a time when the Front's membership was peaking.[68] Toothpaste and others describe Wood Green as a massive collection of "running battles" as fascists and anti-fascists fought wherever gaps broke in police lines. These fights turned dangerous quickly, not least because of police violence against anti-fascists. Toothpaste later reported police siding with the National Front and furiously beating and mocking anti-fascists. Nonetheless, the anti-fascists successfully disrupted and dispersed the fascist procession, but at a high cost: dozens were seriously injured, and police arrested over seventy anti-fascists while neglecting to arrest more than a handful of the fascists, who had come to Wood Green looking for a fight.[69]

In the aftermath of Wood Green, Toothpaste made further calls for punks and queers to organize. In her self-published zine *Jolt*, she promoted the even larger

August counterprotest at Lewisham, where over one hundred people were injured and two hundred arrested protesting five hundred National Front marchers.[70] Copsey and Renton have written that Lewisham was a breaking point; the National Front never organized a protest as large again, and mass anti-fascism only grew over the next two years.[71] Two broad national campaigns emerged at this time: the Anti-Nazi League, one of the largest mass anti-fascist organizations in history, and Rock Against Racism, a broad coalition of bands founded in 1976, which hosted two anti-fascist music festivals in 1978, drawing almost one hundred thousand people.

Historians, however, have neglected the surge in queer anti-fascist activity after Lewisham. Toothpaste continued her organizing: after Rock Against Racism staged several bands with misogynistic lyrics, she created Rock Against Sexism (RAS), a coalition of feminist and queer anti-fascist bands, writing in a 1979 *Spare Rib* article that punk music was the ideal vehicle for exposing young people to queer feminism.[72] In RAS's self-published zine *Drastic Measures*, Toothpaste clarified that the organization's main goals were "to define the right of everyone to determine their own sexuality, whether they be straight, gay, both, or neither," and "to fight sexism in music and to use music to fight sexism at large."[73] For example, RAS campaigned heavily against the Corrie Bill, a parliamentary attempt in 1979 to restrict abortion access, organizing a major benefit show in October 1979 at the University of London, and once again highlighting how queer anti-fascists recognized the need to enact structural change.[74] RAS was successful throughout the United Kingdom and Ireland, featuring bands like Gang of Four, the Mo-dettes, Poison Girls, Soulyard, and the Au Pairs.

RAS's success points to the importance of musical subcultures in queer anti-fascist organizing. Discos, zines, punk shows, installations, street theater, and ska gigs were all vital as links for a queer activist community and as effective fund-raising sources, but these were also contested spaces. Rhoda Dakar, a Black feminist activist and singer for the all-female ska group Bodysnatchers, shared Toothpaste's belief in the importance of anti-fascist music and underground subcultures like ska and punk.[75] Dakar's experience, however, shows how they could also be dangerous for women and people of color. In a 1980 interview conducted by Toothpaste, Dakar spoke about the rise of fascist skinhead culture in the early-1980s punk and ska scenes and the subsequent increase in incidents of hate, intimidation, and violence at gigs.[76] This tension between resistance and recuperation by structures of violence points to the perpetuation of inequalities even within anti-fascist subcultures, as well as their possibilities for real change.

While Toothpaste was working with RAS in the late 1970s, two major queer anti-fascist groups emerged: Gays Against Fascism, a subgroup of the GLF-successor organization Gay Activists Alliance, and Gays Against the Nazis. The latter organized several mass-leafleting campaigns, including at the second Rock Against

Racism festival, where they handed out ten thousand flyers that appropriated the anti-fascist slogan "the National Front is a Nazi Front" but changed to "NF = Nazi Front = No Future for Gays!" The modification connected anti-fascism to the broader struggle of queers against societal repression of gender and sexual minorities. For queer anti-fascists, the National Front could not be separated from the general anti-queer backlash of the late 1970s: the year of the Rock Against Racism festivals also saw Margaret Thatcher co-opting the National Front's racist and queerphobic rhetoric and drawing away its members to the Conservative Party.[77]

Queer anti-fascists consistently pointed out the connections between mainstream conservatism and fascism. In 1979, Gays Against Fascism published their own document: an extended structural analysis of fascism and queer anti-fascist theory and praxis called *An Anti-fascist Handbook*. Intended for both cis-het and queer audiences, the handbook distilled the theoretical contributions of queer anti-fascists into an accessible text while critiquing anti-fascists who separated their activism from structural violence and the rising tide of anti-abortion, anti-queer, and anti-immigrant conservative movements in the late 1970s. To this end, its discussion of fascist groups goes beyond the National Front to include organizations such as the Freedom Association, an early neoliberal think tank devoted to anti-union propaganda; the Nationwide Festival of Light, a queerphobic organization dedicated to the "sanctity of marriage"; and the Society for the Protection of the Unborn Child, an anti-abortion group.[78] Calling these groups fascist was not just rhetoric: the handbook was a serious attempt to broaden definitions of fascism and show its relation to everyday, mainstream forms of oppression.

The pamphlet also continues and develops queer anti-fascism's intersectional praxis. In a section on effective anti-fascist organizing, the pamphlet argues for a coalitional approach of "autonomous organisations centred around particular categories of oppression to enable people to come into an awareness of their own distinct personal/political needs."[79] Queer anti-fascists recognized the need for coalitions of oppressed groups through their own experience and the enduring influence of Black Power and especially Black feminism.[80] While criticizing the marginalization of queers by class-first cis-het anti-fascists, the authors highlight the "need to recognize the validity of *every* form of oppression."[81] Compared with earlier sources, *An Anti-fascist Handbook* shows the continuity in queer anti-fascism and its unity of theory and praxis: fascism was rooted in structural oppression and could be defeated only by a coalitional, democratic movement of autonomous organizations united for a social revolution against white supremacy, capitalism, and heteropatriarchy.

Decline and Legacy

What happened to this queer anti-fascist network? Most of the organizations I have described either did not survive into the early 1980s or abandoned their revolutionary aims. I argue there were two main causes of decline: first, the cis-het Left's marginalization of queer anti-fascists, and second, new political realities arising from neoliberal restructuring, the rightward turn of European governments, and the devastating effects of the AIDS crisis and the subsequent anti-queer backlash. In addition to the traditional denunciations of queer anti-fascism as bourgeois identity politics, cis-het anti-fascists pushed out queer anti-fascists by making them convenient scapegoats in internal activist struggles. In Britain, for instance, cis-het anti-fascists blamed women and queer activists for the collapse of the national coordinating bodies of local anti-fascist groups—the Campaign Against Racism and Fascism and the Anti-Racist, Anti-Fascist Co-ordinating Committee (ARAFCC)—at the ARAFCC Conference on Racism and Fascism in the summer of 1978. In the July 1978 issue of *Searchlight*, Britain's largest anti-fascist publication, the editor Maurice Ludmer wrote: "Certainly those responsible (certain women, Gay and Left groups) must bear a heavy responsibility. They sought continuously to confuse issues and saw the question of 'sexism' as one of the dominant themes of the conference."[82] Ludmer's dismissiveness of social justice issues was emblematic of the cis-het Left's narrower politics. Some anti-fascists took issue with *Searchlight*, such as the Oxford Anti-Fascist Committee, which wrote a reply letter disagreeing firmly with the scapegoating of queer activists.[83] In a response, however, Ludmer doubled down, arguing that queer organizations did not belong in a national coalition of local anti-fascist organizations.[84]

This rejection from the mainstream led to burnout and the demise of many queer groups due to lack of support and resources. Unable to work with the socialist Left, activists had to choose between continuing on their own or joining the new reformist movements that began making substantial headway pursuing a strategy of gay rights over queer socialism. Mieli had noticed these trends as early as 1973 as he saw an influx of moderate cisgender men enter the movement, attracted to revolutionary language but not real social revolution.[85] Against his wishes, FUORI! federated itself in 1974 to the Italian Radical Party, a center-left coalition promising to secure rights for the LGBT+ community. Soon after this, Mieli left to focus on radical queer theater until his death in 1983.[86] As Miguel Malagreca has written, "Whatever remained of the original movement was noteworthy only as a linguistic remembrance."[87]

In Germany, the queer movement split between the majority mainstream, which embraced reform, and an active underground minority. As Van Cleef has written, anti-capitalism declined as moderates took up the mainstream in the mid-1970s.[88] Meanwhile, queer anti-fascists continued in smaller numbers while maintaining their intersectional approach and organizing to protect immigrants and asylum seekers. By the mid-1980s, queers had embraced the tactics and decentralized structure of the autonomists and the black blocks, or "gay blocks" (Schwule Blöcke) as they called themselves. Transgressive and intersectional groups—such as Schwule Antifa, which was active by 1985, and feminist Fantifa groups—continued the tradition of queer anti-fascism into the 1990s, providing models for present-day intersectional antifa organizing.[89] Nonetheless, despite the persistence of exciting grassroots activism, gone were the days when the largest queer organizations were openly anti-capitalist and anti-fascist. Instead, gay rights organizations increasingly sought accommodations with the state and capitalism, reflecting trends general to the LGBT+ movement at the time.

As the German case shows, the 1980s marked a restructuring rather than an endpoint. As European governments shifted to the right, the mass anti-fascist movements of the 1970s went into a period of relative decline before the emergence of new forms of autonomous organizing in the mid-1980s, such as Anti-Fascist Action (AFA). Yet queer anti-fascists had always looked beyond party politics. Like many others, Peter Tatchell, a founder of London GLF and a queer anti-fascist who later marched with AFA, became a radical AIDS activist and continued the tactics pioneered by gay liberation.[90] Increasingly, queer people of color founded their own organizations, such as London's Black Lesbian and Gay Centre.[91] Queers showed what an inclusive and radical anti-fascism should look like and how queers could draw revolutionary, anti-fascist potential from their positionality. Their analysis and organizing laid a foundation and provides a model for today's intersectional anti-fascist movements as well as a warning against marginalization and power imbalances within liberatory movements.

Rosa Hamilton is a doctoral candidate in history at the University of Virginia writing her dissertation on queer anti-fascism in twentieth-century Europe. She is a cofounder of the Far Right and Anti-fascism Group, an interdisciplinary collective in Charlottesville, Virginia, which provides a public platform for research on fascism and anti-fascism, especially for women scholars in a cis-men-dominated field. She received her BA in history from the University of California, Davis, and her MA in history from the University of Virginia.

Notes

1.   I use *queer* for revolutionary, anti-assimilationist gender and sexual minority identities that are diverse and fluid but also shaped by existent social totalities. I use *LGBT+* for broader gender and sexual minority communities.
2.   Charlottesville queer anti-fascists remain active long after the Unite the Right rally; see Montgomery, "Charlottesville Residents."
3.   Griffin, *Nature of Fascism*, chap. 6.
4.   *Transgender, lesbian,* and *gender-nonconforming* are not exclusive terms. The reference highlights the contributions of overlapping identities marginalized within the LGBT+ movement.
5.   Crenshaw, "Intersection."
6.   Vials first used the term for American and German activists who reclaimed the Nazi persecution of LGBT+ people especially in 1980s AIDS activism (Vials, *Haunted by Hitler*, 194–213). Lucy Robinson's work on gay men in the British Left discusses some

queer anti-fascists (Robinson, *Gay Men and the Left*, 110–17). This article decenters gay men and argues for a uniquely queer anti-fascism.

7.   Mark Bray's history of transnational anti-fascism and Emily Hobson's history of the gay and lesbian Left have been particularly significant for me; see Bray, *Antifa*; Hobson, *Lavender and Red*.

8.   Weeks, *Coming Out*, 148.

9.   Vials, *Haunted by Hitler*, 206.

10.   Reich, "What Is Class Consciousness?," 297; Reich, *Mass Psychology of Fascism*, 192.

11.   Shirer, *Rise and Fall*, 120, 122.

12.   Herzog, *Sexuality in Europe*, 61; Herzog, *Sex after Fascism*, 5–7.

13.   Kaiser, *Gay Metropolis*, 203–66.

14.   Power, *No Bath*, 4–5. I use the interviews collected in Power's oral history of London GLF extensively.

15.   Stein, *Loves*, 331–40.

16.   Newton, "Letter from Huey."

17.   Porter, "Rainbow in Black," 372.

18.   London GLF, "Oppression."

19.   London GLF, "Principles."

20.   Power, *No Bath*, 16. On GLF's history, see Walter, *Come Together*.

21.   Angelo, "Black Panthers in London"; Narayan, "British Black Power."

22.   Power, *No Bath*, 17.

23.   Hillel and Iglikowski, "Rights, Resistance, and Racism."

24.   Power, *No Bath*, 62, 79.

25.   Power, *No Bath*, 38.

26.   Power, *No Bath*, 61.

27.   *Lesbians Come Together*, "Free Our Sisters," 1.

28.   *Lesbians Come Together*, "Don't Call Me Mister," 18–19.

29.   *Lesbians Come Together*, "Fascism Is Alive," 2.

30.   *Outcome*, "Gays against Fascism," 20–22.

31.   Manchester GLF, "Facts about Fascism."

32.   MGL, "On Opposition to Fascism."

33.   Power, *No Bath*, 62.

34.   Marcus, *National Front and French Politics*, 131–58; Bray, *Antifa*, 49.

35.   FHAR, *Rapport contre la normalité*.

36.   *Fléau social*, "Le fascisme kotidien," 8.

37.   *Antinorm*, "Des lycéens parlent," 10.

38.   Mieli used *he/him* and *she/her* pronouns interchangeably. English language sources use *he/him* pronouns, so this article does the same.

39.   Mieli, *Gay Communism*, 172.

40.   Mieli, *Gay Communism*, 130.

41.   FUORI!, "Le sterminio," 32.

42.   Van Cleef, "A Tale of Two Movements?," 1.

43.   Van Cleef, "A Tale of Two Movements?," 1; Salmen and Eckert, "Die Neue Schwulenbewegung."

44.   Praunheim, *Nicht der Homosexuelle*, 57.

45.   Praunheim, *Nicht der Homosexuelle*, 56.

46.   Praunheim, *Nicht der Homosexuelle*, 56.

47. Plastargias, *RotZSchwul*, 187–99.

48. HAW, "Grundsatzerklärung."

49. Grau, *Hidden Holocaust?*

50. United States Holocaust Memorial Museum, "Persecution of Homosexuals."

51. HAW Feministengruppe, "Thesenpapier," 1.

52. HAW Feministengruppe, "Rosa Winkel," 13.

53. HAW, "Noch nicht."

54. On French anti-fascism, see Vergnon, *L'anti-fascisme en France*.

55. Gunther, *Elastic Closet*, 46; Sibalis, "Gay Liberation."

56. *Fléau social*, "Fascisme européen," 9.

57. Jackson, "Sex, Politics, and Morality," 87–88.

58. Airone, "Spagna: Fascismo!," 8–9.

59. Pérez-Sánchez, "Queer Nation?," 373.

60. Pérez-Sánchez, "Queer Nation?," 383–86.

61. Pérez-Sánchez, *Queer Transitions*, 187; Pérez-Sánchez, "Queer Nation?," 395.

62. Pérez, " España cumple 40 años."

63. Copsey, *Anti-fascism in Britain*, 114–20.

64. David Landau, interview by Daniel Jones, August 7, 2015, Searchlight Oral Histories Collection.

65. Copsey, *Anti-fascism in Britain*, chap. 4.

66. Lucy Toothpaste, interview by Rosa Hamilton, August 10, 2018.

67. *Gay News*, "ALGG," 10.

68. Renton, "Guarding the Barricades."

69. Renton, *Never Again*, 69.

70. Toothpaste, "Important Message," 6.

71. Copsey, *Anti-fascism in Britain*, 123–25; Bray, *Antifa*, 46–47; Renton, *Never Again*, 69–86.

72. Toothpaste, "Rock Against Sexism," 6.

73. Toothpaste, "Aims," 4.

74. Toothpaste, "Right to Choose," 4–5.

75. Rhoda Dakar, interview by Rosa Hamilton, August 19, 2018.

76. Toothpaste, "Bodysnatchers," 13–14.

77. Pitchford, *Conservative Party*, 4.

78. Gays Against Fascism, *Anti-fascist Handbook*, 3–16, 22–23.

79. Gays Against Fascism, *Anti-fascist Handbook*, 68.

80. For the intersections of 1970s Black and trans feminisms, see Stryker and Bettcher, "Trans/Feminisms."

81. Gays Against Fascism, *Anti-fascist Handbook*, 68.

82. Ludmer, "Editorial," 2.

83. Oxford Anti-Fascist Committee, "Letters," 5.

84. Ludmer, "Letters," 5.

85. Collettivo Redazionale, "Omosessualità e controrivoluzione"; Mieli, "I radical-chic."

86. Malagreca, *Queer Italy*, 102–8.

87. Malagreca, *Queer Italy*, 125.

88. Van Cleef, "A Tale of Two Movements?," 154.

89. Schwule Antifa, "Kampf."

90. Lucas, *OutRage!*
91. Murphy, "Black Lesbian and Gay Centre."

References

Airone, Enrico. "Spagna; Fascismo!" *Fuori!*, no. 1 (1972): 8–9.

Angelo, Anne-Marie. "The Black Panthers in London, 1967–1972: A Diasporic Struggle Navigates the Black Atlantic." *Radical History Review* 2009, no. 103 (2009): 17–35.

Antinorm. "Des lycéens parlent . . . sur la libération sexuelle." *Antinorm*, no. 4 (1973): 11.

Bray, Mark. *Antifa: The Anti-Fascist Handbook*. Brooklyn: Melville House, 2017.

Collettivo Redazionale. "Omosessualità e controrivoluzione." *Fuori!*, no. 7 (February 1973): 2–5.

Copsey, Nigel. *Anti-fascism in Britain*. Basingstoke: Macmillan, 2000.

Crenshaw, Kimberlé. "Demarginalizing the Intersection of Race and Sex: A Black Feminist Critique of Antidiscrimination Doctrine, Feminist Theory, and Antiracist Politics." In *Feminist Legal Theory*, edited by Katharine T. Bartlett and Rosanne Kennedy, 57–80. Boulder, CO: Westview, 1991.

FHAR. *Rapport contre la normalité*. Paris, 1971.

Fléau social. "Fascisme européen." *Fléau social*, no. 1 (June 1972): 9.

Fléau social. "Le fascisme kotidien." *Fléau social*, no. 3 (May 1973): 8.

FUORI! "Le sterminio degli omosessuali nel Terzo Reich." *Fuori!*, no. 14 (Spring 1974): 30–39.

Gay News. "ALGG." *Gay News*, no. 131 (November 17, 1977): 10.

Gays Against Fascism. *An Anti-fascist Handbook*. London, 1979.

Grau, Günter, ed. *Hidden Holocaust? Gay and Lesbian Persecution in Nazi Germany 1933–1945*, translated by Patrick Camiller. Chicago: Fitzroy Dearborn, 1995.

Griffin, Roger. *The Nature of Fascism*. London: Routledge, 1993.

Gunther, Scott. *Elastic Closet: A History of Homosexuality in France, 1942–Present*. Basingstoke: Palgrave Macmillan, 2014.

HAW. "Für Schwule ist das Dritte Reich noch nicht zu Ende." Berlin, April 1974. SL HAW 12–15, folder 12. Schwules Museum.

HAW. "Vorläufige Grundsatzerklärung." Berlin, November 1971. SL HAW 1–6, folder 1. Schwules Museum.

HAW Feministengruppe. "Rosa Winkel," November 1973. SL HAW 16–29, folder 25. Schwules Museum.

HAW Feministengruppe. "Thesenpapier zur Strukturierung der Diskussion über das F-Papier." Berlin, November 1973. SL HAW 16–29, folder 16. Schwules Museum.

Herzog, Dagmar. *Sex after Fascism: Memory and Morality in Twentieth-Century Germany*. Princeton, NJ: Princeton University Press, 2005.

Herzog, Dagmar. *Sexuality in Europe: A Twentieth-Century History*. Cambridge: Cambridge University Press, 2011.

Hillel, Rowena, and Vicky Iglikowski. "Rights, Resistance, and Racism: The Story of the Mangrove Nine." National Archives blog, October 21, 2015. blog.nationalarchives.gov.uk /rights-resistance-racism-story-mangrove-nine.

Hobson, Emily. *Lavender and Red: Liberation and Solidarity in the Gay and Lesbian Left*. Berkeley: University of California Press, 2016.

Jackson, Julian. "Sex, Politics, and Morality in France, 1954–1982." *History Workshop Journal* 61, no. 1 (March 1, 2006): 77–102. doi.org/10.1093/hwj/dbi076.

Kaiser, Charles. *The Gay Metropolis: 1940–1996*. Boston: Houghton Mifflin, 1997.

Lesbians Come Together. "Don't Call Me Mister, You Fucking Beast." *Lesbians Come Together*,
    January 1972, 18–19.
Lesbians Come Together. "Fascism Is Alive and Well." *Lesbians Come Together*, January 1972, 2.
Lesbians Come Together. "Free Our Sisters, Free Ourselves." *Lesbians Come Together*,
    London: January 1972.
London GLF. "The Gay Liberation Front Fights the Oppression of Homosexual People." 1971.
London GLF. "Principles of the Gay Liberation Front." 1970.
Lucas, Ian. *OutRage! An Oral History*. London; New York: Cassell, 1998.
Ludmer, Maurice. "Editorial." *Searchlight Magazine*, no. 37 (July 1978): 2.
Ludmer, Maurice. "Letters." *Searchlight Magazine*, no. 39 (September 1978): 5.
Malagreca, Miguel. *Queer Italy: Contexts, Antecedents, and Representation*. New York: Peter
    Lang, 2007.
Manchester GLF. "A Few Little Known Facts about Fascism." 1973.
Marcus, Jonathan. *The National Front and French Politics: The Resistible Rise of Jean-Marie Le
    Pen*. London: Palgrave Macmillan, 2016.
MGL. "On Opposition to Fascism—a Libertarian Approach." October 1974.
Mieli, Mario. "I radical-chic e lo chic radicale." *Fuori!*, no. 7 (February 1973): 16–17.
Mieli, Mario. *Towards a Gay Communism: Elements of a Homosexual Critique*, translated by
    David Fernbach and Evan Williams. London: Pluto, 2018.
Montgomery, Blake. "Charlottesville Residents Created Their Own Niche Media in Reaction to
    the Unite the Right Violence. Now They're Covering the Aftermath." *BuzzFeed News*,
    December 1, 2018. www.buzzfeednews.com/article/blakemontgomery/charlottesville
    -residents-media-rally-aftermath.
Murphy, Gillian. "The Black Lesbian and Gay Centre." *LSE History* (blog), October 31, 2016.
    blogs.lse.ac.uk/lsehistory/2016/10/31/theblacklesbianandgaycentre.
Narayan, John. "British Black Power: The Anti-imperialism of Political Blackness and the
    Problem of Nativist Socialism." *Sociological Review* 67, no. 5 (September 2019): 945.
Newton, Huey. "A Letter from Huey to the Revolutionary Brothers and Sisters about the
    Women's Liberation and Gay Liberation Movements." *Black Panther*, August 21, 1970.
Outcome. "Gays against Fascism." *Outcome (Manchester)*, no. 38, 345 (December 9, 1977): 20–
    22.
Oxford Anti-Fascist Committee. "Letters." *Searchlight Magazine*, no. 39 (September 1978): 5.
Pérez, Beatriz. "España cumple 40 años sin el delito de homosexualidad." *El periódico*,
    December 26, 2018.
Pérez-Sánchez, Gema. "Franco's Spain, Queer Nation?" *University of Michigan Journal of Law
    Reform* 33, no. 3 (2000). works.bepress.com/gemaperezsanchez/5.
Pérez-Sánchez, Gema. *Queer Transitions in Contemporary Spanish Culture: From Franco to La
    Movida*. Albany: State University of New York Press, 2007.
Pitchford, Mark. *The Conservative Party and the Extreme Right, 1945–75*. Manchester:
    Manchester University Press, 2011.
Plastargias, Jannis. *RotZSchwul: Der Beginn einer Bewegung (1971–1975)*. Berlin: Querverlag,
    2015.
Porter, Ronald K. "A Rainbow in Black: The Gay Politics of the Black Panther Party."
    Counterpoints 367 (2012): 364–75.
Power, Lisa. *No Bath but Plenty of Bubbles: An Oral History of the Gay Liberation Front,
    1970–1973*. London: Cassell, 1995.

Praunheim, Rosa von. *Nicht der Homosexuelle ist pervers, sondern die Situation, in der er lebt*. Berlin: Rosa von Praunheim Filmverlag, 2007.

Reich, Wilhelm. *The Mass Psychology of Fascism*. New York: Noonday, 1970.

Reich, Wilhelm. "What Is Class Consciousness?" In *Sex-Pol: Essays, 1929–1934*, edited by Lee Baxandall, translated by Anna Bostock, Tom DuBose, and Lee Baxandall, 297. New York: Vintage Books, 1972.

Renton, Dave. "Guarding the Barricades: Working-Class Anti-fascism 1974–79." In *British Fascism, the Labour Movement, and the State*, edited by Nigel Copsey and Dave Renton, 141–59. Basingstoke: Palgrave Macmillan, 2005.

Renton, David. *Never Again: Rock Against Racism and the Anti-Nazi League 1976–1982*. London: Routledge, 2018.

Robinson, Lucy. *Gay Men and the Left in Post-war Britain: How the Personal Got Political*. Manchester: Manchester University Press, 2007.

Salmen, Andreas, and Albert Eckert. "Die neue Schwulenbewegung in der Bundesrepublik Deutschland zwischen 1971 und 1987." *Forschungsjournal Neue Soziale Bewegungen* 1, no. 3 (July 1988): 25–32.

Schwule Antifa. "Erinnern wir uns an 1933—Kampf den alten und neuen Nazis." Berlin, January 29, 1985. Antifa, folder 1. Schwules Museum.

Shirer, William. *The Rise and Fall of the Third Reich*. New York: Simon & Schuster, 1960.

Sibalis, Michael. "Gay Liberation Comes to France: The Front Homosexuel d'Action Révolutionnaire (FHAR)." In *French History and Civilization: Papers from the George Rudé Seminar*, edited by Ian Coller, Helen Davies, and Julie Kalman, 1:267–78. Melbourne: George Rudé Society, 2005.

Stein, Marc. *City of Sisterly and Brotherly Loves: Lesbian and Gay Philadelphia, 1945–1972*. Chicago: University of Chicago Press, 2000.

Stryker, Susan, and Talia M. Bettcher. "Introduction: Trans/Feminisms." *Transgender Studies Quarterly* 3, no. 1–2 (May 1, 2016): 5–14. doi.org/10.1215/23289252-3334127.

Toothpaste, Lucy. "Aims of Rock Against Sexism." *Drastic Measures*, no. 1 (1979): 4.

Toothpaste, Lucy. "Bodysnatchers." *Spare Rib*, no. 100 (November 1980): 13–14.

Toothpaste, Lucy. "Important Message." *Jolt*, no. 3 (1977): 6.

Toothpaste, Lucy. "Rock Against Sexism." *Spare Rib*, no. 81 (April 1979): 5–7.

Toothpaste, Lucy. "A Woman's Right to Choose." *Drastic Measures*, no. 3 (1979): 4–5.

United States Holocaust Memorial Museum. "Persecution of Homosexuals in the Third Reich." Holocaust Encyclopedia, n.d. encyclopedia.ushmm.org/content/en/article/persecution-of -homosexuals-in-the-third-reich.

Van Cleef, Ronald. "A Tale of Two Movements? Gay Liberation and the Left in West Germany, 1969–1989." PhD diss., Stony Brook University, 2014.

Vergnon, Gilles. *L'anti-fascisme en France: De Mussolini à Le Pen*. Rennes: Presses Universitaires de Rennes, 2009.

Vials, Christopher. *Haunted by Hitler: Liberals, the Left, and the Fight against Fascism in the United States*. Amherst: University of Massachusetts Press, 2014.

Walter, Aubrey. *Come Together: The Years of Gay Liberation 1970–73*. London: Gay Men's Press, 1980.

Weeks, Jeffrey. *Coming Out: Homosexual Politics in Britain, from the Nineteenth Century to the Present*. London: Quartet Books, 1977.

"No State Apparatus Goes to Bed Genocidal Then Wakes Up Democratic"

Fascist Ideology and Transgender Politics in Post-dictatorship Argentina

Cole Rizki

On March 24, 1976, the Argentine military staged a coup d'état and established a fascist dictatorship that perpetrated genocide for seven years.[1] Following an inauguration ceremony, the military junta dissolved the National Congress, removed all members of the Supreme Court, and suspended political and union activity.[2] Composed of de facto president Army General Jorge Rafael Videla, Navy Admiral Emilio Eduardo Massera, and Air Force Brigadier General Orlando Ramón Agosti, the junta unveiled its sinister "Process of National Reorganization" to "eradicate subversion and promote national economic development."[3] For the next seven years, the authoritarian regime decimated radical leftist movements it deemed subversive threats to the nation while denying all responsibility for mass murder of civilians. Armed and paramilitary forces kidnapped, tortured, and exterminated thirty thousand subjects accused of political subversion.[4] People were disappeared: dragged off the street in broad daylight by *grupos de tarea*, heavily armed gangs of plainclothes officers and military personnel.[5] If there was any doubt as to the military's nefarious plan, in a nationally televised press conference held in 1979, dictator Jorge Rafael Videla declared: "The disappeared is a mystery . . . he has no identity, he's neither dead nor alive, he's disappeared."[6] Videla's shocking statement inaugurated "the

Radical History Review

Issue 138 (October 2020)   DOI 10.1215/01636545-8359271

© 2020 by MARHO: The Radical Historians' Organization, Inc.

Figure 1. The Mothers of the Plaza de Mayo's final march under dictatorship in the Plaza de Mayo on December 8, 1983. Photograph by Mónica Hasenberg-Brennan Quaretti. Image courtesy of the Hasenberg-Quaretti archive.

disappeared" as an identity category that, paradoxically, denied identity and with it the legal, social, and biological coordinates of personhood on which human rights depend. With no public accountability, the military sowed terror, *terrorismo de estado* that targeted the population, espousing a politics of death that aimed to eradicate radical left political projects.[7]

In 1977, in the midst of dictatorship, the Mothers of the Plaza de Mayo emerged with formidable force, protesting their adult children's disappearance (fig. 1).[8] Enlarging their missing sons' and daughters' black-and-white national identity document photographs, the Mothers lifted these images high above their heads, circling the Plaza de Mayo every Thursday, marching in front of the executive mansion to demand justice. The Mothers' use of black-and-white photos of their children cemented photography of the disappeared as an iconic activist genre. By mobilizing the state's own archival imagery, the Mothers demanded that the government take responsibility for its murderous actions. With democratic transition in 1983 following the botched Falklands/Malvinas War, the Mothers continued to march, denouncing government impunity, and they do so to this day, still calling for justice. In consequence, black-and-white headshots have become highly legible to a national viewing public as signifiers for military dictatorship, disappearance, and activist resistance to state terror.[9]

Figure 2. "López como las travas." 2016. Digital
image courtesy of La Brecha La Plata.

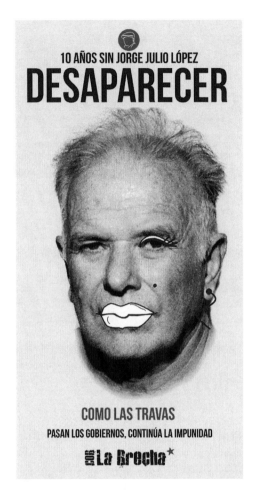

More than thirty years later, in September 2016, a polemic image (fig. 2) of
disappeared activist and trial witness Jorge Julio López appeared online as part of a
contemporary Argentine activist intervention titled Campaña DESAPARECER.
Feminist activists photoshopped this black-and-white portrait of López, layering
his facial features with lush, feminized lips and one stylized eyelid framed by long,
fake lashes. An earring dangles from his ear while one mole à la Marilyn Monroe
further accentuates the image's ludic feminine aesthetic. Yet this disappeared subject, who did not identify as trans, is not only feminized. The image's text and bold
iconography portray him as a *trava* or a *travesti*: a Latin American social category
similar but not identical to transgender. The late, internationally renowned Argentine travesti activist Lohana Berkins glosses this distinction, writing that, as an
English-language signifier and imported identity category, "the word transgender
comes from theoretical work developed within the North American academy."[10]

In contrast, *travesti*, as a Spanish-language signifier, is a "vernacular subject
positionality" specific to Latin America.[11] Travesti subjects often espouse multiple

social and political self-identifications such as indigenous and/or Afro-descendant, migrant, lower-class, and femme, though neither male nor female.[12] As Berkins elaborates: "The term 'travesti' has been and continues to be used [by the public] as a synonym for AIDS-ridden, criminal, scandalous, infectious, and marginal subject[s]."[13] Such negative associations render this photoshopped image of a disappeared person all the more audacious.

Yet what do travesti subjects have to do with the disappeared? This image condenses a series of unlikely relationships between political subversion, travesti identification, and disappearance as a fascist technology of power employed most heavily during Argentina's most recent military dictatorship (1976–83). By creating a composite image layering a travesti silhouette over a disappeared subject, this activist intervention raises a number of provocative questions concerning the targets of historic technologies of state violence: What are the boundaries of disappearance, and who counts as a disappeared subject? How might contemporary political actors stake claims to national belonging by mobilizing histories of fascism and historic anti-fascist visual culture?

This article forms part of an emerging body of scholarship on the sex/gender politics of authoritarian regimes in Latin America, turning specific attention to Argentine trans and travesti politics and rights claims as these articulate with legacies of authoritarianism.[14] Drawing on intelligence archive surveillance documents from the Intelligence Office of the Buenos Aires Provincial Police (DIPPBA), the artist-activist intervention Campaña DESAPARECER, and travesti and transgender testimony, this article argues that enduring social and political legacies of interwar fascism not only persist into the years of the *proceso*, but they also continue to animate and mediate post-dictatorship transgender politics.

The Origins of Fascist Ideology in Argentina

According to historian Federico Finchelstein, "Fascism provided the background for the principles and practices of the violence that the Argentine government unleashed against a group of its citizens in the 1970s" during dictatorship.[15] Like its European counterparts, fascist ideology in Argentina is grounded in anti-Semitism, xenophobia, and racism.[16] Yet Finchelstein and others, including Sandra McGee Deutsch and Alberto Spektorowski, persuasively argue that while "there was a great deal of appropriation, reformulation, and distortion in the Argentine reception of fascism . . . this reception was already 'prepared' by local illiberal ideologies that had predated it"—specifically, Argentine *nacionalista* ideology as it emerged in the 1920s and evolved, incorporating elements of fascist ideology throughout the 1930s and 1940s.[17]

Argentine nacionalista ideology was staunchly invested in rigid gender distinctions. As Deutsch notes, nacionalistas "defined themselves as masculine, which they saw as synonymous with strength. In doing so, they distinguished themselves from women, whom they regarded as inherently weak."[18] The nacionalistas were concerned about "perversion and loss of manhood."[19] They considered themselves "a community of virile men"—"strong, faithful and zealous" and certainly neither "sensual nor effeminate."[20] Common to fascism and shared by neighboring far-right *integralista* ideology in Brazil, such a rigid emphasis on both normative gender roles and sexual practice was deeply embedded within Argentine nacionalista ideology.[21] For nacionalistas, "the enemy was construed in terms of very traditional gender roles and fascist notions of so-called abnormal sexuality."[22] Nonnormatively sexed and gendered subjects, including travestis, represented an internal, degenerate threat to reigning Catholic sexual mores that exalted heterosexuality and racial purity as founding pillars of fascist ideology in Argentina.

The intrinsic belief that nonnormatively sexed and gendered subjects jeopardized the integrity of the state, cemented in the reactionary mixture of fascist and Catholic ideology that emerged during the nacionalista period, continued into subsequent permutations of fascist ideology in Argentina with its culmination in Argentina's military dictatorship of 1976–83. For example, the far-right movement Tacuara, which followed Juan Domingo Perón's populist government (1946–55), espoused many of the ideas that *nacionalismo* championed.[23] The same is true for secret service and intelligence forces, including the Intelligence Office of the Buenos Aires Provincial Police (DIPPBA), which I will discuss shortly.[24] In the early 1970s, after Perón's death, the paramilitary organization Alianza Anticomunista Argentina (or the Triple A) was born; many members of Tacuara were also participants in the Triple A, suggesting ideological continuity between the two organizations. The Triple A's ideology was likewise rooted in nacionalismo and, in addition to espousing extreme anti-Semitism, "advocated for the concentration and physical extermination of gays and lesbians. [It] considered homosexuality to be part of an imaginary Marxist plan against Argentina. [It] also regarded gays as agents of the CIA."[25] An absurd statement in and of itself, here the hyperbolic collapse of Marxism with homosexuality as a threat to the nation is even more unlikely given leftist activist movements' entrenched homophobia during this time period.[26] In the 1970s, for example, in response to right-wing accusations that the Montoneros and the Peronist Youth were "homosexuals and drug addicts," the Peronist Left developed and widely used the chant "we aren't fags, we're not drug addicts: we're soldiers of Perón and Montoneros," thereby disavowing any association with "homosexuality" and "drug addiction."[27] Nevertheless, by linking homosexuality with Marxism and the CIA, the Right insisted that nonnormative sex and gender form part and parcel of both imperial espionage and subversive Marxist plans to restructure Argentine social and political norms. The Triple A capitalized on the homophobia of both the Right and the Left in order to paint Marxism as degenerate while simultaneously implying that nonnormative sex and gender practices were politically subversive and represented threats to be eliminated. Such murderous convictions about nonnormative sexual and gender practices extended into the dictatorship when the state hired Triple A assassins, incorporating them into its brutal repressive apparatus.[28]

The Argentine military dictatorship's origins were rooted in this particular Argentine bent of fascism informed by heteronormative and homo- and transphobic nacionalista ideology, which understood subversion as a threat grounded in part in nonnormative sex and gender practices. Yet the sex/gender politics of "subversion," as a target of state violence, remained relevant to the state beyond fascist dictatorship, as recently declassified state intelligence force archives suggest. The Intelligence Office of the Buenos Aires Provincial Police (DIPPBA) archive evinces traces of both normative and nonnormative gender and sexual practices in its surveillance reporting, highlighting how the sex/gender politics of who counts as a subversive target of state surveillance remained relevant to security forces across dictatorship and democracy.

DIPPBA: The Sex/Gender Politics of Surveillance

From 1956 to 1998, the Intelligence Office of the Buenos Aires Provincial Police (DIPPBA) collected intelligence information used to effect persecution across the population. Spanning nearly half a century, this intelligence archive contains over 4 million pages of detailed reporting of espionage that targeted individuals, political parties, student groups, the armed forces, and religious groups, among others. In addition to ubiquitous written intelligence reports, the archive also contains hundreds of hours of video and audio surveillance—750 VHS tapes and 160 audiocassettes—as well as countless photographs surveilling individuals, protests, and other potentially subversive activities.[29]

The initial priority of the DIPPBA during the 1950s and 1960s responded to national and international imperatives to surveil communist and union activity.[30] Nationally, the Revolución Libertadora—the military coup ending Juan Domingo Perón's presidency in 1955—aimed to eradicate Peronism, a political belief system deeply embraced by unionized workers and the popular class.[31] During this time period, the DIPPBA thus heavily surveilled union activity.[32] With the emergence of the Cold War, Argentine security forces continued to focus on internal enemies: "subversive" ideological agents such as communists whose belief system was deemed threatening to Argentina's dominant social, political, and economic order. During the 1976–83 dictatorship, the DIPPBA's central purpose was to track subversive subjects and civil associations, gathering intelligence that led to disappearances.

While the DIPPBA's stated primary aim during dictatorship was to surveil political "subversion," the DIPPBA also by default surveilled the sexual and gender practices of subversive subjects as part of its espionage activities. As historian Ana Cecilia Solari Paz and author Cristián Oscar Jilberto Prieto Carrasco, of the Comisión Provincial por la Memoria (CPM), which houses the DIPPBA archive, demonstrate, part of gathering intelligence on "subversive subjects" required expanding on particular "puntos" or items of interest, which included a "personal life report."[33] One such intelligence document from 1981 elaborated priorities for surveilling targets' private lives:

The personal life report should consist of the following aspects: 1) nuclear
family: civil status, names of wife, children, and everyone's occupation . . .
3) conduct: public and private; 4) functional: personal and professional
aptitudes and conduct; 5) ethics: moral and religious (values) and customs;
6) ideological: tendency (manifest or detectable) ideology (expressed or
demonstrable).[34]

Intelligence reports and memos such as this one suggest that, in addition to surveilling subjects' expressly political activities, the DIPPBA was concerned with the "private life" and "morality" of its suspects, evincing ongoing nacionalista ideological concerns with normative gender and sexual behaviors under the guise of "nuclear family," "conduct," and "ethics." By virtue of "the personal life report," the DIPPBA's espionage reporting reiteratively mapped heterosexual reproduction through the elaboration and surveillance of nuclear kinship networks to wipe out entire lineages of subversive subjects. Such family surveillance was thus largely undertaken to eliminate the heterosexual reproduction of subversion through its familial transmission. The surveillance of normative sexual and gender practices implicitly policed nonnormative sexual and gender practices, even while this was not the military's primary concern during dictatorship.

Despite Argentina's transition to democracy in 1983, the DIPPBA remained fully operational, continuing its surveillance activities across Buenos Aires Province for another sixteen years until its dissolution. However, democratic imperatives prevented the DIPPBA from explicitly targeting political subversion. While the label *factor subversivo* had to disappear from the filing structure of the DIPPBA archive, the DIPPBA continued to use the language of "subversive delinquent" within its written reports, redefining subversion in part through the lens of nonnormative sex/gender practices.[35]

The advent of the HIV/AIDS crisis in 1982, just one year prior to Argentina's democratic transition, provided one such opportunity. Intelligence forces stepped in ostensibly to track the epidemic's incidence and evolution, generating over six hundred pages of intelligence reporting on the crisis well into the 1980s and mid-1990s. Rather than the heterosexual reproduction of subversive political ideology through its familial transmission, the nonnormative sexual and criminal reproduction of deadly viral loads became a threat endangering national public health. The DIPPBA surveilled HIV/AIDS patients, collected HIV/AIDS organizations' pamphlets on everything from medical precautions to safer sex practices and even newspaper clippings from major Argentine newspapers on evolving cases. In a report

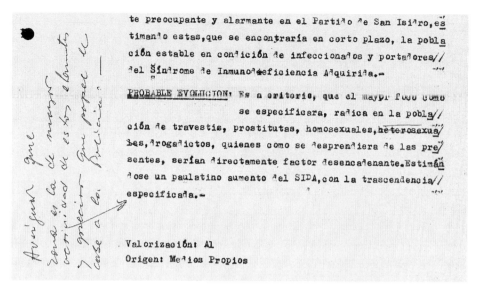

Figure 3. Detail of "Asunto: Producir información." October 3, 1988. CPM-Fondo DIPPBA, División Central de Documentación, Registro y Archivo, Mesa Referencia, Legajo N° 18.398, Tomo 1.

documenting the surge in HIV/AIDS cases in San Isidro municipality in the late 1980s (fig. 3), an unnamed intelligence officer's handwriting reveals the DIPPBA's espionage priorities.

The officer's typed notes track the HIV/AIDS epidemic's "Probable Development," stating that, "It is thought that the greatest focus [of the AIDS epidemic] . . . lies in the travesti, prostitute, homosexual, ~~heterosexual~~, and drug addict populations."[36] Significantly, the word *heterosexual* appears in the above report but is crossed out with blue pen. In the margins, the handwritten text reads: "Check which zone has the greatest activity of these elements and evaluate what role falls to the police." Heterosexuality, as an identity category, is quite literally stricken from the archive, while other social sectors' activities and movements require police surveillance in order to assess "what role" the police will take as the epidemic unfolds. Striking heterosexuality has the further effect of canceling out its relationship not only to HIV infection (a common prejudice in the early days of the HIV/AIDS crisis) but also to perverse subjects, rendering travestis, prostitutes, homosexuals, and drug addicts the proper targets of surveillance. Though cancelled out, heterosexuality importantly remains visible, reflecting the importance this category has in relation to the others; indeed, in superseding all other listed categories, heterosexuality here regulates how these categories ought to be understood. Through sleight of hand, heterosexuality becomes a privileged site of reproductive normativity, whereas nonnormative sexual and criminal practices are rendered the reproductive locus of an epidemic.

The DIPPBA's interest in surveilling sex and gender went beyond the HIV/ AIDS epidemic. Indeed, between 1983 and 1998 a number of intelligence files appear in the DIPPBA archive mentioning travesti subjects, detailing cases including homicide,[37] sex work,[38] and other crimes such as narco trafficking[39] or kidnapping.[40] At the same time, in this period we also witness the onset of formally organized travesti and trans activism, such as the Travesti Association of Argentina (ATA) and the Association for the Fight for Travesti and Transexual Identity (ALITT).[41] Travesti political activities did not go wholly unnoticed by the DIPPBA, which at times saw the organizing of nonnormative sex and gendered subjects as a threat to civil order, underscoring the ways in which sexuality and gender continued to matter to projects of surveillance in democracy. Interestingly, it is precisely in the Mothers' activism as it resists forms of illiberal state violence that travesti and trans activism finds some of its inspiration. Travesti activist Berkins states in an interview with Mothers of the Plaza de Mayo Association president Hebe de Bonafini that, from the Mothers' influence, travestis recognized that they had to become political subjects by organizing collectively instead of seeking recognition on an individual basis.[42] Travesti activists such as Berkins embraced and politicized travesti identification in part by drawing on an emergent conception of human rights developed by the Mothers, even as travesti activists were not always recognized as such by leftist activists, including the Mothers writ large, as Berkins reminds.[43]

Nascent travesti activism thus began to stake political demands in the early 1990s, and intelligence office files appear surveilling travesti subjects' explicitly political demands that could lead to further organizing. In one file titled "Solicitud de Personería Jurídica," dated October 26, 1994, an unnamed intelligence officer from Mar del Plata sent a report to the DIPPBA summarizing five newspaper articles concerning travesti activists.[44] The report describes the growth of an emerging travesti organization, the Mar del Plata Travesti Organization, and details travesti demands for *personería jurídica*—a juridical category that would confer legal status on the organization. Citing the newspaper articles, the unnamed officer writes that upward of "60 travestis" live in Mar del Plata. "They [travestis] denounce police activity that they *consider* discriminatory, [noting] how much they *feel* pursued. . . . Likewise, distinct news outlets made reference to the discrimination that travestis *suffer*, echoing travesti denunciations, in which travestis indicate that the situation is very serious" (emphasis mine). As is clear from the report, the officer characterizes the travestis' demands as a matter of perception and feeling rather than fact, while the passive grammatical construction—"the discrimination travestis *suffer*"—erases the perpetrator: police officers. The travestis further "denounce physical aggression," accusing the Buenos Aires Police of excessive force. The report ends with the officer's evaluations, which indicate why this report might further matter to the DIPPBA:

In conclusion, it is thought that given the emphasis placed on protest by the members of this group, that they will persist with their stance towards gaining legal status, in order to obtain equality in living and working conditions. Such a situation could provoke greater frictions between residents and "travestis" which would result in a greater number of police reports, without discounting that something of greater magnitude could come to pass due to any of the involved sectors.[45]

As the report's language makes clear, such activist demands not only denounced police violence but were also perceived by the police force as a threat to civil obedience warranting surveillance.[46] Such monitoring of political organizations suggests an expanded target of surveillance that, at times, includes travestis as social agents whose political demands for "equality" might implicate the police forces in contemporary human rights abuses. Yet such human rights abuses during democracy also serve to underscore the violence that becomes possible in the context of a liberal state, which aims to assign "state violence" to an illiberal past.

Campaña DESAPARECER and State Violence under Liberalism

Examining artist-activist interventions and archives similarly reveals the shifting (if distinct) politics of sex/gender in activist responses to state terror and its afterlife. The artist-activist intervention Campaña DESAPARECER organized for the tenth anniversary of Jorge Julio López's disappearance highlights such transformations by giving visual form to the fantasy of liberal democracy as free from state violence. Indeed, Jorge Julio López—the subject whose face appears in the image at the start of this article (fig. 2)—was disappeared twice: once in 1976 and again in 2006. His final disappearance remains unsolved, and Campaña DESAPARECER emerged in response one decade later, as I will discuss shortly.

On October 27, 1976, Jorge Julio López was disappeared in Los Hornos, kidnapped during the dictatorship in the middle of the night by a task force composed of members of the armed forces, security forces, and paramilitary groups under the command of Miguel Osvaldo Etchecolatz, police commissioner general and general director of investigations of the Buenos Aires Provincial Police.[47] Jorge Julio López was an *albañil*, or bricklayer, and member of the "Juan Pablo Maestre"[48] unit affiliated with the radical left activist group Peronist Youth, once located on the corner of 68th and 142nd Streets in La Plata's Los Hornos neighborhood.[49] After that night, López was officially disappeared. Over the next year, he passed through multiple clandestine detention centers under the La Plata Group's control within the Clandestine Detention Centers (CCD) circuit subzone 1-1 including el Pozo de Arana, the Fifth and Eighth Comisarías, and the Unidad 9.[50] La Plata Group's territory contained 43 percent of all operational CCDs in Argentina, rendering La Plata and its outskirts a particular hotbed of repression.[51]

In 1977, for unknown reasons, López's disappearance was "legalized." He was officially labeled a political prisoner and his family informed of his whereabouts. On June 25, 1979, he was suddenly released.[52] Following his release, López kept to himself. Until dictatorship ended in 1983, it remained a veritable death sentence to discuss any aspect of one's disappearance, in the extremely rare circumstance that one resurfaced alive. López soon joined the group Ex-Detenidos Desaparecidos, or Formerly Detained and Disappeared Persons, formed in 1984. Yet it was not until 2006 that he would have the opportunity to testify in a trial against his torturer Etchecolatz in an attempt to find justice where none had been served. In September 2006, in Case 2251/06, Etchecolatz was sentenced for the illegal privation of liberty of Jorge Julio López and Nilda Emma Eloy; the murder of Diana Esmeralda Teruggi de Mariani; and the kidnappings, torture, and murder of Ambrosio Francisco De Marco, Patricia Graciela Dell'Orto, Elena Arce Sahores, Nora Livia Formiga, and Margarita Delgado, who all remain disappeared.[53] The day of Etchecolatz's sentencing, September 19, 2006, student, labor, and political organizations filled La Plata's central plaza, Plaza Moreno, where Etchecolatz's sentencing and verdict were projected onto a giant screen.[54] The courtroom was so packed that not even the trial lawyers could get through to take their places.[55]

Yet as Judge Carlos Alberto Rozanski read Etchecolatz's verdict aloud, Jorge Julio López was not in the courtroom. Indeed, López failed to meet plaintiff Nilda Eloy at 9:00 that morning as they had promised one another; he was nowhere to be seen.[56] As the days passed, it became clear that on September 18, 2006, the then seventy-seven-year-old López was disappeared for a second time, twenty-three years after dictatorship ended and in *plena democracia*. His body has never resurfaced and the investigation remains open, if stalled. López's accusations along with Eloy's had resulted in Etchecolatz's arrest: Etchecolatz had personally tortured López in La Plata's Eighth Comisaría.[57] López's crucial testimony at the Tribunal Oral Federal 1 of La Plata in one of the first trials to open against *genocidas* identified at least sixty-two military and police officials who had tortured, detained, kidnapped, and disappeared people.[58]

Perversely, as journalist Adriana Meyer remarked on the tenth anniversary of López's disappearance, López's second and final disappearance "reinstalled the collective perception that one could disappear in democracy."[59] Indeed, López remains the only former survivor—a previously disappeared person—now disappeared for a second time after providing testimony in one of the nation's most high-profile trials.[60] López's disappearance violently called into question the boundary between liberal and illiberal state formations and their attendant ideologies, underscoring material and ideological continuities between the two.[61]

Immediately following López's second and final disappearance in 2006, stenciled images of López were graffitied in public spaces across the nation. In La Plata, the response was particularly sharp. Activist groups quickly painted an enormous bust of López on the bricks forming Plaza Moreno, La Plata's central plaza. Interventions like these certainly have an impact—especially those staged in such a central location as Plaza Moreno—but in 2016, after ten years of the same collective demand, some activists felt that the call for López's "¡aparición con vida!" or "appearance alive" had lost its initial punch. In particular, activists from the united political front La Brecha decided to take action. La Brecha's chapters exist in eleven Argentine provinces and, as an umbrella, the political front includes organizations such as Marabunta, a socialist feminist organization; FOL (Frente de Organizaciones en Lucha), a territorial and *piquetero*[62] organization; and Hagamos lo Imposible, a youth and cultural organization. Acting in concert under the banner "La Brecha," these organizations are able to make collective demands with increased presence and political heft. In an interview with La Brecha La Plata members, the communications team explained that the local chapter is intimately linked to the piquetero movements and has strong representation in ten La Plata neighborhoods with deep ties to union and neighborhood activist groups, or *activismos barriales*, in largely marginalized and popular-class neighborhoods.[63] La Brecha's local communications team is predominantly concerned with generating the visual aesthetics for large-scale protests and marches such as those that occur each year in the city to mark López's second disappearance and for massive marches that occur annually, such as the national March 24 protest marking the coup d'état. The team disseminates the images nationally through La Brecha's broad provincial network of chapters located throughout Argentina.

La Brecha's interventions are designed to *hacer ruido*, or "make noise," within a human rights environment dominated, in part, by the Madres, Abuelas, and HIJOS.[64] These trail-blazing activist movements remain absolutely vital to human rights struggles in Argentina. Nevertheless, their predominance at times limits the potential of activist visual culture such as photography of the disappeared by fixing the disappeared as a stock group of subjects targeted during dictatorship. As a result, visual culture images of the disappeared have come to form a static archive whose meaning has calcified.[65] La Brecha thus attempts to disrupt this activist imagery's meanings in part by introducing new subjects and resignifying disappearance. As one member[66] explained, La Brecha's image-making process is, in response, "like a search to destabilize" some of these more iconic activist images.[67] By drawing on a historic visual archive of national icons and genres such as photography of the disappeared, La Brecha destabilizes meaning by creating unexpected equivalencies between social sectors that call into question crystallized social, historical, and activist relations, as with the Campaña DESAPARECER. In 2016, for the tenth anniversary marking Jorge Julio López's disappearance, La Brecha thus turned its attention to López's image, employing these same disruptive tactics.

Indeed, after ten years, Jorge Julio López's image was at risk of banalization. So La Brecha did something unthinkable: they digitally altered photographer Helen

Figure 4. "Campaña DESAPARECER." 2016. Courtesy of La Brecha La Plata's Communications Team.

Zout's iconic portrait of Jorge Julio López, photoshopping his image with stereotypical visual marks (fig. 4) that immediately call to mind multiple marginalized collectives such as indigenous subjects, at-risk adolescents from popular-class neighborhoods, and travesti subjects as with the image of "López como las travas" (fig. 2) with which I began this article.

Here, La Brecha plays with not only the subject but also the conventions of portraiture of the disappeared. In these six images, moving from left to right, López's portrait appears variously layered with hats, hair, and other visual signifiers including lush lips and mole, a *trarilongko* or indigenous Mapuche ceremonial headband, and a keffiyeh, a mass-produced Palestinian headscarf worn by Argentine *piqueterxs* to protect themselves during protest.[68] In each case, López appears represented as a particular collective subject—sex-trafficked women, marginalized adolescents targeted by police violence, travestis, indigenous subjects, and *piqueterxs*. In layering López's portrait with several marginalized collectivities, this intervention frames multiple social issues as intersecting and suggests that contemporary practices of state violence and oppression are continuous across social sectors in democracy.

In highlighting the reemergence of disappearance by mobilizing López's image, La Brecha further challenges the figuration of democracy as nonviolent to its citizenry. La Brecha's activist intervention thus productively puts pressure on the juxtaposition of "fascist" versus "democratic" by spawning open-ended provocations that underscore the violence that liberalism itself generates. As La Brecha wryly reminds in an interview: "No state apparatus goes to bed genocidal then wakes up democratic."[69] Indeed, the mobilization and alteration of these historic visual archives draw attention to the fantasy of liberal democracy as panacea rather than perpetrator of state violence. Returning to "López like the travestis" (fig. 2), in which López's headshot appears layered over with a travesti silhouette, Campaña

DESAPARECER raises a series of questions directly related to travesti identity: Are travesti subjects experiencing illiberal forms of state violence presently? Can travesti subjects be considered "disappeared" during dictatorship?

Testimony: Trans and Travesti Experiences of State Terror

Since 2012, following the passage of Argentina's Gender Identity Law, travestis and trans women such as Valeria del Mar Ramírez have begun to come forward, articulating their experiences of detention during dictatorship as disappearance.[70] Indeed, as Valeria Canal, one of Ramírez's lawyers, has stated, the Gender Identity Law is in part what facilitated Ramírez's decision: "Now, as Valeria, she has come forward, because the person who was a kidnapping and torture victim was not [name assigned at birth] but instead Valeria. Now with her new DNI [national identity document] and her rectified birth certificate she decided to present herself as a complainant."[71] Without her rectified DNI, Ramírez would have had to discuss intimate details of her detention and torture as if she were a masculine subject, addressed with masculine pronouns and a masculine name assigned at birth. Testifying under such circumstances would have further perpetuated the sexual and gender violence her torturers physically and psychologically inflicted. With her new DNI in hand, however, Ramírez became the first travesti witness in Argentina in a trial prosecuting crimes against humanity when she testified concerning crimes committed in the Pozo de Banfield concentration camp,[72] where she was detained in both 1976 and 1977.[73]

As Ramírez recounts in her official judicial testimony signed by her lawyers María Valeria Canal and Carlos Federico Gaitán Hairabedian, it was not uncommon for her to be detained; police operatives from the Monte Grande and Avellaneda Brigadas de Moralidad, or Morality Brigades, typically arrested Ramírez and transferred her to the *comisarías* or police headquarters. However, on one night between 1976 and 1977, the Buenos Aires Police detained Ramírez along with other travestis and trans women including Romina, la Hormiga, la Sonia, and la Mono. Police officers registered their fingerprints and asked them to wait in an office. Rather than release them or take them to a comisaría as was typical, the police officers transferred them to the clandestine torture and detention center El Pozo de Banfield, where Ramírez first spent two days. She describes her detention in which she was repeatedly raped by multiple guards: "Each one of us was in a cell that measured 1×2 meters, with a cement bench, a lightbulb, and the only ventilation was the slot in the door for food. They made me have sexual relations with the guards and my food and ability to use the bathroom depended on it."[74] In September 1977, she was transferred and detained again in el Pozo de Banfield where she was held fourteen days and suffered the same torture: "The same uniformed man of robust build perpetuated abuses and rape as before . . . multiple guards raped me almost every day, up to four times in a single day. I was made to perform oral sex through the food slot in the door, I was anally raped without a condom by a young police officer. I was systematically physically and psychologically tortured."[75]

Ramírez's testimony and multiple detentions make clear that the extreme sexual and psychological torture she suffered was systematic. Of the travesti and trans women detained in El Pozo de Banfield with Ramírez, Ramírez is the only survivor. According to Ramírez, security forces targeted, kidnapped, and tortured her because of her gender identity:

> At that time, they arrested you just for being a travesti. If you were walking on the road at night practicing prostitution or if you were in the bakery buying bread it was all the same, you always had to hide from the police. . . . We lived by night. If we went out during the day there was no way to hide ourselves. We even knew that we shouldn't go on paved roads where the patrol cars and Ford Falcons circulated. Always like that, in hiding, getting together in our friends' houses, helping one another between ourselves so that others could be who they are without shame. We passed information to one another if someone was detained in a police station. We told each other if there was a police raid. We helped each other hide. That was our activism. We fought for our identity in spite of the police and a society that didn't understand us.[76]

Her testimony draws parallels between her experience and those of other non-trans and non-travesti activists: "We lived by night. If we went out during the day there was no way to hide ourselves. . . . We told each other if there was a police raid. We helped each other hide." Her emphasis on a networked response to such terror suggests the systemic persecution that she and other trans women and travestis faced during dictatorship. Reflecting on the reason for her constant detentions, Ramírez stated: "I was always Valeria and 'being Valeria' caused me to experience persecution, discrimination, abuses, rapes, and it also led me to be kidnapped and tortured in a clandestine detention center."[77]

A historic ruling on May 17, 2018, corroborates Ramírez's allegations. On that day, Carolina Boetti of Rosario, Santa Fe Province, became the first trans woman in Argentina to successfully draw on the same legal apparatus that grants pensions to victims of dictatorship under Santa Fe's Provincial Law 13.298 (2012) to receive economic reparations. The 2012 law extends a monthly pension to people who were illegally detained between March 24, 1976, and December 10, 1983, "due to political, union, or student reasons."[78] Previously, trans women and travestis were unable to access the pension, because gender identity was not considered a primary reason for detention.[79] Yet, for the first time, in 2018, Argentine judges in Santa Fe Province reinterpreted the 2012 law by recognizing that, in trans woman Carolina Boetti's case, she was "illegally detained and persecuted" during dictatorship "because of her gender identity," ruling in her favor.[80] While this ruling is currently effective only at the provincial level, such a move opens the door for trans women and travestis detained during dictatorship to receive national economic reparations under the same legislation currently in place for non-trans and non-travesti *desaparecidas/os*. By granting Boetti economic reparations, the judges implicitly ruled that trans and travesti gender identification was (and is) political, that gender identification can be considered a primary cause for detention; and that travestis and trans women can be considered desaparecidas. The ruling set a new legal precedent and, in response, Boetti stated: "I'm very happy because justice was served. My story is that of many trans women who suffered dictatorship, where we were detained and were victims of violence and aberrations. This monthly pension is a historic reparation. . . . Never again."[81] Boetti stresses that this moment is historic, and she ends with "Nunca más" or "Never again"—the refrain often repeated in reference to genocide. In granting Boetti reparations, perhaps most importantly, the state claimed responsibility for her detention, recognizing the continuities in detention during dictatorship due to "political, union, or student reasons" and "gender identity."

Conclusion

Taken together, the DIPPBA archival documents, La Brecha's Campaña DESAPARECER, and trans women's and travestis' testimony all ask us to contend with questions about the targets of dictatorship—a dictatorship undergirded by Argentina's fascist nacionalista ideology whose expression takes as its most extreme form torture and extermination in the Argentine concentration camps. Yet, as these trans and travesti testimonies make clear, illiberal state violence targeted a range of marginalized subjects during dictatorship. The sex/gender politics of surveillance and glimmers of sex and gender practices evinced by traces in the DIPPBA archive further suggest the latent import of sex/gender to security forces.

Similarly, La Brecha's visual activism gives visual form to the reemergence of disappearance and contemporary forms of state violence targeting a number of minoritarian subjects. La Brecha's Campaña DESAPARECER cites the Mothers' historic visual culture archive to mobilize photography of the disappeared, layering photographer Helen Zout's headshot of López with representations of other collectives to suggest that Argentine history is a palimpsest. Like La Brecha's image composition itself, palimpsests overlay past with present. Yet the past juts up, texturing the present to produce unexpected meanings that might alter historical interpretation, productively challenging the targets of fascist state violence during dictatorship. In so doing, this activist intervention troubles the boundaries of fascist nacionalista ideology, state violence, and its subjects.

At the same time, reparations, testimony, and activist interventions such as La Brecha's highlight how activists are mobilizing the past in the present to mediate contemporary political demands. That is, in democracy, the persistent afterlife of fascism creates conditions of possibility for activists to mobilize the language of anti-fascism and shared memories of fascist violence—namely dictatorship, genocide, and disappearance—in the service of contemporary rights claims. Activists are working against and working with the memory and afterlife of fascism as a shifting ideology and set of material practices that persist into the present. As testimonies of trans women and travestis such as Valeria del Mar Ramírez and Carolina Boetti suggest, trans subjectivity is contoured in the present by historic forms of state violence. As these testimonies further demand, we must continue to grapple with illiberal state violence and such violence's deadly imbrications with the politics of sex and gender. Rather than memorialize anti-fascist responses to such violence in order to remember a distant illiberal past, we must identify the ways in which liberalism itself perpetuates violent state practices in order to contest them. Such a move will require mobilizing a broad coalitional politics rooted in the shared material and symbolic stakes of our ongoing collective struggles to combat the enduring legacies of fascism.

Cole Rizki is assistant professor of Spanish at the University of Virginia. He is a coeditor of the *TSQ: Transgender Studies Quarterly* special issue "Trans Studies en las Américas," and his work appears in journals such as *TSQ*, *GLQ*, and the *Journal of Visual Culture*, among others. His research focuses on transgender politics and cultural production throughout the Americas.

Notes

I thank my colleagues Chase Gregory, Ella Fratantuono, Carolyn Laubender, Michael Becker, Robyn Wiegman, Erica Rand, and Antonio Viego for their critical generosity and rigorous commentary on drafts of this essay. Two anonymous reviewers' insights and this issue's guest editors greatly improved the quality of this manuscript. Special thanks to historian Ana Cecilia Solari Paz and author Cristián Oscar Jilberto Prieto Carrasco of the Comisión Provincial por la Memoria for their archival assistance; to the activists of La Brecha for their bold interventions; and to the trans women and travesti activists whose fierce activism continues to rewrite history.

1. While the Argentine case does not meet the United Nation's criteria for genocide, Argentine Federal Court decisions and activists name the violence perpetrated during this period (1976–83) as such. I therefore use the term *genocide* throughout in recognition of national politics and activist epistemologies. See Rozanski, *Etchecolatz, Miguel Osvaldo*; Feierstein, *El genocidio como práctica social*. All translations from Spanish are mine unless otherwise noted.

2. *La opinión*, "Gobierna la junta militar"; Radio Nacional Argentina, "Comunicado Número 1°"; *Boletín oficial número 23.372*.

3. "Acta fijando el propósito y los objetivos básicos para el proceso de reorganización nacional"; Radio Nacional Argentina, "Comunicado Número 1°."

4. For the authoritative National Commission on the Disappearance of Persons (CONADEP) report on state terror published in 1984, see CONADEP, *Nunca más*. While CONADEP lists only 8,960 disappearances, the commission acknowledges that

"we have reason to believe that the true figure is much higher. Many families were reluctant to report a disappearance for fear of reprisals. Some still hesitate, fearing a resurgence of these evil forces" (CONADEP, *Nunca más*, 447, 5). Prominent human rights groups estimate thirty thousand people were disappeared, and I use thirty thousand throughout in recognition of activist claims.

5. According to the CONADEP report, the armed forces created 340 Clandestine Torture, Detention, and Extermination Centers (CCDTyE) throughout the country to murder its citizens (CONADEP, *Nunca más*, 447). Of those detained, 86.6 percent were taken from their homes and off the streets (CONADEP, *Nunca más*, 11). Of the disappeared, 81.39 percent were between the ages of sixteen and thirty-five, while 70 percent of the total disappeared were men and 30 percent women. An estimated 3 percent of these women were pregnant at time of disappearance (CONADEP, *Nunca más*, 285–86).

6. Jinkis, "Ni muerto ni vivo." Videla uses the masculine form *desaparecido*, where the masculine folds both men and women into his statement.

7. Prior to the coup and throughout the early 1970s, radical leftist activist groups such as the left-wing Peronist Montoneros and the Marxist-Leninist People's Revolutionary Army (ERP) had formed, and these groups set out to undertake an armed revolution. The Montoneros and ERP targeted government and police officials, killing at least eight hundred prior to the 1976 coup. CONADEP, *Nunca más*, xii. These targeted assaults included the assassination of former Argentine president Pedro Eugenio Aramburu, whom the Montoneros kidnapped and executed on June 1, 1970. Catela, "Juicio y muerte a Aramburu." As Marguerite Feitlowitz notes, armed leftists, while active in the early 1970s, had largely been eliminated prior to the 1976 coup, and their numbers were widely exaggerated by the armed forces. Feitlowitz, *Lexicon of Terror*, 313.

8. For an authoritative account of the Mothers of the Plaza de Mayo, see Ulises Gorini's two-volume history: *La rebelión de las madres*; *La otra lucha*. See also publications by the Mothers including Hebe de Bonafini's speeches: de Bonafini, *Seguir pariendo*. It is of note that, over internal conflicts, the Mothers split into two lines in January 1986: Línea Fundadora and Asociación. For an overview of major distinctions between the Mothers' activisms, see Rosenblatt, "Politics of Grief."

9. For an excellent account of the Mothers' use of visual culture, including portraiture of the disappeared, see Longoni, "Photographs and Silhouettes."

10. Berkins, "Travestis."

11. Cornejo, "*Travesti* Dreams Outside in the Ethnographic Machine," 457.

12. Guimaraes García, *La roy*, 56; Rizki, "Latin/x American Trans Studies," 149. For superb recent scholarship on travesti social and political formations, see Cornejo, "*Travesti* Dreams Outside in the Ethnographic Machine"; Di Pietro, "Decolonizing *Travesti* Space in Buenos Aires"; and Sabsay, *Fronteras sexuales*. The latter two works focus on Argentine travesti politics, identifications, and activisms.

13. Berkins, "Travestis." *Travesti* is a highly politicized term. As Berkins elaborates, in the 1990s, as travesti activism emerged in Argentina, travesti activists "decided to give new meaning to the word *travesti* and link it with political struggle, resistance, dignity, and happiness." In this way, *travesti* has been reclaimed as a potent site of political possibility. For foundational studies on Argentine travesti identity, see Berkins, *Cumbia, copeteo y lágrimas*; Programa de Género y Diversidad Sexual and Bachillerato Popular Mocha Celis, *La revolución de las mariposas*.

14. See Cowan, *Securing Sex*; Manzano, *Age of Youth in Argentina*; Manzano, "Sex, Gender, and the Making of the 'Enemy Within'"; Green, "(Homo)sexuality, Human Rights, and Revolution"; Insausti, "Los cuatrocientos homosexuales desaparecidos"; Figari, "Queer Argie"; Carvajal, "Image Politics and Disturbing Temporalities"; Rizki, "Familiar Grammars of Loss and Belonging"; and Hiner and Garrido, "Antitrans State Terrorism." The latter four articles in particular pay nuanced attention to trans and travesti experiences of authoritarianism and the politics of visibility in Argentina and Chile.
15. Finchelstein, *Ideological Origins of the Dirty War*, 1.
16. Finchelstein, *Ideological Origins of the Dirty War*, 7.
17. Finchelstein, *Ideological Origins of the Dirty War*, 7; Finchelstein, *Transatlantic Fascism*, 8; Spektorowski, *Origins of Argentina's Revolution of the Right*; Deutsch, *Las derechas*; Finchelstein, *Fascismo, liturgia e imaginario*.
18. Deutsch, *Las derechas*, 4.
19. Deutsch, "Contra 'el gran desorden sexual,'" 133.
20. Deutsch, "Contra 'el gran desorden sexual,'" 133, 134.
21. Deutsch, *Las derechas*. See in particular chap. 11, "Brazil: A Revolution of the Heart and Soul," 282–89. On the cross-fertilization of integralista, fascist, and nacionalista ideology more broadly, see Bertonha and Bohoslavsky, *Circule por la derecha*.
22. Finchelstein, *Ideological Origins of the Dirty War*, 58.
23. On continuities between Tacuara and nacionalismo see Lvovich, *El nacionalismo de derecha*.
24. Finchelstein, *Ideological Origins of the Dirty War*, 111–12.
25. Finchelstein, *Ideological Origins of the Dirty War*, 115.
26. As a paradigmatic example, Nuestro Mundo, the first homosexual organization in Argentina, understood sex and gender as both political and intrinsic to radical left political projects. In attempting to align with dominant left political parties, Marxist activisms, and the Peronist Left alike, however, the group was consistently rejected due to pervasive homophobia. See Insausti, "Los cuatrocientos homosexuales desaparecidos," 66.
27. Insausti, "Los cuatrocientos homosexuales desaparecidos," 66.
28. Finchelstein, *Ideological Origins of the Dirty War*, 120.
29. "Guía de archivos y fondos documentales." The archive was declassified in 2003 and is now open to the public and family members who use the archive to search for information surrounding their loved ones' disappearance and last known whereabouts. The archive is also actively used as evidence for trials prosecuting crimes against humanity.
30. "Comisión Provincial por la Memoria."
31. While it is outside the scope of this article to provide a detailed account of Peronist political ideology, for a selection of foundational work, see Di Tella and Lucchini, *América Latina*; Germani, *Authoritarianism, Fascism, and National Populism*, in which Germani compares the conditions of Latin American authoritarianism and European fascism. For reflections on Peronism, see chap. 5 of Germani's text: "Political Traditions and Social Mobilization at the Root of a National Populist Movement: Argentine Peronism." See also Brennan, *Peronism and Argentina*; James, *Resistance and Integration*. For a consideration of Peronism's populist and fascist undercurrents see chap. 4, "Peronist Populism and Fascism," in Finchelstein, *Ideological Origins of the Dirty War*.
32. "Comisión Provincial por la Memoria."
33. Solari Paz and Prieto Carrasco, "Cuerpos disidentes," 2.

34. CPM-Fondo DIPPBA, División Central de Documentación, Registro y Archivo, Mesa Doctrina, Legajo N° 207. I thank Solari Paz and Prieto Carrasco for directing me to this document.

35. Comisión por la Memoria, *Historia institucional de la DIPPBA*, 19.

36. I thank Solari Paz and Prieto Carrasco for directing me to this document.

37. See CPM-Fondo DIPPBA, División Central de Documentación, Registro y Archivo, Mesa "D(s)," Carpeta Varios, Legajo N° 28.139; CPM-Fondo DIPPBA, División Central de Documentación, Registro y Archivo, Mesa "D(s)," Carpeta Varios, Legajo N° 35.337; and CPM-Fondo DIPPBA, División Central de Documentación, Registro y Archivo, Mesa "D(s)," Carpeta Varios, Legajo N° 35.850.

38. See for example CPM-Fondo DIPPBA, División Central de Documentación, Registro y Archivo, Mesa "D(s)," Carpeta Varios, Legajo N° 30.594 and CPM-Fondo DIPPBA, División Central de Documentación, Registro y Archivo, Mesa "D(s)," Carpeta Varios, Legajo N° 31.213.

39. CPM-Fondo DIPPBA, División Central de Documentación, Registro y Archivo, Mesa "D(s)," Legajo N° 31.119.

40. CPM-Fondo DIPPBA, División Central de Documentación, Registro y Archivo, Mesa "D(s)," Legajo N° 35.333.

41. Fernández, *Cuerpos desobedientes*, 116–17; Berkins, "Un itinerario político del travestismo," 129–31; Berkins, *La gesta del nombre propio*; Guimaraes García, *La roy*, 25.

42. Lohana Berkins (travesti activist, Buenos Aires), interview by Hebe de Bonafini.

43. As she states on another occasion, although travesti activism was influenced by the Mothers' demands, this influence and understanding was uneven. Berkins, "Un itinerario político del travestismo," 132. This hostility was not unique to the Mothers. The entrenched homophobia of leftist activist movements during the 1970s through the 1990s such as the Juventud Peronista, to which López belonged before his first disappearance, also led such groups to be openly hostile toward nonnormatively sexed and gendered subjects. After dictatorship during the consolidation of democracy, leftist hostility endured. As James N. Green notes, across Latin America following authoritarianism, "when public debates occurred, representatives of leftist groups argued that personal or sexual questions remained secondary considerations in the process of defeating dictatorships . . . and in the efforts to expand democracy" (Green, "(Homo)sexuality, Human Rights, and Revolution in Latin America," 143).

44. CPM-Fondo DIPPBA, División Central de Documentación, Registro y Archivo, Mesa "D(e)", Factor Social, Año 1994, Legajo N° 824. The city of Mar del Plata is located in Buenos Aires Province and fell under the DIPPBA's jurisdiction.

45. Quotes around *travesti* appear in the original report.

46. While the policing of nonnormative sexual and gender practices is hardly uncommon and exists across fascist and post-fascist states as well as those that were never fascist, my point here is to draw attention to the particular national histories and ideological constructions that might subtend or fuel such policing practices.

47. Brienza, "Variaciones sobre López," 35.

48. The group named their collective "Juan Pablo Maestre" after a member of Fuerzas Armadas Revolucionarias (Armed Revolutionary Forces) who was shot and killed in July 1971 after leaving his partner Mirta Misetich's parents' house located in Buenos Aires's Belgrano neighborhood. Asuaje, "Lo que el pueblo tiene que saber," 17.

49. Asuaje, "Lo que el pueblo tiene que saber," 21.

50. Brienza, "Variaciones sobre López," 35.

51. Brienza, "Variaciones sobre López," 35.

52. Brienza, "Variaciones sobre López," 35.

53. Rozanski, *Etchecolatz, Miguel Osvaldo*, 92–93.

54. Graziano, *En el cielo nos vemos*, 41.

55. Graziano, *En el cielo nos vemos*, 41.

56. Rosende and Pertot, *Los días sin López*, 23.

57. Brienza, "Variaciones sobre López," 37–38.

58. Brienza, "Variaciones sobre López," 37.

59. Meyer, "Diez años sin López."

60. Meyer, "Otro aniversario sin Jorge Julio López."

61. While the phrase "disappeared in democracy" cropped up around López's disappearance, López's is not the only high-profile case of disappearance to occur. Most recently, on August 1, 2017, Santiago Maldonado, a twenty-eight-year-old tattoo artist and anarchist, was disappeared from the indigenous Mapuche community Pu Lof en Resistencia in the Cushamen Department of Chubut Province, Argentina. Maldonado had joined a Mapuche road blockade demanding the release of Mapuche activist and leader Facundo Jones Huala, wanted by the Chilean government on terrorism charges. Politi and Londoño, "Police and Protestors Clash." After breaking up the blockade, Argentina's National Gendarmerie stormed and terrorized the adjacent community, and Maldonado was disappeared during the ensuing military raid. Barreiro, "La desaparición de un joven." Maldonado's disappearance resulted in massive protests and similarly served as a flashpoint, making clear the persistent reemergence of disappearance in democracy.

62. The identity category *piquetero* emerged to describe protestors from the popular class forming part of the Argentine unemployed movements that reached their height in the early 2000s, after the 2001 economic crisis that sent over half of the country's population spiraling beneath the poverty line. Borland and Sutton, "Quotidian Disruption and Women's Activism," 701.

63. La Brecha Communications Team, Skype interview by author, May 5, 2018.

64. Founded in 1995, HIJOS or Sons and Daughters for Identity and Justice Against Forgetting and Silence emerged when, through DNA testing, the Grandmothers (Abuelas de Plaza de Mayo) recuperated them from military or complicit families who had kidnapped them at birth. HIJOS activism is defined by its *escraches*, or ludic public protests, that occurred largely during the 1990s, aiming to *escrachar* or publicly identify and shame those involved with dictatorship. Taylor, "'You Are Here.'"

65. La Brecha Communications Team, interview.

66. I withhold La Brecha's Communications Team members' names out of privacy concerns.

67. La Brecha Communications Team, Skype interview by author, May 5, 2018.

68. The *x* is used to modify *piqueteros*, signaling that non-trans, travesti, and trans subjects all participate in this movement. Well-known travesti activist Diana Sacayán, for example, participated tirelessly in piquetero movements before her 2015 murder in an unrelated hate crime.

69. La Brecha Communications Team, Skype interview by author, May 5, 2018.

70. *Identidad de Género 2012*, Ley Público Núm. 26.743 (2012). Travesti and trans people living in Argentina are presently able to change their name and gender markers on all documents through free bureaucratic procedures without pathologizing diagnoses or invasive surgical or hormonal requirements. Further, in reframing "gender identity" as a

universal right to which all persons should have access free of diagnoses, bureaucratic hurdles, or unwanted medical-psychiatric management and interference, the Argentine Gender Identity Law remains one of the most progressive national gender identity laws to date. For more on the politics of the Gender Identity Law, see de Mauro Rucovsky, "The Travesti Critique of the Gender Identity Law in Argentina."

71. I have intentionally chosen to use "[name assigned at birth]" out of respect for Ramírez even though the newspaper article includes her name assigned at birth. Meyer, "'Ser Valeria me llevó a ser secuestrada.'"

72. Sociologist Pilar Calveiro, among others, has argued persuasively for the use of the term *concentration camp* in reference to the 340 clandestine detention, torture, and extermination centers operational in Argentina during dictatorship due to the systematized logic of killing employed in such spaces. See Calveiro, *Poder y desaparición.*

73. Meyer, "'Ser Valeria me llevó a ser secuestrada.'"

74. Meyer, "'Ser Valeria me llevó a ser secuestrada.'"

75. Meyer, "'Ser Valeria me llevó a ser secuestrada.'"

76. Meyer, "'Ser Valeria me llevó a ser secuestrada.'"

77. Meyer, "'Ser Valeria me llevó a ser secuestrada.'"

78. *Pensión para presos políticos, gremiales o estudiantiles (1976–1983).*

79. It is of note that even leftist activists do not always agree that resources should be shared with travestis and trans subjects also detained during dictatorship. Máximo and Prieto, "¿Dónde está la memoria LGBTI?" Thus, although the Santa Fe Province government awarded Carolina Boetti reparations, this was not a move without controversy.

80. Agencia Presentes, "Por primera vez, el Estado repara a una trans sobreviviente de la dictadura."

81. Agencia Presentes, "Por primera vez, el Estado repara a una trans sobreviviente de la dictadura."

References

"Acta fijando el propósito y los objetivos básicos para el proceso de reorganización nacional." Reproduced in "Para el Proceso de Reorganización Nacional: Propósitos y objetivos básicos." *La Opinión*, March 24, 1976.

Agencia Presentes. "Por primera vez, el Estado repara a una trans sobreviviente de la dictadura." *Agencia Presentes*, May 18, 2018. agenciapresentes.org/2018/05/18/por-primera -vez-el-estado-repara-a-una-trans-sobreviviente-de-la-dictadura.

Asuaje, Jorge Pastor. "Lo que el pueblo tiene que saber." In *Jorge Julio López: Memoria escrita*, edited by Jorge Caterbetti, 13–32. Buenos Aires: Marea Editorial, 2012.

Barreiro, Ramiro. 2017. "La desaparición de un joven durante un conflicto con mapuches moviliza a Argentina." *El país*, August 8, 2017. elpais.com/internacional/2017/08/07 /argentina/1502124830_768290.html.

Berkins, Lohana, ed. *Cumbia, copeteo y lágrimas: Informe nacional sobre la situación de las travestis, transexuales y transgéneros.* 2nd ed. Buenos Aires: Ediciones Madres de Plaza de Mayo, 2015.

Berkins, Lohana. *La gesta del nombre propio. Informe sobre la situación de la comunidad travesti en la Argentina.* Buenos Aires: Ediciones Madres de Plaza de Mayo, 2005.

Berkins, Lohana. Interview by Hebe de Bonafini, Auditorio Juana Azurduy, June 11, 2012. YouTube video, posted by Madres de Plaza de Mayo, June 18, 2012. www.youtube.com /watch?v=wk1W2ug7otE.

Berkins, Lohana. "Travestis: Una identidad política." Paper presented at the conference "VIII Jornadas Nacionales de Historia de las Mujeres/III Congreso Iberoamericano de Estudios de Género DiferenciaDesigualdad: Construirnos en la diversidad," Villa Giardino, Córdoba, Argentina, October 25–28, 2006. hemisphericinstitute.org/en/emisferica-42/4-2 -review-essays/lohana-berkins.html#_edn2 (accessed September 15, 2019).

Berkins, Lohana. "Un itinerario político del travestismo." In *Sexualidades migrantes: Género y transgénero,* edited by Diana Maffía, 127–37. Buenos Aires: Scarlett, 2003.

Bertonha, João Fábio, and Ernesto Lázaro Bohoslavsky, eds. *Circule por la derecha: Percepciones, redes y contactos entre las derechas sudamericanas, 1917–1973.* Buenos Aires: Ediciones UNGS, Universidad Nacional de General Sarmiento, 2016.

Boletín oficial número 23.372. March 26, 1976. www.infoleg.gob.ar/?page_id=216&id=23372 (accessed November 19, 2019).

Borland, Elizabeth, and Barbara Sutton. "Quotidian Disruption and Women's Activism in Times of Crisis, Argentina 2002–2003." *Gender and Society* 21, no. 5 (October 2007): 700–722.

Brennan, James P., ed. *Peronism and Argentina.* Wilmington, DE: SR Books, 1998.

Brienza, Hernán. "Variaciones sobre López." In *Jorge Julio López: Memoria escrita,* edited by Jorge Caterbetti, 33–40. Buenos Aires: Marea, 2012.

Calveiro, Pilar. *Poder y desaparición: Los campos de concentración en Argentina.* Buenos Aires: Colihue, 1998.

Carvajal, Fernanda. "Image Politics and Disturbing Temporalities: On 'Sex Change' Operations in the Early Chilean Dictatorship." *TSQ* 5, no. 4 (2018): 621–37.

Catela, Sonia. "Juicio y muerte a Aramburu." *Página/12,* September 15, 2017. www.pagina12 .com.ar/62881-juicio-y-muerte-a-aramburu.

"Comisión Provincial por la Memoria." Archival Finding Aid and Description. www .comisionporlamemoria.org/archivos/archivo/cuadroclasificacion/ (accessed June 18, 2019).

Comisión Provincial por la Memoria. *Historia institucional de la DIPPBA: La inteligencia policial a través de sus documentos.* www.comisionporlamemoria.org/archivos/archivo /historia-institucional-dippba/historia-institucional-dippba.pdf (accessed September 1, 2019).

CONADEP (Comisión Nacional sobre la Desaparición de Personas). *Nunca más: The Report of the Argentine National Commission on the Disappeared* (English translation). New York: Farrar, Straus, Giroux, 1986.

Cornejo, Giancarlo. "*Travesti* Dreams Outside in the Ethnographic Machine." *GLQ* 25, no. 3 (2019): 457–82.

Cowan, Benjamin. *Securing Sex: Morality and Repression in the Making of Cold War Brazil.* Chapel Hill: University of North Carolina Press, 2016.

De Bonafini, Hebe. *Seguir pariendo: Discursos de Hebe de Bonafini 1983–2012.* Buenos Aires: Ediciones Madres de Plaza de Mayo, 2013.

De Mauro Rucovsky, Martín. "The *Travesti* Critique of the Gender Identity Law in Argentina." *TSQ* 6, no. 2 (2019): 223–38.

Deutsch, Sandra McGee. "Contra 'el gran desorden sexual': Los nacionalistas y la sexualidad, 1919–1940." *Sociohistórica,* no. 17–18 (2005): 127–50. www.sociohistorica.fahce.unlp.edu .ar/article/view/SHn17-18a05.

Deutsch, Sandra McGee. *Las Derechas: The Extreme Right in Argentina, Brazil, and Chile, 1890–1939.* Stanford: Stanford University Press, 1999.

Di Pietro, Pedro José Javier. "Decolonizing *Travesti* Space in Buenos Aires: Race, Sexuality, and Sideways Relationality." *Gender, Place & Culture: A Journal of Feminist Geography* 23, no. 5 (2016): 677–93.

Di Tella, Torcuato Salvador, and Cristina Lucchini, eds. *América Latina. Sociedad y estado, conceptos teóricos y transformaciones históricas*. Buenos Aires: Editorial Biblos, 2008.

Feierstein, Daniel. *El genocidio como práctica social: Entre el nazismo y la experiencia argentina*. Buenos Aires: Fondo de Cultura Económica de Argentina, 2007.

Feitlowitz, Marguerite. *A Lexicon of Terror: Argentina and the Legacies of Torture*. 2nd ed. New York: Oxford University Press, 2011.

Fernández, Josefina. *Cuerpos desobedientes: Travestismo e identidad de género*. Buenos Aires: Edhasa, 2004.

Figari, Carlos. "Queer Argie." *American Quarterly* 66, no. 3 (2014): 621–31.

Finchelstein, Federico. *Fascismo, liturgia e imaginario: El mito del General Uriburu y la Argentina nacionalista*. Buenos Aires: Fondo de Cultura Económica, 2002.

Finchelstein, Federico. *The Ideological Origins of the Dirty War: Fascism, Populism, and Dictatorship in Twentieth Century Argentina*. Oxford: Oxford University Press, 2014.

Finchelstein, Federico. *Transatlantic Fascism: Ideology, Violence, and the Sacred in Argentina and Italy, 1919–1945*. Durham, NC: Duke University Press, 2010.

Germani, Gino. *Authoritarianism, Fascism, and National Populism*. New Brunswick, NJ: Transaction Books, 1978.

Gorini, Ulises. *La otra lucha, 1983–1986*, vol. 2 of *Historia de las Madres de Plaza de Mayo*. La Plata: Editorial de la Universidad Nacional de La Plata, 2017.

Gorini, Ulises. *La rebelión de las madres, 1976–1983*, vol. 1 of *Historia de las Madres de Plaza de Mayo*. La Plata: Editorial de la Universidad Nacional de La Plata, 2017.

Graziano, Miguel. *En el cielo nos vemos: La historia de Jorge Julio López*. Buenos Aires, Argentina: Peña Lillo, Ediciones Continente, 2013.

Green, James N. "(Homo)sexuality, Human Rights, and Revolution in Latin America." In *Human Rights and Revolutions*, edited by Jeffrey N. Wasserstrom et al., 139–53. Lanham, MD: Rowman and Littlefield, 2007.

"Guía de archivos y fondos documentales." Andar, August 6, 2013. www.andaragencia.org/guia -de-archivos-y-fondos-documentales.

Guimaraes García, Florencia. *La roy: Revolución de una trava*. Buenos Aires: Puntos Suspensivos Ediciones, 2017.

Hiner, Hillary, and Juan Carlos Garrido. "Antitrans State Terrorism: Trans and Travesti Women, Human Rights, and Recent History in Chile." *TSQ* 6, no. 2 (2019): 194–209.

Identidad de Género, 2012, Ley Público No. 26.743 (2012). servicios.infoleg.gob.ar /infolegInternet/anexos/195000-199999/197860/norma.htm.

Insausti, Santiago Joaquín. "Los cuatrocientos homosexuales desaparecidos: Memorias de la represión estatal a las sexualidades disidentes en Argentina." In *Deseo y represión: Sexualidad, género y Estado en la historia Argentina reciente*, edited by Débora D'Antonio, 63–82. Buenos Aires: Imago Mundi, 2015.

James, Daniel. *Resistance and Integration: Peronism and the Argentine Working Class, 1946–1976*. London: Cambridge University Press, 1988.

Jinkis, Jorge. "Ni muerto ni vivo." *Página/12*, August 3, 2006. www.pagina12.com.ar/diario /psicologia/9-70866-2006-08-03.html.

La opinión. "Gobierna la junta militar." March 24, 1976.

Longoni, Ana. "Photographs and Silhouettes: Visual Politics in the Human Rights Movement of Argentina." *Afterall: A Journal of Art, Context, and Enquiry* 25, no. 1 (2010): 5–17.

Lvovich, Daniel. *El nacionalismo de derecha: Desde sus orígenes a Tacuara.* Buenos Aires: Capital Intelectual, 2006.

Manzano, Valeria. *The Age of Youth in Argentina: Culture, Politics, and Sexuality from Perón to Videla.* Chapel Hill: University of North Carolina Press, 2014.

Manzano, Valeria. "Sex, Gender, and the Making of the 'Enemy Within' in Cold War Argentina." *Journal of Latin American Studies* 47, no. 1 (2015): 1– 29.

Máximo, Matías, and Cristián Prieto. "¿Dónde está la memoria LGBTI?" *Página/12*, March 18, 2016. www.pagina12.com.ar/diario/suplementos/soy/subnotas/4447-595-2016-03-18.html.

Meyer, Adriana. "Diez años sin López." *Página/12*, September 18, 2016. www.pagina12.com.ar/diario/elpais/1-309682-2016-09-18.html.

Meyer, Adriana. "Otro aniversario sin Jorge Julio López." *Página/12*, September 19, 2014. www.pagina12.com.ar/diario/elpais/1-255650-2014-09-19.html.

Meyer, Adriana. "'Ser Valeria me llevó a ser secuestrada.'" *Página/12*, January 8, 2013. www.pagina12.com.ar/diario/elpais/1-211380-2013-01-08.html.

Pensión para presos políticos, gremiales o estudiantiles (1976–1983), Ley Provincial No. 13.298/2012 (2012). www.santafe.gov.ar/normativa/item.php?id=109765&cod=485d49d7501754d378b4c841bdae459c.

Politi, Daniel, and Ernesto Londoño. 2017. "Police and Protesters Clash over Disappearance of Argentine Activist." *New York Times*, September 2, 2017. www.nytimes.com/2017/09/02/world/americas/argentina-protests-santiago-maldonado.html.

Programa de Género y Diversidad Sexual del Ministerio Público de la Defensa de la Ciudad Autónoma de Buenos Aires and Bachillerato Popular Mocha Celis, eds. *La revolución de las mariposas: A diez años de "La gesta del nombre propio."* Buenos Aires, Argentina: Ministerio Público de la Defensa de la Ciudad Autónoma de Buenos Aires, 2017. www.mpdefensa.gob.ar/biblioteca/pdf/la_revolucion_de_las_mariposas.pdf.

Radio Nacional Argentina, "Comunicado Número 1° de la Junta de Comandantes de las Fuerzas Armadas." March 24, 1976. Transcribed and reprinted by Secretaría de Estado de Prensa y Difusión. In *De memoria: Testimonios, textos y otras fuentes sobre el terrorismo de Estado en Argentina*. Disc 2, "1976," " Folder "b," File "b010.jpg." Edited by Memoria Abierta, la Secretaría de Educación, and la Subsecretaría de Derechos Humanos del Gobierno de la Ciudad de Buenos Aires, 2005.

Rizki, Cole. "Latin/x American Trans Studies: Toward a Travesti-Trans Analytic." In "Trans Studies *en las Américas*," edited by Claudia Sofía Garriga-López, Denilson Lopes, Cole Rizki, and Juana María Rodríguez. Special issue, *TSQ* 6, no. 2 (2019): 145–55.

Rizki, Cole. "Familiar Grammars of Loss and Belonging: Curating Trans Kinship in Post-dictatorship Argentina." *Journal of Visual Culture* 19, no. 2 (2020): 197–211.

Rosenblatt, Adam. "The Politics of Grief." In *Digging for the Disappeared: Forensic Science after Atrocity*, 83–122. Stanford: Stanford University Press, 2015.

Rosende, Luciana, and Werner Pertot. *Los días sin López: El testigo desaparecido en democracia*. Buenos Aires: Planeta, 2013.

Rozanski, Carlos Alberto. *Etchecolatz, Miguel Osvaldo*. Case 2251/06. Federal Criminal Tribunal Número 1, La Plata, Argentina. September 19, 2006.

Sabsay, Leticia. *Fronteras sexuales: Espacio urbano, cuerpos y ciudadanía*. Buenos Aires: Paidós, 2011.

Solari Paz, Ana Cecilia, and Cristián Oscar Jilberto Prieto Carrasco. "Cuerpos disidentes en la mira de la Dirección de Inteligencia de La Policía de La Provincia de Buenos Aires (DIPPBA)." Paper presented at the conference "IX Seminario Internacional Políticas de la Memoria," Centro Cultural Haroldo Conti, Buenos Aires, Argentina, November 3, 2016.

Spektorowski, Alberto. *The Origins of Argentina's Revolution of the Right.* Notre Dame, IN: University of Notre Dame Press, 2003.

Taylor, Diana. "'You Are Here': H.I.J.O.S. and the DNA of Performance." In *The Archive and the Repertoire: Performing Cultural Memory in the Americas*, 161–89. Durham, NC: Duke University Press, 2003.

Global Fascism?

The British National Front and the Transnational Politics of the "Third Way" in the 1980s

Benjamin Bland

In September 1988, three leading members of the British neofascist party the National Front (NF) traveled from London to the Libyan capital of Tripoli. They were there, ostensibly, to learn from the example of Libya's dictator, Colonel Muammar Qathafi, who had come to power in 1969 on the back of a revolutionary military coup. Having deposed the Western-backed monarchy, he led the transformation of Libya into, first, a republic and, from 1977, a unique form of socialist state—a *Jamahiriya* (literally "state of the masses"). Qathafi envisioned the Jamahiriya as the solution to what he cited in *The Green Book* (the ideological handbook he wrote to explain and promote his vision) as "the prime political problem confronting human communities," namely "the instrument of government." Particularly troublesome, Qathafi explained, were parliaments: "The mere existence of a parliament means the absence of the people," he argued, before emphasizing his belief that "true democracy exists only through the direct participation of the people, and not through the activity of their representatives."[1] This interpretation of true democracy infiltrated (at least theoretically) every element of life in Qathafi's Libya, from the rule of law to the running of supermarkets, and was at the heart of what Qathafi believed to be his own unique ideological synthesis: Third Universal Theory.

The NF observers, reporting on their Libyan visit in one of their party journals, suggested that Qathafi's implementation of these ideas had transformed his

Radical History Review
Issue 138 (October 2020)   DOI 10.1215/01636545-8359443
© 2020 by MARHO: The Radical Historians' Organization, Inc.

country into "a progressive and forward-thinking nation" that was naturally "of great interest to National Revolutionaries throughout Europe."[2] At first glance this might seem strange. Qathafi's aforementioned vision of a supposedly pure democracy was always full of many of the same contradictions as those visible in fascism, not least in that its populism and supposed investment of power in the hands of the people ultimately translated into severe authoritarianism.[3] Qathafi's thought was also undeniably anti-Semitic and, like fascism, reached for an approach to political economy that went beyond what was envisaged by either capitalism or communism.[4] It would, however, be a stretch to brand Qathafi's ideology as fascist. Even acknowledging the existence of some crossover between Third Universal Theory and fascism does not, however, necessarily explain how members of an organization like the NF could declare themselves admirers of the Libyan dictator. After all, during the 1970s, the NF made its name through a crude form of racist populism that briefly threatened to attract major support from those Britons opposed to nonwhite immigration—a threat that was ultimately curtailed by a series of party splits and by the strength of anti-fascist opposition.[5] More fundamentally, as contemporaneous research by the social psychologist Michael Billig demonstrated, the 1970s NF was at its core not just neofascist but essentially neo-Nazi, in a mimetic sense. Behind its populist attacks on immigration, the most dedicated members of the NF were largely committed to a worldview dominated by an almost fetishistic faith in and adherence to Hitler's political program and, crucially, to anti-Semitic conspiracy theory.[6]

There was, of course, some degree of alliance between the Third Reich and select Islamic regimes in the Middle East during the Second World War. Fundamentally, however, such collaborations were marriages of convenience, reliant upon the Nazi regime's shift toward pragmatism as the tide of the war turned against them in the early 1940s.[7] Thus, while Nazi-Arab alliances may have, in Jeffrey Herf's words, "leapt over the seemingly insurmountable barriers created by [the Nazi] ideology of Aryan racial superiority," this was essentially a process in which existing Nazi anti-Semitic propaganda was adapted according "to the religious traditions of Islam and the regional and local political realities of the Middle East and North Africa," not one in which Nazism became significantly influenced by the ideas of Arab leaders.[8] Ultimately, contextually useful though they may have been, the NF interest in Libya and the ideas of Qathafi did not stem from these limited Nazi-Arab collaborations at all. Certainly, the NF's interest in the creation of transnational alliances with Qathafi (and others, discussed later) acted as a continuation of long-term fascist tendencies toward building supranational links to try and shift the balance of global hegemony.[9] Alongside this basic ideological motivation, however, there was a unique convergence of several domestic and international political factors in the 1980s that prompted the NF to take on an (ultimately unrequited) fascination with not only Qathafi but also the Nation of Islam (NOI) leader Louis Farrakhan and the Ayatollah Khomeini of Iran. It is worth briefly sketching out these factors before continuing.

Within Britain, the political context was dramatically altered by Margaret Thatcher's willingness to employ anti-immigration rhetoric, swiftly endorsed by the tabloid press, which presented her position as moderate compared to the NF, even if her suggestion that Britons felt "swamped" by immigrants was not far short of the language used by British fascists and legitimized racism by depicting immigrants themselves as "the source of racial antagonisms."[10] On the eve of Thatcher's election, the cultural theorist Stuart Hall famously branded Thatcherism as a form of "authoritarian populism," suggesting not that her political philosophy was fascist but that it represented a "swing to the Right" that effectively removed the need for fascism through, among other things, its emphasis on authority and its transformation of NF ideas about race into "a more respectable discourse."[11] Historian Eric Hobsbawm, meanwhile, suggested that there was something almost "semi-fascist" about the way Thatcher turned what could have been an extremely minor conflict with Argentina over the Falkland Islands into "a dramatic victorious war" in 1982.[12] On an international level, of course, Thatcherism was part of a broader shift toward what is today recognized as neoliberalism. As Quinn Slobodian has recently emphasized, neoliberal thought emerged in a "specifically post-fascist context" and was rooted in "the tension . . . between advocating democracy for its peaceful change and condemning its capacity to upend order."[13] Equally, Slobodian notes, neoliberalism had an important "postcolonial context," with "the tension between the nation and the world" also highly significant in determining neoliberal strategies of "militant globalism" based on a "perceived . . . need to constrain nation-states and set limits on their exercise of sovereignty" in order to maintain the "holistic integrity" of the "world economy."[14] These longer-term global processes, alongside the shorter-term sense of political rupture within Britain, necessitated changes in the British neofascist program—even if it was only a small group of young radicals in the NF who recognized this fact. The search for new ideological inspiration led, perhaps inevitably, to exemplars like Qathafi's Libya, which consciously resisted the globalist slant of burgeoning neoliberalism (especially as represented by the United States, Britain's chief ally in both a diplomatic and ideological sense in the period under discussion).[15]

I will return to Qathafi and Libya later. First it is important to sketch a brief time line of changes within the NF. The radicals (who became known as "political soldiers" after one of their more important ideological handbooks) gradually gained control over the movement beginning in 1983.[16] They were more cognizant than the old guard of the practical need for the party to expand its political vocabulary so as to become less reliant on popular anti-immigration sentiments. Crucially they were also somewhat less beholden to essentially mimetic neo-Nazi ideals. This latter element was partly responsible for another major split in 1986, which saw the most radical members of this younger generation left in control of the party proper (or rather, what was left of it), while dissidents splintered off to form the National Front Support Group (NFSG). The NFSG, along with the equally NF-descended British National Party (BNP), continued along much the same path as in the 1970s but with severely decreased returns.[17] This left the NF to pursue an ultimately deeply flawed and almost completely unsuccessful new form of neofascism that it generally referred to as the politics of the *Third Way* (or *Third Position*).[18] Its failure notwithstanding, the ideological synthesis that the NF pursued in the mid to late 1980s was a significant and distinctive variant of far-right extremism that empha-sized different elements of classic fascist ideology than those favored by the majority of neofascist (especially neo-Nazi) organizations. Thus, this article assesses the Third Way NF less through judging its success or failure—although, as shall be seen, this is not irrelevant to the discussion provided here—than in terms of what it can reveal about the mutating character of postwar fascisms, particularly in the specific context of the 1980s. It contributes to ongoing debates about neofascist transnationalism and on the capacity of the extreme right to absorb new ideas and form new ideological models. In part, the point here is historiographical, designed to demonstrate the continued postwar ability of fascism to draw together (even if only vaguely coherently) a wide range of disparate ideological influences. Equally, however, there is a rather more subtle historical point to be made here about neo-fascism's relationship (and potential ability to collaborate with or learn from) other anti-globalist forms of politics. This is a transnational story, first and foremost in the general sense that it "explore[s] connections between peoples, societies and events usually thought of as distinct and separate."[19] More specifically, however, the anal-ysis here is focused on an example of transnational politics, with regard both to the circulation of ideas across borders and continents and to the fact that the NF's Third Way ideas could only ever be realized through change on a global scale: specifically the destruction of capitalism and communism and the reshaping of international politics along ethnonationalist lines.

Fittingly, the NF's Third Way approach emerged not in a vacuum but as part of more widespread changes across the European neofascist underground. Of par-ticular note to this case study were connections between British and Italian extrem-ists, developed in the early to mid-1980s, which were a central prerequisite to the development of NF ideological transnationalism. The first section of the article focuses on these connections and highlights their importance in influencing the NF radicals. Moreover, it shall provide some clarity as to the Third Way NF's rela-tionship with fascism as a generic phenomenon.

Fascism, the NF Italian Connection, and the Third Way

Readers will no doubt be aware that fascism can, at its very core, be considered a body of thought that promotes a "Third Way" of sorts: one that supposedly avoided the problems perceived by extreme rightists as inherent in both capitalism and communism or socialism. Richard Griffiths emphasizes that many of the energies that ultimately produced fascist dictatorships stemmed from a more general interwar desire to reject the materialist worldviews of capitalism and communism.[20] Roger Eatwell—in one of the most oft-cited definitions in a crowded field—identifies fascism as seeking "to create a 'new man' . . . who would forge a holistic nation and radical Third Way state."[21] For Ruth Ben-Ghiat, "the 'third way' may be viewed as one response to the perceived 'crisis of the West'" in the interwar period, but, as she has expertly demonstrated with reference to the Italian case, the new path that it represented was not merely political or socioeconomic. "The fascists," she affirms, "argued that their revolution . . . was spiritual" and thus would not cause "harm to individual identity or national traditions."[22] These aspects of classic fascism were, as shall be apparent from the examples provided, still important to the Third Way proffered by the NF in the late 1980s, albeit with some minor caveats, especially as it regards Eatwell's fascist minimum. For Eatwell, fascism is "holistic because [it seeks] to homogenize the nation rather than celebrate diversity within it" and represents a "Third Way because [it seeks] to synthesize aspects of both capitalism and socialism."[23] The Third Way NF certainly sought to homogenize the nation, and in the latter years of the 1980s, it saw the championing of other separatisms (including the pan-Arabic nationalism of Qathafi and the radical black nationalism of Farrakhan) as a method by which this could be accomplished. This was partly due to continental influences drawn from the Nouvelle Droite (or European New Right; not to be confused with the Anglo-American neoliberal New Right), which has long sought to "absolve its thinkers of any racialist bias through the adoption of the ambiguous formulation known as the 'right to difference.'"[24] Moreover, the Third Way NF did not look to blend capitalism and socialism but to reject them outright—although it is, of course, debatable if this element of the organization's thinking was ever even remotely realistic. In a sense, however, the practicality or otherwise of Third Way visions of a future economy was beside the point. Behind the NF's rejection of materialist doctrines lay a convoluted array of motivations, of which anti-Semitic conspiracy theory was a central pillar.[25]

The NF Third Way program also had important—and quite specific—roots in some of the more radical and esoteric variants of Italian neofascism that had emerged in the 1960s and 1970s. The key figure in making connections between Britain and Italy in this regard was Roberto Fiore, a young Catholic from Rome who in 1978 had cofounded an organization called Terza Posizione (Third Position, TP). Unlike some other Italian neofascist groups, TP showed little nostalgic interest in Mussolini and the Fascist past. Instead it purported to offer a radically new path between orthodox radicalisms of left and right, an approach clearly indicated in its logo (a *Wolfsangel*, a traditional German symbol associated with branches of the SS, overlaid with a fist holding a hammer) and its slogan ("Neither red front nor reaction, armed struggle for the Third Position!").[26] In the oft-divided Italian neo-fascist underground of the late 1970s and early 1980s, TP's views regularly caused controversy. Gianni Alemanno, a future mayor of Rome who was a member of the orthodox neofascist Movimento Sociale Italiano (Italian Social Movement) in this period, recalled in a 2004 interview that those active on the extreme right of Italian politics in this period often found the innovative approach of TP confusing and alienating. "Sometimes we had more clashes with those of the Third Position than those on the left," he admitted.[27] In many ways, the eclectic range of ideas present in TP's approach—and the ambiguous ways in which it presented them in its logo alone—made the organization a perfect example of a strange form of hypersyncretism. It has long been widely accepted that fascism is "a unique syncretic ideology," defined to a not insignificant extent by the "major ambiguities" discernible in its combination of "among other ideas anti-Marxism, populist ultra-nationalism, syndicalism, corporatism and socialism."[28] It is important to affirm at this juncture that this syncretism was neither wholly genuine nor necessarily damaging to attempts to present a coherent whole. George L. Mosse, describing fascism as "a scavenger which attempted to co-opt all that had appealed to people in the nineteenth and twentieth-century past," stressed the cynicism of this tendency while also emphasizing that "all these fragments . . . were integrated into a coherent attitude toward life through the basic fascist nationalist myth."[29]

TP was no less cynical than any other fascist movement in its picking of ideological meat off the bones of historical (and indeed contemporaneous) radicalisms, but it was a fair deal less coherent. This is not surprising. As Roger Griffin has argued, neofascism(s) have often become largely "faceless" phenomena, adapting to the less favorable context provided by the postwar world in a bewildering variety of different ways, with ideological coherence sometimes prone to becoming an inevitably secondary concern as a result.[30] For Griffin, transnationalism—"an aspect of fascism that was comparatively underdeveloped during the interwar years"—has been one of the central innovations, with "the dominant forms of fascism now see[ing] the struggle for national or ethnic rebirth in an international or supranational context." Griffin refers to "Third Positionism" as a key example here, describing this particular branch of extremism as an "ideological Third Way [that] looks forward to an entirely new economic system and international community . . . its struggle against the world system foster[ing] a solidarity with non-aligned countries such as Libya."[31] Third Way neofascism's shift of emphasis toward sculpting a new global system of political economy made it more flexible—in the case of the Third Way NF, to the point of undermining the racism that had always been a core part of British neofascist thought—while also creating new problems and ambiguities for activists and ideologues. In this sense, Third Way neofascism can be considered a fascist variant that prioritizes demonstrating its antagonistic relationship with existing national and global power structures over asserting national and racial superiority.

The lengths to which TP itself was prepared to go were apparent from its connections with the militant Nuclei Armati Rivoluzionari (Armed Revolutionary Nuclei, NAR), members of which were found guilty of carrying out the infamous Bologna railway station bombing of August 1980. In the aftermath, numerous NAR members fled Italy under fear of arrest. Roberto Fiore was one. He arrived in London in late 1980, and despite a vocal campaign by the anti-fascist journal *Searchlight* (which accused Fiore of leading the NF toward terrorism), successfully avoided multiple extradition requests from the Italian government.[32] Sharing a flat with NF activist Michael Walker, Fiore became close friends with many of the younger, more intellectually minded figures on the British extreme right, especially the Cambridge graduate Nick Griffin and the intensely Catholic (and somewhat eccentric) Derek Holland. Fiore would introduce NF radicals to several of his major influences, the most important of which was Julius Evola, the Italian philosopher who had critiqued fascism from the right and inspired a whole generation of postwar extremists in his home country.[33] This "fervent critic of US-style liberal democratic modernity and . . . advocate of European spiritual rebirth" was also beloved by the Nouvelle Droite, whose ideas were conveniently being circulated in Britain at precisely the same time by Walker, whose journal the *Scorpion* (initially *National Democrat*) "became the leading proponent of Nouvelle Droite thought in Britain throughout the 1980s."[34]

Fiore worked with Holland to produce a journal, *Rising*, which sought to convert NF members to a more spiritual form of activism, inspired not only by Evola but also the likes of Corneliu Codreanu, leader of the Eastern Orthodox interwar Romanian Iron Guard. In 1984 Holland also produced a major ideological statement for NF radicals: *The Political Soldier*. While both *Rising* and *The Political Soldier* served a purpose in spreading radical ideas within the NF (and thus helping to take over the party, albeit partly by alienating some long-term members to the point that they left), these publications also worked, alongside *The Scorpion*, to attempt to tackle the problems caused for the extreme right by the renewed ascendance of globalization fueled by the successes of the neoliberal Anglo-American New Right. In doing so, they absorbed elements of other bodies of thought that were influential in the NF around this time. These included "Strasserism" (the more overtly anti-capitalist Nazism associated with Gregor and Otto Strasser) and distributism (an economic ideology, based on the redistribution of land and industry, that emerged from Catholic social teaching and was particularly associated in Britain with Hilaire Belloc and G. K. Chesterton), filtering them through the spiritual anti-materialism of Evola, whose largely untranslated works would have been explained by Fiore.[35]

Crucially, the NF radicals saw the newly invigorated free market capitalism of the 1980s as just one side of a coin whose other face featured communism. This perspective had its roots in anti-Semitic conspiracy theory, which attacked a shadowy "internationalist Establishment . . . with sectional, international and/or alien interests and loyalties" promoting capitalism and communism "towards the same end of a world monopoly of economic and political power."[36] Crucially, for Evola-influenced radicals like Fiore and Holland, resisting the power of this euphemistic internationalism necessitated detachment from the orthodox sociopolitical realm and the values associated with it. This could be found in a state that Evola referred to as *apolitìa*, a vague concept that Evola scholar Paul Furlong describes as "the interior quality that preserves one's being from being corrupted by interaction with a world that is increasingly unstructured and lacking in values of any kind."[37] The introduction to the second issue of *Rising* made clear the importance of this concept to the new NF radicalism:

> On a practical level today we see our "new man" as one whose character is fundamentally opposed to the influences which created the bourgeois and Marxist outlooks.
>
> In the world today there is a pervasive network of factors all preventing people from waking up, from looking at themselves and the world and appreciating the true relationship which one bears to the other. These factors include television, advertising, the work ethic, the greedy ideals of acquisitive society, and the ineffectual game of the democratic party system.
>
> All these factors work together in an effort to enslave people to the idea that the object of life is pleasure, which comes from buying things. So why don't we break away from all this—by building our own houses; educating our own children; creating our own communities which could be the basis for a new world![38]

In essence, then, *Rising* argued that true radicals needed to genuinely disentangle themselves from the web of materialism in order to adequately pursue revolutionary nationalist goals.

Ideas of this nature had been circulating for some time in the Italian fascist underground, where they were essentially utilized as a justification for terrorism.[39] In the British context, however, what these ideas might justify was less important. Instead the focus was, in a classic fascist sense, on the creation of a prototypical New Man who would be able to resist the decadence of contemporary materialism and move forward to help create an altogether new world system. As the next section of the article will demonstrate, it was this anti-materialist, but authentically fascist, element of NF Third Way ideas that would lead to the radicalized party's interest in Islamic radicalism.

Islamic Radicals, Racial Separatism, and the Evolution of the Third Way

It was clear from the beginning that the NF Third Way project was necessarily transnational. *Rising* clarified that it was Europe, not just Britain, which needed "to be reborn."[40] Similarly *The Political Soldier* emphasized that it was "the death of Europe" that needed to be prevented, as this would "signal the end of the White peoples forever" and leave "Britain . . . a vague, unimportant memory."[41] Unsurprisingly, then, *Rising* stressed that "no single European nation can stand up to Zionism, U.S. Capitalism or Soviet Imperialism by itself. Our independent nations must learn to co-operate—or else lose their independence forever. We speak the gospel of Nationalism, that is the gospel of the real Europeans!"[42] For all that *Rising* emphasized its Europeanness, however, it also prefigured the ostensible softening of attitudes toward race that would become a central part of the Third Way NF's approach. In its very first issue *Rising* informed its readers:

The African or the Asian man who strives to create his own national identity deserves our respect. Our enemy is he who seeks to destroy the difference between races and who suffocates traditions. A yankee who, with his blonde hair and blue eyes, when representing the mercantilist Coca-Cola ideology, is doubtless a more dangerous enemy. The White capitalist who promotes the influx of cheap coloured labour to this country for mere economic reasons is our major adversary.[43]

This mirrored the Nouvelle Droite's tendency "to blame capitalism rather than immigrants for the problems associated with immigration."[44] Far from being simply a cynical trick, this (and indeed all of *Rising*'s pronouncements) must be read as genuine attempts to reorient the views of NF activists, since this was a purely underground journal intended for circulation only within extreme right circles. In this case, by presenting immigration as a by-product of capitalism, *Rising* sought to persuade readers to channel their racial prejudice through opposing globalization. On one level, this represented the continuation of anti-Semitic conspiracy theory, with the forces of materialism being portrayed as engaged in a secretive plot to undermine ethnic distinctions. At the same time, however, this rhetoric should be taken at face value, insofar as it established that the endorsement of nonwhite racial separatisms was a potentially useful route toward the collapse of the multiracial society the NF so abhorred. It therefore enabled, or even encouraged, activists to recognize and endorse examples of such separatisms.

In the context of these developments, Farrakhan, Khomeini, and Qathafi were relatively obvious influences for the NF to adopt. All were authoritarian figures fundamentally opposed to globalization and to the political consensus represented by the Anglo-American New Right. They shared the NF's distaste for racially diverse societies and, by virtue of the core role of Islam in their political philosophies, they also promoted a worldview rooted in timeless, spiritual values. Early examples of NF praise for this trio of figures reflected these elements of loose crossover. In one, published in the ideological journal *Nationalism Today*, Holland critiqued Britain and the United States for their censuring of Iran, praising the

Khomeini regime for promoting "a view of the world which rejects the crass materialism and despiritualization of Yankee imperialism on one hand and the exploitative tyranny of Soviet communism on the other."[45] Soon after, in the midst of the Libyan embassy siege in London, similar arguments were discernible in an article that attacked the numerous British Conservatives publicly calling for the fall of the Qathafi regime.[46] Griffin, upon returning from a trip to the United States in 1985, was effusive in his praise for Farrakhan, in particular endorsing the NOI leader's diagnosis of white society as "mortally sick."[47] Of course it was also not entirely coincidental that these three regimes and leaders were vocal critics of Israel, and indeed the radical NF's endorsement of each should be seen as also appropriating the cause of Palestinian nationalism in the mid to late 1980s, especially after the afore discussed party split of 1986.[48]

Predictably, this split also allowed the NF to support these alternative ideological touchstones more explicitly. A *Nationalism Today* editorial directly after said split alerted readers—under the heading "Farrakhan Aid"—to the inclusion in the journal of an article by Abdul Wali Muhammad, then editor of the NOI newspaper the *Final Call*. This, readers were reassured, marked nothing less than "a new stage in the fight against multi-racialism." For the purposes of clarity, the editorial then emphasized:

> The current leadership of the NF is not interested in the mindless bigotry or nihilism of the past. . . . We are ready and willing to work with those of other races who wish to maintain their separateness and identity. Black Power and White Power are *not* enemies. They are allies in the struggle to resist and defeat the race and nation destroying Capitalism that is engulfing the globe. Unity in diversity is *not* a slogan, it is a Way of Life.[49]

This amounted to a dramatic progression of the views on race expressed in *Rising* four years earlier. Now the NF radicals did not merely request respect for nonwhite racial separatists, they demanded that members of the party actively engage with individuals and groups promoting such ideas. As per the Third Way's discursive focus on globalization, this shared racial struggle was presented as part of a struggle against capitalism—the pitting of one way of life against another. Muhammad's contribution hinted at these themes, but was predominantly an advertisement for the NOI and its leader. Much of the focus was on portraying Farrakhan as the true, popular voice of black Americans. It also highlighted the NOI's militancy—in the form of its armed wing, the Fruit of Islam—as well as its leader's virulent anti-Zionism (in reality anti-Semitism) and supposed willingness to collaborate with American white supremacists. A brief, sanitized rundown of the NOI's core beliefs was also provided.[50]

Unsurprisingly, no mention was made here of the depth of the NOI's racial views, which were not merely separatist but were predicated on "the genetically given divinity of the black man and the genetically given evilness of the white man," an idea that would, of course, have been anathema to all *Nationalism Today*'s readers, including the leading proponents of the Third Way.[51] Of course the fact that radical NF leaders were prepared to overlook this element of NOI belief can be seen as proof of the genuineness of their respect for Farrakhan and his ideas. This respect was no doubt strengthened by an additional factor, related to Farrakhan's ability (or otherwise) to visit supporters in Britain. In January 1986 the Conservative government decided to ban Farrakhan from entering the country after he was invited to speak in London by the Hackney Black People's Association. The issuing of the invitation indicated the growing global reach of the NOI's appeal to disenfranchised black communities, while the ban—on account of perceived anti-Semitism and largely as a result of the British-Israeli group in Parliament—proved that those in power saw Farrakhan's politics as genuinely divisive.[52] This enabled the NF to position Farrakhan and the NOI as presenting a real threat to the established political order—in other words, a worthy ally. Equally, of course, for the NF, the process behind the ban also fitted neatly into its conspiratorial worldview, as clarified in an earlier *Nationalism Today*: "The thought of anybody—Black or White—exposing Jewish power and demanding racial separation and racial freedom is an horrific challenge to the 'Powers That Be.'"[53]

By the autumn of 1987 the NF was distributing leaflets in support of Farrakhan, bearing the slogan "Louis Farrakhan: He Speaks for His People, We Speak for Ours."[54] This was the realization of the radical leadership's earlier call to fully commit to strategies of engagement with black separatists, or as *National Front News* put it, to engage in "*political* action designed to replace the capitalist system and the corrupt politicians who imported millions of coloured immigrants into our land."[55] Crucially, this was now part of a broader discourse of supposed anti-imperialism. "Imperialism is the domination of one nation by another," the party newspaper declared. "Since all peoples have an inbuilt preference for rule by their own kind, such a policy can only be maintained by oppression and by cultural and even national genocide," it continued, before emphasizing that such drastic means "inevitably [lead] to the mixing of the different populations and to 'subject peoples' being brought back to the 'mother country' as cheap labour . . . the result of which is the disastrous immigration which is destroying the identity of our own country."[56] If the long history of British imperialism figured at all in this perspective, it was stripped of its national specificity and its racial dimension was inverted. *National Front News* readers were warned about Soviet imperialism ("the most brutal . . . of all time"), but it was the American empire—cited as being heavily influenced by the "hidden power" of Zionist imperialism—that was established as the chief threat to Britain, and indeed Western Europe more generally. Cultural Americanization through Hollywood was presented as part of a chain that included "mass immigration and forced multi-racialism," all as part of "the drive of American capitalists to create a rootless, coffee coloured world of mindless consumers." Through this philosophy of "Profit [as] God," the radicals concluded, the American model was *the most dangerous empire of all time.*[57]

This expanded anti-capitalist rhetoric can be cast as a natural extension of that which appeared in *Rising* and *The Political Soldier* earlier in the decade. This time, however, there was a greater—and more global—purpose. This became apparent in March 1988, when *National Front News* placed Farrakhan, Khomeini, and Qathafi on its front page and declared that there was now a "New Alliance" ready to replace the "Old Order." The paper elaborated by asserting:

Revolutionary nationalist groups, racial separatists and the anti-Zionist nations of the Middle East, are beginning to recognize a common set of interests and enemies which make closer co-operation both beneficial and inevitable.

Against our common enemies—Capitalism and Communism—we are at last beginning to develop a credible alternative: the *Third Way.*[58]

The clear implication here was that it was only through a globally oriented alliance of Third Way forces that the materialist doctrines of capitalism and communism could be defeated. The globalist imperialism that the NF saw as being maintained by these two competing bodies of thought could be overridden, and distinct nations could be saved—but the process by which this could be accomplished was inherently transnational in itself. There was, of course, a caveat. Despite the impression given by the bulk of the article, *National Front News* admitted that there remained a need for "common interest [to] be turned into practical co-operation."[59] In effect, this was an admission that its actual relationships with those it now held up as key allies were relatively insubstantial. If the so-called New Alliance existed in fact, then the NF was scarcely part of it.

What was less limited was the willingness of radical NF activists to introduce ideas from Libya, in particular, into the NF. Holland, by far the most influential ideologue in the party in the late 1980s, had clearly devoured *The Green Book* and saw a synergy between its key ideas and those of his political soldier program. More specifically, Holland saw in Qathafi's Third Universal Theory a set of ideas that he believed would make it possible to realize the unclear utopian vision he had of an alternative postrevolutionary society. Particularly appealing, in this regard, was Qathafi's vision of a "society of all people, where all men are free and equal in authority, wealth and arms, so that freedom may gain the final and complete triumph."[60] Writing in the same 1986 issue of *Nationalism Today* that featured Muhammad's article on the NOI, Holland explained that he felt this aspect of Qathafi's thought was the route to ensuring "the subordination of the State to the Nation." What this amounted to was, in effect, securing the tyranny of the majority. By arming the people, a process that Holland accepted would only occur gradually after "our people have . . . be[en] re-educated into the responsible use of their new freedoms" (thus individually becoming Holland's version of the prototypical fascist "New Man"), the population would be able to defend their own interests against the despotism of capital, which was enforced via the concentration of arms within the arsenal of the state. Accordingly, Holland asserted, "Only those—like Thatcher and Gorbachev—who have something to fear from ordinary folk will be against arming the people."[61]

Qathafi's broader vision of direct democracy also gained significant stamps of approval from the NF over the following months, particularly his excoriation of parliaments and "establishment of Popular Congresses and People's Committees."[62] The NF thus began to call for "People's Democracy," based on Third Universal Theory principles. This would be realized through various tiers of democratic engagement—from "Street Councils" to a "National People's Council"—in which "*all* people [would] have the facility to debate issues affecting themselves, their families and their property, and to take part in the decision-making process at the end of such debate."[63] Such a process would also, *Nationalism Today* noted, require new ways of thinking, fully achievable only "when the centralized mass media of today is transformed into the Media of the Masses."[64] This was another nod to Qathafi, who saw "the continuing problem of press freedom" as "a product of the problem of democracy" and therefore argued that alongside the implementation of "popular rule" must come the implementation of a "democratic press . . . issued by a popular committee."[65] The global dissemination of Qathafi's thought through *The Green Book* and other methods—including newspapers such as *Arab Dawn* in Britain—was one outcome of this process as it was applied in Libya. The NF leadership undoubtedly saw their output in a similar light, and they took seriously the education of those who read their publications, encouraging them to buy works including *The Green Book* and *Islam and Revolution*, an essay collection introducing Khomeini's thought to the West. Such was the hero worship of the Libyan leader that the NF even sold T-shirts bearing the slogan "Death to Imperialism" alongside Qathafi's portrait.[66]

One can only speculate, but the NF's increased promotion of Qathafi's philosophy may well have been what secured three NF directorate members—Holland, Griffin, and Patrick Harrington—their invitation to Libya in September 1988. Despite the party's best efforts, however, the trip was a minor disaster. In a likely unintentional embodiment of the trip's failure, Griffin and Holland were pictured on the front of *National Front News* standing in front of a giant billboard of Qathafi when, no doubt, they harbored hopes of being introduced to the man himself.[67] The center pages continued the NF's pro-Qathafi propaganda campaign—with the damage done to Libya by American air strikes being billed as a "TORY WAR CRIME"—and provided a brief account of some of the activities the trio had participated in, from discussing the economic situation in Libya with shopkeepers to visiting the ruins of the ancient Roman city of Sabrata Magna.[68] The NF's hopes that the visit might provide the beginning of a real partnership were, however, misguided. It was clear from the coverage in *National Front News* that the trio had ultimately been treated as tourists rather than potential partners. Now unavailable internal party documents seen by one researcher apparently suggested that not only did the visit to Tripoli secure no funding for the NF's activities in Britain, but also that the Libyans paid only half the trio's plane fares.[69] It is worth acknowledging here that the NF's visit to Libya came only two years after the British-aided 1986 US air strikes on Tripoli and Benghazi. In retaliation, Qathafi had elected to resume his previous policy of providing arms for the Irish Republican Army (IRA), massively increasing the dissident organization's firepower in the process.[70] It would make sense that any potential alliance with the NF would have had similar motivations: to sponsor activity designed to undermine the United States and its allies. The NF, however, was not a paramilitary organization like the IRA, and it did not have the ideological or practical structure to enable any transition in this direction. It must have been quickly apparent to the representatives of the regime that the trio met in Tripoli that the NF had no serious hopes of destabilizing the British political establishment in the way that Qathafi might have desired.

The party's contacts with the NOI ultimately proved similarly meaningless. While Matt Malone, an NF contact in the United States, did pursue contacts with the NOI, Farrakhan's organization showed no real interest in the NF in return.[71] By mid-1989, stung by these effective rejections, the NF was falling apart. The potential that its radical leadership saw in the ideas of the Third Way never materialized. The party undoubtedly suffered from appalling timing—the Lockerbie bombing took place in December 1988 (although Libya was not directly implicated until 1991), and the Ayatollah issued his fatwa against the British Indian novelist Salman Rushdie in February 1989. The NF was also, however, the victim of its own poor decision-making, spending much of the late 1980s attempting to run before it could walk. Explaining its vigorous support for Qathafi behind closed doors and in ideological journals was one thing. Having to publicly defend itself (as an organization with some links to Northern Irish loyalists) for applauding a man known to have a long history of supporting the IRA was another.[72]

Assessing the Third Way NF: Transnationalism and Radicalism

For all of the potential that the transnationalism of the Third Way NF had to open new doors for the party, it can also be seen as contributing to its eventual collapse, which followed swiftly in the wake of Harrington declaring—in a statement issued to the Board of Deputies of British Jews—that the NF was an organization open to Jews and explicitly opposed to anti-Semitism. He only succeeded in receiving a swift rebuttal, with the *Jewish Chronicle* suggesting the statement was nothing more than a deception.[73] His decision, made without the approval of the rest of the NF directorate, led to Griffin and Holland (not to mention Fiore) quitting the NF and moving on to new pastures. After all, as has been shown, the precepts of the Third Way ideology they had helped craft were strongly rooted in euphemistic anti-Semitism, and this was not easily overcome. Harrington, left with a small handful of activists, soon gave up the ghost, allowing the National Front Support Group to regain the party name. By this time, however, the NF had shrunk dramatically. As Ryan Shaffer's brief summary illustrates, all this occurred at least in part because many ordinary members were perplexed or offended by the idea of endorsing the likes of Farrakhan, Khomeini, and Qathafi.[74] Some of the ideas that the Third Way NF absorbed from these figures did continue to resonate in a variety of ways in other, later groups. These included the various projects of onetime NF political soldier and later national anarchist Troy Southgate, Patrick Harrington's more moderate post-NF group (conveniently entitled Third Way), and the International Third Position (ITP), cofounded by Holland, Griffin, and Fiore.[75] Crucially, however, none of these organizations made any even vaguely significant impact. This, aligned with the collapse of the Third Way NF at the end of the 1980s, raises the possibility that—sincerity notwithstanding—certain forms of overt transnationalism, especially those that seek to supersede fascist interpretations of racial hierarchy, can be an actively damaging addition to neofascist political programs, even when they may appear to offer potential new routes forward. As if to demonstrate that they had learned this lesson, both Griffin and Fiore reached a new level of prominence after 9/11 (and in the midst of the Qathafi rapprochement with the West) as the leaders of (and members of the European Parliament for) unambiguously nationalist, deeply Islamophobic parties: the BNP and Forza Nuova.[76]

It can scarcely be denied that the Third Way NF aspired to a truly transnational form of political action and thought. It is clear from the examples gathered above that many of the NF radicals devoted much of their intellectual energies to the absorption of ideas from abroad (not least from Italy and Libya), which they consciously tried to fit into their preexisting ideological framework. For Andrea Mammone, a study of transnational neofascism will tend to focus on "forgotten people crossing borders, and neglected cultural transfer," the effect of which is to provide analysts with a route in to the "interconnected neofascist web" that may spread across nations and, indeed, continents.[77] These features can certainly be seen to neatly characterize the NF in the 1980s, with its many overseas contacts (of which only the most ideologically significant have been referred to today) and its importing and, on a far smaller scale, exporting of ideas (in the latter case chiefly through post-NF movements such as the ITP). In this sense, moving away from the overly definitional realm of the fascist minimum that was briefly entered at the beginning of the article, the 1980s NF can be regarded as a transnational movement because it consistently engaged in "fascist processes of global circulation, adaptation and reformulation," which Federico Finchelstein rightly cites as being at least as important as the "aspects of fascism" that many scholars tend to reify.[78]

What is less clear-cut is the extent to which the NF's incorporation of its myriad of new foreign influences created an authentically transnational ideology. Finchelstein, following Benjamin Zachariah, notes that most existing scholarship on fascism remains doggedly Eurocentric, again largely because of its overly definitional slant, not just in that it focuses on European case studies but also in that it continues to foreground "'top-down' Eurocentric frameworks" that render non-European forms or adaptations of fascism purely mimetic.[79] While the major problem this creates is the sidelining of studies that seriously consider the spread of fascist ideas outside Europe, there is also another potential side effect: the dismissal—out of hand—of the possibility that elements of contemporary fascism may in fact have important origins outside Europe. This may be said to be especially pertinent in the case of the Third Way NF, and not only because of its fascination with select Islamic radicals. Evola, for all that he believed in the need for European regeneration, was deeply influenced by traditions from outside the continent. As he was a pagan, something that makes his magnetic appeal for so many fervently Catholic neofascists a little strange, Evola took a deep interest in a range of spiritual practices, particularly Buddhism (which he credited with helping to save his life when he considered suicide in the early 1920s).[80] He also, however, praised elements of Islam—particularly its dual conception of internal and external "Holy Wars"—and characterized it as "a tradition at a higher level than both Judaism and the religious beliefs that conquered the West."[81]

Both Finchelstein and Zachariah suggest that, in place of the classic fascist minimum, scholars should utilize what the latter calls a "fascist repertoire," a selection of fascistic qualities "from which ideologues have the agency to choose."[82] The Third Way NF may be said to have expanded this repertoire to include ideas borrowed from the likes of Farrakhan, Khomeini, and, of course, Qathafi. In this it would, in some senses, be following Evola in seeking inspiration from a wider array of sources than most orthodox fascists would ever consider. Just as Evola's interest in Buddhism and Islam should not be taken to mean that either of these religions should be reinterpreted as fascist, so the NF's appropriation of ideas from the aforementioned trio does not necessitate the branding of any of these figures as "Islamo-fascists."[83] We should also, of course, avoid taking Evola's incorporation of selected elements of Buddhism and Islam into his worldview as evidence that the Italian was, in some meaningful sense, a practitioner of either of these philosophies. Similarly, there is a need to note the limitations of the Third Way NF's transnational development. As has been clear throughout, while NF radicals participated in processes of exchange and networking, these were often ineffective and one-sided—as is particularly clear in the sections that deal with the NF's borrowing from Qathafi. Moreover, it must be acknowledged that, in most cases, the NF used new ideas from such sources chiefly to fill gaps in its preexisting ideology. As Alan Sykes suggests, Qathafi's philosophy provided "a revolutionary solution" to the central problem left unresolved by distributism: "the need for, but threat from, the state."[84] While this verdict underestimates the real affinity that some (no doubt not all) NF radicals felt for Qathafi's politics, it is accurate insofar as it recognizes that the NF's adoption of elements of Third Universal Theory never quite got beyond a focus on how structures and ideas from Libya could be applied in Britain.

In effect, then, the NF added the ideas of Qathafi (and, to a lesser extent, others like Farrakhan and Khomeini) to their fascist repertoire. Even if a full, intensive fusion of ideas never quite took place, there was enough overlap between the Third Way NF's core beliefs—essentially those Holland had outlined in his writings, meshed with anti-Semitic conspiracy theory—to leave open this possibility. The *apolitic* resistance to materialism that was at the center of Third Way ideology prompted NF radicals to believe that they were capable of becoming a revolutionary elite, but the actual vision that the likes of Griffin and Holland had for their future utopia was ultimately rather foggy, beyond the fact that it would be ethnically homogenous and free of supposedly malignant Jewish influence. In this, in fact, some further comparisons could be drawn with the reality of both Third Universal Theory and, even more so, with Khomeinism. In a 1980 interview, later distributed more widely via its inclusion in *Islam and Revolution*, Khomeini explained that the success of the revolution that had brought him to power was in large part because "the people were ready for revolution: they were dissatisfied with their government and discontented with their lives, and—most importantly—God had brought about a spiritual transformation in them." This spiritual basis for the revolution was then acted upon through the guidance of "the religious leaders, who are capable of arousing the people and inspiring them to self-sacrifice."[85]

This was almost precisely how the political soldiers saw the situation. They believed that the majority of people in the West were, at heart, ready for change and that all they needed were spiritual guides (essentially enablers of radicalization) in the form of the NF's revolutionary elite. It is impossible to see how, in practice, the NF's Third Way revolution would have ended up all that different from that of Khomeini's or Qathafi's, which both relied on demagoguery and dictatorship even if they lacked many of the classic fascist features that no doubt would have resurfaced within a more powerful NF.

Conclusion

One of Margaret Thatcher's most oft-used slogans was "There is no alternative," by which she meant that globalist capitalism was the only route the world could take. In this context, looking to nations like Iran and Libya made sense for the NF precisely because, at the historical moment in which politicians like Thatcher were rapidly embarking on a newly vigorous program of globalization, these were among the few nations combining vocal opposition to American-dominated global capitalism with alternative (albeit poorly realized) "Third Ways" of their own. Nonetheless, the NF's interest in these alternative models must also be seen as an early example of what Paul Gilroy has cited as a wider blurring of ideological divisions and undermining of "racial solidarities" engendered by "a new geopolitical context that increasingly lacks even the possibility of imagining an alternative to capitalism."[86] In effect, context is crucial here. The 1980s produced a situation in which the neofascist radicals that populated the Third Way NF recognized that the various discontents produced by globalization could exacerbate opposition to materialist ideologies and multicultural societies in certain national and, potentially, diasporic environments. We can be thankful that their attempts to build alliances with the likes of Qathafi failed to make any serious headway, but we should also accept the potential for new forms of collaboration between racial separatists of many stripes today. Such a threat is only made more likely by the impasse of political economy that continues to furnish us with global and national forms of desperate inequality so as to maintain the cynical structures of consumerist late capitalism. Thus, while this article has shown the limitations of radical transnational reorientations of neofascism, it has also demonstrated the potential crossover that can be identified between the extreme right and other non-Western anti-globalist ideologies. A truly global fascism may well be an oxymoronic concept, but there is a need for us to remain vigilant about the idea of a transnationally oriented fascism engaging seriously with other forces—particularly those centered on racial separatism—in pursuit of common, anti-globalization goals. After all, the context of the moment once again seems potentially favorable to such a meeting of ideas and perspectives.

Benjamin Bland recently completed a PhD at Royal Holloway, University of London, funded by the Arts and Humanities Research Council, in the cultural history of British right-wing extremism. He is currently a visiting lecturer in politics and international relations at the University of Hertfordshire and a teaching associate in history at Queen Mary, University of London.

Notes

1. Qathafi, *Green Book*, 5–7. For an introduction to the Qathafi regime and the difference between theory and practice in Libya, see Vandewalle, *Modern Libya*, 96–172.
2. *Nationalism Today*, "Libya," 8–9.
3. Vandewalle, *Modern Libya*, 5–6.
4. Eatwell, "Fascism and Political Racism," 229.
5. For an introduction to the NF and its opponents in the 1970s, see Renton, *Never Again*.
6. Billig, *Fascists*.
7. Motadel, *Islam and Nazi Germany's War*, 7–8.
8. Herf, *Nazi Propaganda for the Arab World*, 1–3.
9. See, for an example, the links between Fascist Italy and Argentina, as discussed in Finchelstein, *Transatlantic Fascism*.
10. Smith, *New Right Discourse*, 179–80.
11. Hall, "Great Moving Right Show," 14–20.
12. Hobsbawm, "Falklands Fallout," 15.

13. Slobodian, *Globalists*, 19.

14. Slobodian, *Globalists*, 19.

15. Vandewalle, *Modern Libya*, 130.

16. For a brief summary, see Copsey, *Contemporary British Fascism*, 29–35.

17. For a concise account of this split, see Shaffer, *Music, Youth, and International Links*, 123–26. The NFSG was also known as the Flag Group after its newspaper the *Flag*.

18. The terms *Third Way* and *Third Position* were often used interchangeably. The latter was probably used more regularly, but I have preferred the term *Third Way* in this article to avoid confusion with organizations using the term *Third Position* in their names.

19. Curthoys and Lake, "Introduction," 6–7.

20. Griffiths, *Fascism*, 59–71.

21. Eatwell, *Fascism*, xxiv.

22. Ben-Ghiat, "Italian Fascism," 311.

23. Eatwell, *Fascism*, xxiv.

24. Bar-On, "Ambiguities," 344–45.

25. For an informative analysis of the discursive overlap of these concepts and others in francophone Third Way thought, see Bastow, "Neo-Fascist Third Way," 354–61.

26. Quoted in Osservatorio sul Fascismo a Roma, "Terza Posizione."

27. Alemanno, quoted in Telese, *Cuori neri*, 628.

28. Bar-On, *Where Have All the Fascists Gone?*, 99.

29. Mosse, *Fascist Revolution*, 23.

30. Griffin, *Fascist Century*, 181–202.

31. Griffin, *Fascist Century*, 195.

32. The British government's files relating to these extradition requests have been retained by the Home Office; my Freedom of Information requests have been refused on grounds related to international relations, personal information, and national security. Many of the *Searchlight* accusations were compiled in a booklet entitled *From Ballots to Bombs*.

33. For a brief summary of Evola's influence in postwar Italy, see Drake, "Julius Evola."

34. Copsey, "Au Revoir to 'Sacred Cows'?," 289–90, 292.

35. On Strasserism, distributism, and the NF, see Sykes, *Radical Right*, 116–19. This account, like several others both contemporaneous and subsequent, overstates the influence of the Strasser brothers while failing to recognize the primacy of Evola.

36. *Nationalism Today*, "What We're Fighting For," 20.

37. Furlong, *Social and Political Thought of Julius Evola*, 98. See also Wolff, "Apolitìa and Tradition."

38. *Rising*, "Introduction," 2.

39. See Wolff, "Evola's Interpretation."

40. *Rising*, "Men and Doctrines," 6.

41. Holland, *Political Soldier*, 7–8.

42. *Rising*, "Folk-Community," 4.

43. *Rising*, "Racial Question," 10.

44. Bar-On, "Alternative Modernity," 47.

45. Holland, "Iran's National Revolution," 12.

46. Bell, "Gadaffi and the 'Right-Wing' Patriots," 14.

47. Griffin, "Deadly Trap / Let My People Go." 17.

48. On this see Bland, "Holocaust Inversion," 92–96.

49. *Nationalism Today*, "Farrakhan Aid," 2.

50. Muhammad, "Nation of Islam," 16–20.

51. Gardell, *In the Name of Elijah Muhammad*, 348.

52. Gibson, *History of the Nation of Islam*, 99–100.

53. *Nationalism Today*, "Louis Farrakhan," 7.

54. The flyer and a variation of it can be seen in various NF publications around this time, but the original is most easily found in *Searchlight*, "New Axis," 3.

55. *National Front News*, "Fight Racism," 4. Emphasis in original.

56. *National Front News*, "Death to Imperialism," 4.

57. *National Front News*, "Death to Imperialism," 4–5. Emphasis in original.

58. *National Front News*, "New Alliance," 1. Emphasis in original. Interestingly, this front cover followed a similar one by *Searchlight*, suggesting that the NF leadership was unconcerned by the potential ammunition its new focus would give to anti-fascists (*Searchlight*, "New Axis," 1).

59. *National Front News*, "New Alliance," 1.

60. Qathafi, *Green Book*, 68–69.

61. Holland, "Armed People," 22–23.

62. *Nationalism Today*, "People Not Parliaments," 10–11.

63. *Nationalism Today*, "Principles of Democracy," 6.

64. *Nationalism Today*, "Media for the Masses," 15.

65. Qathafi, *Green Book*, 38–39.

66. Catalogues were regularly included as inserts or adverts in issues of *National Front News*.

67. *National Front News*, "NF Chiefs Visit Libya," 1.

68. *National Front News*, "The Shame and the Anger," 4–5; *National Front News*, "Mad Dogs and Englishmen," 5.

69. O'Hara, "Creating Political Soldiers?," 252–53.

70. On Qathafi and the IRA, see Moloney, *Secret History of the IRA*, 6–15.

71. Gardell, *In the Name of Elijah Muhammad*, 275–77.

72. The NF, of course, seized on the hollow Libyan disavowal of IRA violence—largely conducted with weapons gifted by Qathafi—in 1988 (*National Front News*, "Libya Condemns the IRA," 6).

73. Harrington, quoted in *Jewish Chronicle*, "NF About-Turn," 21.

74. Shaffer, *Music, Youth, and International Links*, 135–38.

75. On Southgate, see Macklin, "Troy Southgate." On the ITP, see Shaffer, "Pan-European Thought," 85–91.

76. Wodak, *Politics of Fear*, 199. For an analysis of Griffin's BNP, see Copsey, *Contemporary British Fascism*. For Fiore's thoughts on Third Position thought at the turn of the century, see Adinolfi and Fiore, *Noi, Terza Posizione* (*We, Third Position*).

77. Mammone, *Transnational Neofascism*, 26.

78. Finchelstein, *From Fascism to Populism*, 54.

79. Finchelstein, *From Fascism to Populism*, 55; Zachariah, "Voluntary Gleichschaltung."

80. Furlong, *Social and Political Thought of Julius Evola*, 3–4.

81. Evola, *Revolt against the Modern World*, 118, 245.

82. Zachariah, "Voluntary Gleichschaltung," 67.

83. This is not to say there are no parallels worth discussing, merely to acknowledge that the terminology of Islamo-fascism is hopelessly tarnished by its use in the early twenty-first century during the so-called War on Terror, during which—as Tony Judt emphasized—the term was used to perpetuate the idea of a "worldwide civilizational struggle" between

East and West (Judt, *Reappraisals*, 19). For a thoughtful recent take, see Bar-On, "'Islamofascism.'"

84. Sykes, *Radical Right*, 120.
85. Khomeini, *Islam and Revolution*, 336–39.
86. Gilroy, *Between Camps*, 209–10.

References

Adinolfi, Gabriele, and Roberto Fiore. *Noi, Terza Posizione (We, Third Position)*. Rome: Settimo Sigillo, 2000.

Bar-On, Tamir. "The Ambiguities of the Nouvelle Droite, 1968–1999." *European Legacy* 6, no. 3 (2001): 333–51.

Bar-On, Tamir. "The French New Right's Quest for Alternative Modernity." *Fascism* 1, no. 1 (2012): 18–52.

Bar-On, Tamir. "'Islamofascism': Four Competing Discourses on the Islamism-Fascism Comparison." *Fascism* 7, no. 2 (2018): 241–74.

Bar-On, Tamir. *Where Have All the Fascists Gone?* Farnham: Ashgate, 2007.

Bastow, Steve. "A Neo-Fascist Third Way: The Discourse of Ethno-Differentialist Revolutionary Nationalism." *Journal of Political Ideologies* 7, no. 3 (2002): 351–68.

Bell, Donald. "Gadaffi and the 'Right-Wing' Patriots." *Nationalism Today*, no. 24 (1984): 14.

Ben-Ghiat, Ruth. "Italian Fascism and the Aesthetics of the 'Third Way.'" *Journal of Contemporary History* 31, no. 2 (1996): 293–316.

Billig, Michael. *Fascists: A Social Psychological View of the National Front*. London: Harcourt Bruce Jovanovich, 1978.

Bland, Benjamin. "Holocaust Inversion, Anti-Zionism, and British Neo-fascism: The Israel-Palestine Conflict and the Extreme Right in Post-war Britain." *Patterns of Prejudice* 53, no. 1 (2019): 86–97.

Copsey, Nigel. "Au Revoir to 'Sacred Cows'? Assessing the Impact of the Nouvelle Droite in Britain." *Democracy and Security* 9, no. 3 (2013): 287–303.

Copsey, Nigel. *Contemporary British Fascism: The British National Party and the Quest for Legitimacy*. Basingstoke: Palgrave Macmillan, 2008.

Curthoys, Ann, and Marilyn Lake. "Introduction." In *Connected Worlds: History in Transnational Perspective*, edited by Ann Curthoys and Marilyn Lake, 5–20. Canberra: ANU Press, 2005.

Drake, Richard H. "Julius Evola and the Ideological Origins of the Radical Right in Contemporary Italy." In *Political Violence and Terror: Motifs and Motivations*, edited by Peter H. Merkl, 61–90. Berkeley: University of California Press, 1986.

Eatwell, Roger. *Fascism: A History*. London: Pimlico, 2003.

Eatwell, Roger. "Fascism and Political Racism in Post-war Britain." In *Traditions of Intolerance: Historical Perspectives on Fascism and Race Discourse in Britain*, edited by Tony Kushner and Kenneth Lunn, 218–38. Manchester: Manchester University Press, 1989.

Evola, Julius. *Revolt against the Modern World*, translated by Guido Stucco. Rochester, VT: Inner Traditions, 1995.

Finchelstein, Federico. *From Fascism to Populism in History*. Oakland: University of California Press, 2017.

Finchelstein, Federico. *Transatlantic Fascism: Ideology, Violence, and the Sacred in Argentina and Italy, 1919–1945*. Durham, NC: Duke University Press, 2010.

Furlong, Paul. *Social and Political Thought of Julius Evola*. Abingdon: Routledge, 2011.

Gardell, Mattias. *In the Name of Elijah Muhammad: Louis Farrakhan and the Nation of Islam*. Durham, NC: Duke University Press, 1996.

Gibson, Dawn-Marie. *A History of the Nation of Islam: Race, Islam, and the Quest for Freedom*. Santa Barbara, CA: Praeger, 2012.

Gilroy, Paul. *Between Camps: Nations, Cultures, and the Allure of Race*. London: Routledge, 2004.

Griffin, Nick. "The Deadly Trap / Let My People Go." *Nationalism Today*, no. 29 (1985).

Griffin, Roger. *A Fascist Century: Essays by Roger Griffin*, edited by Matthew Feldman. Basingstoke: Palgrave Macmillan, 2008.

Griffiths, Richard. *Fascism*. London: Continuum, 2005.

Hall, Stuart. "The Great Moving Right Show." *Marxism Today* 23, no. 1 (1979): 14–20.

Herf, Jeffrey. *Nazi Propaganda for the Arab World*. New Haven, CT: Yale University Press, 2009.

Hobsbawm, Eric. "Falklands Fallout." *Marxism Today* 26, no. 1 (1983): 13–19.

Holland, Derek. "The Armed People." *Nationalism Today*, no. 39 (1986).

Holland, Derek. "Iran's National Revolution." *Nationalism Today*, no. 21 (1983): 12.

Holland, Derek. *The Political Soldier*. London: International Third Position, 1994.

Jewish Chronicle. "NF About-Turn is 'Not Serious.'" October 13, 1989.

Judt, Tony. *Reappraisals: Reflections on the Forgotten Twentieth Century*. London: Vintage, 2009.

Khomeini, Imam. *Islam and Revolution: Writings and Declarations of Imam Khomeini (1941–1980)*, edited and translated by Hamid Algar. North Haledon, NJ: Mizan, 1981.

Macklin, Graham D. "Co-opting the Counter Culture: Troy Southgate and the National Revolutionary Faction." *Patterns of Prejudice* 39, no. 3 (2005): 301–26.

Mammone, Andrea. *Transnational Neofascism in France and Italy*. Cambridge: Cambridge University Press, 2015.

Moloney, Ed. *A Secret History of the IRA*. London: Penguin, 2007.

Mosse, George L. *The Fascist Revolution: Toward a General Theory of Fascism*. New York: Howard Fertig, 1999.

Motadel, David. *Islam and Nazi Germany's War*. Cambridge, MA: Harvard University Press, 2014.

Muhammad, Abdul Wali. "Nation of Islam." *Nationalism Today*, no. 39 (1986): 16–20.

National Front News. "Death to Imperialism." No. 88 (1987).

National Front News. "Fight Racism." No. 88 (1987).

National Front News. "Libya Condemns the IRA." No. 110 (1988).

National Front News. "Mad Dogs and Englishmen." No. 111 (1988).

National Front News. "The New Alliance." No. 103 (1988).

National Front News. "NF Chiefs Visit Libya." No. 111 (1988).

National Front News. "The Shame and the Anger." No. 111 (1988).

Nationalism Today. "Farrakhan Aid." No. 39 (1986).

Nationalism Today. "Libya: A Study of the Third Position in Practice." No. 44 (1988).

Nationalism Today. "Louis Farrakhan: Pointing the Way for Black America." No. 37 (1986).

Nationalism Today. "A Media for the Masses." No. 42 (1987).

Nationalism Today. "People Not Parliaments." No. 41 (1987).

Nationalism Today. "Principles of Democracy." No. 42 (1987).

Nationalism Today. "What We're Fighting For." No. 1 (1980).

O'Hara, Lawrence. "Creating Political Soldiers? The National Front 1986–1990." PhD diss., Birkbeck, University of London, 2000.

Osservatorio sul Fascismo a Roma. "Terza Posizione." March 24, 2018. www .osservatoriosulfascismoaroma.org/terza-posizione.

Qathafi, Muammar Al. *The Green Book*. Tripoli: Public Establishment for Publishing, 1980.

Renton, David. *Never Again: Rock Against Racism and the Anti-Nazi League 1976–1982*. Abingdon: Routledge, 2019.

Rising. "The Folk-Community." No. 2 (1982).

Rising. "Introduction." No. 2 (1982).

Rising. "Men and Doctrines." No. 1 (ca. 1981–82).

Rising. "The Racial Question." No. 1 (ca. 1981–82).

Searchlight. From Ballots to Bombs: The Inside Story of the National Front's Political Soldiers. London, 1989.

Searchlight. "The New Axis." No. 147 (September 1987).

Shaffer, Ryan. *Music, Youth, and International Links in Post-war British Fascism: The Transformation of Extremism*. Basingstoke: Palgrave Macmillan, 2017.

Shaffer, Ryan. "Pan-European Thought in British Fascism: The International Third Position and the Alliance for Peace and Freedom." *Patterns of Prejudice* 52, no. 1 (2018): 78–99.

Slobodian, Quinn. *Globalists: The End of Empire and the Birth of Neoliberalism*. Cambridge, MA: Harvard University Press, 2018.

Smith, Anna Marie. *New Right Discourse on Race and Sexuality: Britain, 1968–2000*. Cambridge: Cambridge University Press, 1994.

Sykes, Alan. *The Radical Right in Britain: Social Imperialism to the BNP*. Basingstoke: Palgrave Macmillan, 2005.

Telese, Luca. *Cuori neri (Black Hearts)*. Milan: Sperling and Kupfer, 2006.

Vandewalle, Dirk. *A History of Modern Libya*. Cambridge: Cambridge University Press, 2012.

Wodak, Ruth. *The Politics of Fear: What Right-Wing Populist Discourses Mean*. London: Sage, 2015.

Wolff, Elisabetta Cassina. "Apolitìa and Tradition in Julius Evola as a Reaction to Nihilism." *European Review* 22, no. 2 (2014): 258–73.

Wolff, Elisabetta Cassina. "Evola's Interpretation of Fascism and Moral Responsibility." *Patterns of Prejudice* 50, no. 4–5 (2016): 478–94.

Zachariah, Benjamin. "A Voluntary Gleichschaltung? Perspectives from India towards a Non-Eurocentric Understanding of Fascism." *Transcultural Studies* 2 (2014): 63–100.

Rank-and-File Antiracism

Historicizing Punk and Rock Against Racism

Stuart Schrader

Ian Goodyer, *Crisis Music: The Cultural Politics of Rock Against Racism.*
Manchester, UK: Manchester University Press, 2009.

Roger Huddle and Red Saunders, eds., *Reminiscences of RAR: Rocking against
Racism 1976–1982.* London: Redwords, 2016.

Daniel Rachel, ed., *Walls Come Tumbling Down: Rock Against Racism, 2 Tone and
Red Wedge.* London: Picador, 2017.

David Renton, *Never Again: Rock Against Racism and the Anti-Nazi League 1976–
1982.* New York: Routledge, 2019.

Syd Shelton, ed., *Rock Against Racism.* London: Autograph ABP, 2015.

Raucous and countercultural": RAR or *RHR*?[1] The movement and this journal
actually shared a point of origin. Rock Against Racism, founded in London in
1976, was an effort to reorient pop music toward a substantive commitment to antiracism, which included concerts, fanzines, records, and mass protest, as well as support for self-defense against street violence by the Far Right. Rock Against Racism
demanded that music, particularly punk and reggae, not be escapes from the

Radical History Review
Issue 138 (October 2020)   DOI 10.1215/01636545-8359468
© 2020 by MARHO: The Radical Historians' Organization, Inc.

everyday, the street, and politics, but be deeply informed by and answerable to these domains. Rock Against Racism attempted to make explicit the implicit promise of agency and social transformation that punk rock's inchoate subcultural rebellion promised.

Analogously, *Radical History Review*, originally a newsletter for the Mid-Atlantic Radical Historians' Organization (MARHO), which was founded in New York City in 1973, represented an effort to shift historical research toward the political margins and to appreciate the agency of the less powerful. Not only was social history compelling for the New Left generation to study, but the soundest way to bridge a divide between "the academy and active experience" was to foreground "an awareness of the institutional and ideological determinations of the societies in which we work" so that historical analysis could be a tool for transforming those determinations, used by and for people at the margins.[2]

E. P. Thompson and other British social historians expressed this underpinning commitment to the agency of common people. According to Ian Goodyer, it is with these intellectuals that the shared origins of RAR and *RHR* can be discovered. Dissident Communist and New Left historians influenced the formation of MARHO and the creation of this journal, as well as the radicals who founded Rock Against Racism. They attempted to "rescue the history of working people from obscurity in order to reinstate workers as subjects, rather than mere objects, of history." This effort, dovetailing with what Goodyer labels "humanist Marxism," meant rejecting methodological orthodoxies and hierarchical approaches to historiography. It also called for a disposition that was open to idiosyncratic forms of political and cultural expression.[3]

For its part, Rock Against Racism, whose original organizers orbited the Socialist Workers Party (SWP), also aimed to challenge ossified beliefs—not least by insisting that mass culture was a central terrain for working-class struggle and antiracist politics. Lasting five years in its original guise, Rock Against Racism proclaimed that young people whose consciousness had not yet been pricked by left-wing organizers might yet retain political agency worth understanding and engaging. At the same time, "many of the key figures" who founded RAR "stayed loyal to their overarching commitment to the labour movement and revolutionary socialism," an orientation diminishing among historians through the 1980s.[4] Notably, Thompson himself nastily dismissed an attempt by the Anti-Nazi League, co-organized by the SWP alongside RAR, to curry his support.[5]

Rock Against Racism almost immediately became a topic of scholarly debate, largely based on personal experience and anecdotal accounts.[6] Although participants largely remember it in positive terms, much of the original scholarship on it was negative. Today, some histories based in the archives revise these accounts: *Crisis Music* by Goodyer and *Never Again* by David Renton.[7] Additionally, a handsome photo book called *Rock Against Racism* and two compilations featuring recollections of key participants, as well as some documents from the time period, are available. (Renton cites these four other recent books.) *Crisis Music* rebuts many of the cynical early analyses of Rock Against Racism and the punk rock explosion more broadly. And *Never Again* explains how Rock Against Racism and the broader Anti-Nazi League substantially advanced antiracist politics, as Renton delves into the internal history of the National Front.

Reading these books with Donald J. Trump in the White House, who has expressed support for public demonstrations by right-wing extremists and opposition to antifa, it is difficult not to try to apply their messages to the present. My focus, however, is on the unique sociohistorical conjuncture that gave rise both to punk rock itself and Rock Against Racism, in an effort to historicize the turn to culture as political battleground amid the shifting fortunes of mass Left politics. If the turn to culture among historians today lacks the spark of excitement it once did, a reinvigoration of the labor movement as a key node in the fight against the resurgent Far Right is welcome today: these books suggest that the battle against it will not be won in the cultural realm alone.

SWP versus NF via RAR

Goodyer locates the core of Rock Against Racism's approach within the particularities of the Socialist Workers Party. Founders of RAR such as David Widgery drew on SWP resources and were party members on its dissident edge. RAR's six-member elected organizing committee, as well as the collective that produced its fanzine *Temporary Hoarding*, did sometimes conflict with SWP leadership, but Goodyer draws on internal records to show that the leadership mostly took a hands-off approach. These upstarts were trying to prove that punk aesthetics and antiracist political organizing might cohere. To them, popular culture mattered, it was vibrant, and it was politically up for grabs. Practically, according to Syd Shelton, a member of the organizing committee and RAR's most prolific photographer, "The SWP did supply troops on the ground: people to put out leaflets; put up posters; sell badges and our fanzine."[8] As a result of these efforts, circulation of *Temporary Hoarding* peaked at over twelve thousand copies, and more than one hundred thousand people attended each of the two London "carnivals" RAR organized in 1978. Thompson's fellow social historian Raphael Samuel described the first RAR carnival as "the most working-class demonstration I have been on" and a unique enough event "to have sensibly changed the climate of public opinion."[9]

Other analyses deemphasize the Socialist Workers Party in Rock Against Racism's trajectory. Renton has previously written about the Anti-Nazi League, the SWP's effort to form a united front and ally with the Labour Party and smaller leftist organizations against the growing Far Right. He offers evidence, which Goodyer confirms, that the party's energies were more focused on the League than RAR.[10] Critical of the Anti-Nazi League but fond of Rock Against Racism, Paul

Gilroy acknowledges SWP's "important" role while remaining skeptical of its "approach to culture and mistaken tendency to imagine RAR as a redemptive infusion of socialist ideology into the nihilistic misery of Punk."[11] Unlike other left-wing organizations, such as the Communist Party of Great Britain, the SWP did not aim to ally against the Far Right with centrists who did not share other aspects of their political program. Instead, it would confront the National Front directly.

Formed as a reconfiguration of the International Socialists, the Socialist Workers Party maintained several aspects that would contribute to the rise of Rock Against Racism, according to Goodyer. As Trotskyists, meaning relatively free of the Stalinist hangover, the SWP did not dismiss US mass culture out of hand. Rock and roll was legitimate.[12] More importantly, the SWP "oriented itself upon the militant minority within the working class" and fostered rank-and-file activism "as an alternative to what many saw as conservative and bureaucratic union leaderships."[13] This orientation toward "socialism from below" and the possibility of rank-and-file self-activity informed RAR. In the September 1976 open letter published in the music press to announce RAR's founding, which attacked Eric Clapton's racist endorsements of Enoch Powell, Red Saunders called for a "rank and file movement against the racist poison in rock music."[14]

Rank-and-file militancy shaped the labor movement of the early 1970s, with waves of strikes, including unofficial or wildcat actions. In 1977, punk's explosion coincided with a labor convulsion. The number of working days lost to strikes in the United Kingdom peaked that year, after declining for the prior two. But material gains for workers were limited.[15] As Goodyer astutely points out, the SWP orientation toward such often youthful and exuberant pushes for control over both union programs and the labor process itself "reached its apogee at precisely the moment when such a perspective became fatally undermined." The reasons are complex and affected most industrialized countries simultaneously, while also having specific coordinates in the United Kingdom. There, trade unions and the Labour Party had been engaged in a delicate effort to stabilize industries and foster productivity, while inviting "overt intrusion of the state" into management of the labor-capital relation.[16] Many unions empowered their leadership to facilitate coordination with management, opening a gulf between rank-and-file demands and the perspectives at the top. Yet these efforts were insufficient amid a global economic crisis of Fordism that revealed the limits of Keynesian policy instruments. A nationally based workers' movement was no match for the transnationalization of capital. Austerity-oriented demands from both voters and International Monetary Fund technocrats grew in tandem with unemployment rates, often affecting the very same young workers who might otherwise have been part of rank-and-file movements.

Beyond fascist appeals by rock stars like Clapton and David Bowie, numerous marches and local electoral wins testified to growing support for the National Front, as did a scourge of racist attacks across Britain. The Front expanded its membership throughout the 1970s, even recruiting some former leftists. Its ideological development was uneven, as members and leaders wavered on how firmly to embrace Nazism or Nazi imagery. On the one hand, the effort to gain respectability and with it to win elections called for distancing the party from its flirtations with Hitler. On the other hand, it was the nasty imagery and language that seemed to attract new supporters. Fascist imagery disenchanted some older party members who recalled World War II vividly, but it was an aphrodisiac to street hooligans. The National Front by 1977 had grown three times as large as the SWP, and its "supporters were predominantly male, relatively young and unafraid of using violence."[17] The destruction in the 1970s of some vestiges of the British empire gave fodder to the Front. Campaigns denouncing political transformations in Rhodesia as well as the arrival of migrants from Kenya, Malawi, and Uganda pulled in supporters.[18] The Front tried to organize among workers too, offering support for efforts to strengthen racialized wage hierarchies and sending white strikebreakers when Asian workers walked off the job. But the Front's primary activities outside its electoral campaigns consisted of provocative marches that often ended in street violence. Under cover of night, there were also bombings of both left-wing and Asian and Black sites, as well as constant daubing of racist graffiti. Although some of the Front's leadership tried to steer the party away from violence, the effort was futile. Meanwhile groups like Rock Against Racism and the Anti-Nazi League amplified any Front linkage to outright Nazism that could be found, stymied Front marches and rallies, and tried to push racists out of trade unions.

Rock Against Racism helped weaken, discredit, and fragment the National Front in three ways. First, RAR staged hugely successful protests and concerts in London and elsewhere in Britain. The size of these events far outmatched even the largest National Front rallies. Second, RAR gave prominent voice to antiracist politics at a time when the Tories were moving right, racist street violence was spiking, and mainstream musicians were openly expressing racist sentiments. By insisting both that the Front was extreme and that it was continuous with a long history of imperialist racism, RAR provided a new antiracist language to many whom socialists and other left-wing activists otherwise may not have reached. RAR fostered interracial solidarity and organizing. Third, RAR gave tangible resources, bodies in number, and spiritual courage to the fight for self-defense against both right-wing mobilizations and physical violence, including by police. These efforts were not always successful, to be sure, and they necessarily relied on coalition with those who did not need RAR's exhortations to galvanize them to fight for their lives against neo-Nazis, whether the Indian Workers' Association or the predominantly West Indian group Peoples Unite.[19]

Rock Against Racism and the Anti-Nazi League did defeat the National Front as such. The 1979 elections, meant to be pivotal for the Front, marked a resounding loss in support, causing the party's leadership to splinter. Although the party's membership declined by nine-tenths by 1985 and electoral wins became elusive, racist street violence continued, with fifteen thousand attacks officially recorded annually. Moreover, Margaret Thatcher and the Tories adopted much of the Front's program regarding immigration. Renton points out how RAR linked the growth of right-wing street violence to racist policing and to the state's nationalism more broadly, including its ongoing disavowal of the violence of imperialism. In this way, contrary to some conservative claims, Thatcher did not neutralize the Front, which RAR and the League had already weakened, but instead laundered its ideas and integrated them with widely shared racial discourses.[20]

For its part, the Socialist Workers Party had theorized that deepening everyday discontent and the fracturing of a socioeconomic consensus were opening the door for neofascist political organizing. The SWP believed that if the party's activists did not attempt to win people over to antiracist politics, the National Front might win them over to the opposite perspective. In advance of Rock Against Racism's creation, the SWP already was focusing on issues of race and gender in its agit-prop. SWP and its predecessors published papers in Bengali (*Pragati*), Punjabi (*Chingari*), and Urdu (*Chingari*), plus magazines specifically dedicated to reaching women (*Women's Voice*) and Black people (*Flame*).[21] The SWP promulgated a campaign to reverse growing unemployment, but changing conditions dictated a move toward reaching the already unemployed and hopeless, rather than focusing on the rank-and-file in unionized sectors—and even those workers faced an onslaught of neofascist appeals within their unions. Antiracists dedicated themselves to pushing these workers out. But macroeconomic trends were already achieving what badges, banners, and brawling could not.

Debating Rock Against Racism

A great deal of the preceding debate about the relationship of the Socialist Workers Party and Rock Against Racism to the punk explosion has been predicated on whether RAR represented an organic tendency within punk or was externally imposed on it. A subsidiary topic in this debate is whether RAR shot itself in the foot, so to speak, by trying to organize an antiracist movement through a cultural phenomenon that was, at best, uninterested in antiracism, and at worst, incipiently or quietly racist. The books under review, particularly Goodyer's, which deals extensively with the existing literature on RAR, indicate that authors such as Simon Reynolds, Roger Sabin, and Simon Frith and John Street missed the mark.[22] For every claim that punk was predominantly white, or that it was replete with racists, or that RAR did not reach the correct audiences, or that the SWP was parasitic and used the inauthentic RAR as a Trojan horse (perhaps the most common critique), there is a photograph by Syd Shelton showing interracial groups of punks wearing RAR badges, dancing together, or chasing neo-Nazis down the street.[23]

The focus of both Goodyer and Renton on London, Rock Against Racism's epicenter, and on the first few years of the organization, however, precludes assessment of its wider effects, while weakening possible rebuttals to existing criticisms. For instance, RAR's central committee diversified after the first couple of years, when two members of Alien Kulture, both Asian, were elected to it.[24] Further, there were over a hundred local RAR branches, plus autonomous subcultural initiatives of organic antiracism. The synergies between DIY punk's spread to the hinterlands of Britain and RAR's organizational infrastructure remain to be elucidated.[25] Renton briefly analyzes Rock Against Sexism, formed by some of RAR's key members, and Daniel Rachel's volume includes a fascinating discussion of how RAR promoted opposition to homophobia.[26] Numerous offshoots and related campaigns emerged as well, including Rock Against Racism outfits in several other countries: Rock Against Reagan (US), Rock Against Sexism (Sweden), Rock Against Prisons (Canada), Rock Against Police (France), Rock Against Religion (Netherlands), and others. Although RAR's founders grew tired of these spin-offs, believing they diluted the core antiracist message and mission, their popularity indicates that a deeper investigation is warranted. What can they tell us about the Left at the moment the workers' movement was crumbling?

Punk and the 1970s Crisis of Capitalism

Long absent from any historical accounting of the punk explosion is an answer to the most basic question about it: Why did it happen when it happened? Why did punk grab hold of urban and suburban youth in the United Kingdom and United States around 1977, and within months, spread across Europe and across the globe to Japan, Mexico, Australia, and other places, though the components of its sound had been available for years? To answer these questions might require looking at and listening to punk more closely than these books allow, focused as they are on Rock Against Racism. But Goodyer's analysis of the socioeconomic conjuncture that gave birth to RAR, highlighting rank-and-file militancy, which reached far beyond the Socialist Workers Party, can help explain punk itself.

Punk was a rank-and-file movement. It was an autonomous explosion from below of political and cultural energy that expressed and took advantage of the foreclosure of more traditional forms of radical militancy wrought by changes in capitalism, exhaustion of extant left-wing organizations, and transformations in political common sense that are widely now associated with neoliberalization.[27] As deindustrialization, offshoring, financialization, and the expansion of the service sector hollowed out communities once bound together by work, music offered new communalisms. Precisely when institutional and overtly political avenues of struggle were becoming foreclosed, the domain of culture, which had always been a site of political contestation, became the primary site. In the 1977 words of The Desperate

Bicycles, "The medium was tedium, the outlets were clogged / The rats were fighting cats again and everyone was stuck." It was not simply that militants turned to music; it was that music was one of the few arenas of struggle that seemed readily available as the institutional Left was in retreat and other organizing methods became exhausted. The rise of punk rock, with all of its political confusions and its contradictory nihilistic romanticism, evidenced the turn away from prior forms of working-class organization toward other modalities of struggle. Yet even as punk represented an extension or culmination of the revolt against Fordism that the New Left and the global revolution of 1968 began, punk risked the replacement of Fordism's stultifying mass cultural and economic seriality with post-Fordism's marketized, individualistic, and consumer-based freedom. Organizations like Rock Against Racism tried to channel punk's energy and prevent this outcome.

Further, the punk explosion was an explosion of broader cultural ferment that mostly took shape through music but generally represented a type of autogestion. Its sound was not only the sound of punk rock and reggae but also that of punk-adjacent "UK DIY," second-wave ska, the "new wave of British heavy metal," industrial, and, of course, rap (first in the United States). The extent and reach of this wave indicates that it had deep, impersonal causes. Punk and rap most directly sought to adequate themselves to a postindustrial economic situation of endless deskilling and unemployment, while reappropriating obsolescent technologies.[28] It is plausible to impugn punk as too white or too middle-class only if analyzed narrowly in time and space and divorced from these sibling cultural phenomena that occurred at the same time.[29]

. . . . .

Historians now understand their field's turn to culture itself, along with the fetish of agency, as consonant with transformations in capitalism that commenced in the 1970s. Although not all scholarly critics of Rock Against Racism and punk were historians, they participated in what William H. Sewell Jr. has called "a culture mania" that "swept across a broad range of fields in the human sciences." This mania transformed social history's focus on agency as experience into agency as freely willed activity, as if the ordinary people who engaged in these movements could have done simply anything they wanted, untethered from historical circumstance.[30] Advancing a structural interpretation of the conditions of possibility for cultural phenomena was never the goal of criticisms of Rock Against Racism or punk, which often cherry-picked texts to suit prefabricated interpretations that masqueraded as hard-nosed realism. The critics' rejection of the new type of militancy that punk represented cannot be explained within the critics' own terms because they were allergic to reflexivity about shared conditions for critique and its object alike.

Scholarly attacks on Rock Against Racism's and punk's shortcomings were themselves part of a broader rejection of collective action that was not market optimizing (whether on the shop floor or in the domain of culture). Claims that punk was too exclusionary, insufficiently solidaristic, or incompletely indigenous to the interracial working class ultimately come across as bad-faith dismissals of a unique effort to fashion a political riposte out of a new form of social collectivity once older forms proved incapable of withstanding the onslaught of capitalist crisis and the political arrival of Ronald Reagan and Margaret Thatcher. Further, critics mistakenly took punk's political volatility as a drawback rather than recognizing, as did Rock Against Racism and many punks unaffiliated with it, that punk, like other cultural phenomena, was a strategic terrain for political battle. To imply that RAR failed to transform politics more broadly because punk was predisposed to accept far-right pleading is empirically incorrect and theoretically wooden. Ultimately, the Left in the United States and the United Kingdom was on its heels by the late 1970s and throughout the 1980s. Apart from a few notable exceptions, the mass movement that the older Marxist Left desired did not take the forms it would have likely recognized, but many anti-Marxist critics also misrecognized what was happening. This mass movement took on new contours, outside workplaces, mixing horizontal networking with entrepreneurialism in production and circulation, earning the label "DIY" but perhaps better considered rank and file, without either bosses or union stewards.

Reconstruction of left-wing strategic decisions is painstaking historical work, and criticism of political strategy for the purpose of refining it is important. Yet that is not what most critics of RAR sought. They ricocheted between voluntarism and cynicism—in retrospect, in accordance with neoliberal ideology itself. Critics blamed the victim while also upbraiding it for not achieving the impossible given the circumstances: thanks to the SWP's ideological proclivities, RAR failed because it did not entirely desegregate a music industry that had been segregated since its inception, et cetera. When attempts to replicate RAR occurred in subsequent decades, their failure should have been predictable, but existing analyses made them difficult to explain. If the SWP were the problem, then without the SWP, they should have succeeded. If punk was the problem, then without punk, they should have succeeded. But the problem was the conjuncture.

With the large amount of source material now available in the books edited by Rachel and by Roger Huddle and Red Saunders, plus the scholarly histories by Goodyer and Renton, misleading accounts of Rock Against Racism should finally be put to rest. At the same time, Goodyer helps to indicate why an internalist history of phenomena like RAR or punk itself will no longer suffice. Renton concludes his analysis by arguing that it is unlikely there will be "any return to the anti-fascism of the 1970s, with its youth, its scepticism of authority and its physical daring, without their prerequisite: an independent cultural movement following its own rules."[31] He is correct. I would add that the possibility of such an independent cultural movement was itself historically specific, fostered but not determined by a crisis of capitalism that augured the culmination of a particular regime of accumulation. That regime and its crisis will not be replicated. Saying "never again" to the birth of fascism requires also recognizing that the period of Fordism-Keynesianism that followed it will never happen again either. Fascism and its resistance today will have different proximate enabling conditions. That should be the basic lesson of a radical history. The tougher lesson is that, as in punk rock, there are no spectators in history, only participants, including historians themselves.

Stuart Schrader is associate director of the Program in Racism, Immigration, and Citizenship and lecturer at Johns Hopkins University. He is the author of *Badges without Borders: How Global Counterinsurgency Transformed American Policing* (2019). He has been writing about punk and other music in fanzines for twenty-five years, and he edits shit-fi.com.

Notes

1. Novick, *That Noble Dream*, 460.
2. Thompson, "Agenda for a Radical History," 362.
3. Goodyer, *Crisis Music*, 106, 157.
4. Goodyer, *Crisis Music*, 110.
5. Renton, *Never Again*, 90.
6. The most well-known analysis is Gilroy, *"There Ain't No Black in the Union Jack."*
7. The largest and most important archive, belonging to Red Saunders, was destroyed in a fire, severely limiting the possibilities for further historical research on the internal organization of RAR.
8. Rachel, *Walls Come Tumbling Down*, 31.
9. Quoted in Renton, *When We Touched the Sky*, 121.
10. Renton, *When We Touched the Sky*. *Never Again* replicates some of this prior book's analysis, though it focuses more directly on RAR and the National Front (RAR was founded about a year before the Anti-Nazi League).
11. Gilroy, "Rebel Souls," 25. For a sharp analysis that emphasizes how RAR echoed the politics of C. L. R. James (once a Trotskyist) but deemphasizes SWP, see Dawson, "'Love Music Hate Racism.'"
12. The Communist Party of Great Britain struggled on this point: Smith, "Are the Kids United?"
13. Goodyer, *Crisis Music*, 54–55.
14. Quoted in Goodyer, *Crisis Music*, 61, and Renton, *Never Again*, 52. Saunders and his comrades had already been planning to create RAR before Clapton's outburst.
15. Callinicos, "Fire This Time."
16. Goodyer, *Crisis Music*, 54, 56.
17. Renton, *Never Again*, 88.
18. RAR's peak coincided with Rhodesia's dissolution, but RAR produced a sticker that declared "Rock Against Racism Zimbabwe Coming Soon!" (A Sex Pistols single was released in Rhodesia in 1977, but Rhodesia came to ban *Punk Rock* magazine and Bob Marley albums alike.) RAR also supported the fight to decolonize Northern Ireland; Rachel, *Walls Come Tumbling Down*, 154–60.
19. Huddle and Saunders, *Reminiscences of RAR*.

20. Renton, *Never Again*, 162, 56–57, 169–71.

21. Goodyer, *Crisis Music*, 58.

22. Reynolds, *Rip It Up*; Sabin, "'I Won't Let That Dago By'"; Frith and Street, "Rock Against Racism and Red Wedge"; Savage, *England's Dreaming*. Savage criticizes RAR from an ultra-left perspective, claiming that it attempted to "codify" and homogenize what could otherwise have been more radical and anarchic (*England's Dreaming*, 484). A more recent collection that attempts to reconsider punk and race, touching on RAR, is Duncombe and Tremblay, *White Riot*; but see Nikpour, "White Riot: Another Failure."

23. Renton credulously accepts National Front claims about the number of punk bands under its wing. Not investigating these bands more closely represents a missed opportunity to rebut the widespread argument that punk was indifferent to antiracist politics or susceptible to the Front. A misspelling of the band name Beyond The Implode appears in both Renton's books, based on an article in an antiracist magazine repeating Front reports claiming the band as its own (*When We Touched the Sky*, 158–59; *Never Again*, 121–22). Not just a gaffe, the claim was untrue. The band was unaware of the Front's claim and had even broken off a relationship with an old friend who joined the British National Party at the time. Lyrics to one of the band's songs, cataloging "midnight adventures," mention fascists, in an observational tone, which an eagle-eyed Front member must have taken as an endorsement. See Forbes and Stampton, *White Nationalist Skinhead Movement*, 21–22; *Searchlight*, "Head-Banging for Hitler."

24. Author interviews with Pervez Bilgrami (2011) and Ausaf Abbas (2008), in author's possession.

25. See Savage, *England's Dreaming*, 484.

26. Rachel, *Walls Come Tumbling Down*, 145–54.

27. I have explored this line of analysis in Schrader, "Rotten Legacy?"; Schrader, "Fiendens Musik"; Schrader, "I Don't Wanna Be a Mercenary"; and Schrader, "New Wave vs. Black Lung?!"

28. In turn, "Punk's narrowed focus on guitar, bass, and drums had filled British junkshops with banged-up horns, reeds, violins, accordions, harmonicas, and more exotic noise-making gear that graced innumerable DIY disks with gleeful disregard for what was or was not cool" (Warner, "Messthetics #103").

29. The most astringent critiques along these lines were Sabin, "'I Won't Let That Dago By,'" and Frith and Street, "Rock Against Racism and Red Wedge." The latter two authors suggested, in a quotation that represents the evidentiary problems of their analysis: "Both heavy metal and disco bands were excluded from RAR line-ups, for example, presumably on the grounds that they were a form of false consciousness" ("Rock Against Racism and Red Wedge," 76). A 1979 *New Musical Express* interview with RAR collective members specifically addressed why metal and disco bands did not appear on RAR bills; false consciousness was not the problem. Widgery asserted, "We don't have any ideological bans on any kind of music" (Renton, *Never Again*, 152).

30. Sewell, "Political Unconscious of Social and Cultural History," 54; Eley, *Crooked Line*; Goswami, "Remembering the Future."

31. Renton, *Never Again*, 172.

References

Callinicos, Alex. "The Fire This Time." *International Socialism* (first series) 104 (January 1978): 5–8.

Dawson, Ashley. "'Love Music Hate Racism': The Cultural Politics of the Rock Against Racism Campaigns, 1976–1981." *Postmodern Culture* 16, no. 1 (2005): n.p.

Duncombe, Stephen, and Maxwell Tremblay, eds. *White Riot: Punk Rock and the Politics of Race*. New York: Verso, 2011.

Eley, Geoff. *A Crooked Line: From Cultural History to the History of Society*. Ann Arbor: University of Michigan Press, 2005.

Forbes, Robert, and Eddie Stampton. *The White Nationalist Skinhead Movement: UK & USA, 1979–1993*. Port Townsend, WA: Feral House, 2015.

Frith, Simon, and John Street. "Rock Against Racism and Red Wedge: From Music to Politics, From Politics to Music." In *Rockin' the Boat: Mass Music and Mass Movements*, edited by Reebee Garofalo, 67–80. Boston, MA: South End, 1992.

Gilroy, Paul. "Rebel Souls: Dance-Floor Justice and the Temporary Undoing of Britain's Babylon." In *Rock Against Racism*, edited by Syd Shelton, 23–26. London: Autograph ABP, 2015.

Gilroy, Paul. *"There Ain't No Black in the Union Jack": The Cultural Politics of Race and Nation*. Chicago: University of Chicago Press, 1991.

Goodyer, Ian. *Crisis Music: The Cultural Politics of Rock Against Racism*. Manchester, UK: Manchester University Press, 2019.

Goswami, Manu. "Remembering the Future." *American Historical Review* 113, no. 2 (2008): 417–24.

Huddle, Roger, and Red Saunders, eds. *Reminiscences of RAR: Rocking Against Racism 1976–1982*. London: Redwords, 2016.

Nikpour, Golnar. "White Riot: Another Failure." *Maximum Rocknroll*, January 17, 2012. maximumrocknroll.com/white-riot-another-failure.

Novick, Peter. *That Noble Dream: The "Objectivity Question" and the American Historical Profession*. New York: Cambridge University Press, 1988.

Rachel, Daniel, ed. *Walls Come Tumbling Down: Rock Against Racism, 2 Tone and Red Wedge*. London: Picador, 2017.

Renton, Dave. *Never Again: Rock Against Racism and the Anti-Nazi League 1976–1982*. New York: Routledge, 2019.

Renton, Dave. *When We Touched the Sky: The Anti-Nazi League 1977–1981*. Cheltenham: New Clarion, 2006.

Reynolds, Simon. *Rip It Up and Start Again: Postpunk 1978–1984*. New York: Penguin, 2006.

Sabin, Roger. "'I Won't Let That Dago By': Rethinking Punk and Racism." In *Punk Rock: So What? The Cultural Legacy of Punk*, edited by Roger Sabin, 199–218. New York: Routledge, 2002.

Savage, Jon. *England's Dreaming: Anarchy, Sex Pistols, Punk Rock, and Beyond*. New York: St. Martin's Griffin, 2001.

Schrader, Stuart. "Fiendens Musik." *Shit-Fi*, August 2015. shit-fi.com/fiendens-musik.

Schrader, Stuart. "I Don't Wanna Be a Mercenary: Punk Rock versus the Mercenary Movement in the 1970s." *Shit-Fi*, June 2015. shit-fi.com/mercenaries.

Schrader, Stuart. "New Wave vs. Black Lung?!" *Shit-Fi*, January 2010. shit-fi.com/new_wave_vs_black_lung.

Schrader, Stuart. "A Rotten Legacy?" *Brooklyn Rail* (December–January 2009–2010).

Searchlight. "Head-Banging for Hitler." November 19, 1979.

Sewell, William H., Jr. "The Political Unconscious of Social and Cultural History; or, Confessions of a Former Quantitative Historian." In *Logics of History: Social Theory and Social Transformation*, 22–80. Chicago: University of Chicago Press, 2005.

Smith, Evan. "Are the Kids United?: The Communist Party of Great Britain, Rock Against Racism, and the Politics of Youth Culture." *Journal for the Study of Radicalism* 5, no. 2 (2011): 85–117.

Thompson, E. P. "Agenda for a Radical History." In *Making History: Writings on History and Culture*, 358–64. New York: New Press, 1994.

Warner, Chuck. 2007. "Messthetics #103." CD liner notes, Hyped 2 Death.

Strategies of Ambivalence

Cultures of Liberal Antifa in Japan

Vivian Shaw

On the evening of June 30, 2014, I arrived at the Tokyo Metropolitan Governor's Office expecting to find a dozen or so activists staging their weekly rally against hate speech. I had been following the group, Tokyo Action for Anti-Discrimination (TA4AD), for the past several weeks, since coming to the city earlier in the summer for fieldwork. Instead, the space—an expanse of sidewalk next to a bus shelter lit up by bright street lights—was empty. I waited for forty minutes and then checked social media. TA4AD had retweeted an announcement of an urgent protest in front of the prime minister's residence. That night an estimated ten thousand people would camp out in the streets surrounding the residence to oppose the impending reinterpretation of Article 9 of the constitution, a segment that prohibited Japan from military action. Japan already had a military force, the Self-Defense Forces, but the reinterpretation would enable Japan to alter the meaning of "self-defense" and enter into combat assertively.

The perimeter surrounding the prime minister's residence and the National Diet was an area I visited regularly. The two buildings are at the center of the nation's capital and a major site of protest, including a series of Friday-night antinuclear rallies that began in 2012 and continue to this day. Before arriving at the Article 9 antiwar protest, I was accustomed to an orderly scene—protesters, mostly in their sixties and seventies, corralled behind metal barricades alongside a courteous yet firm police presence. That evening, however, the crowd spilled into the

Radical History Review

Issue 138 (October 2020)   DOI 10.1215/01636545-8359482

© 2020 by MARHO: The Radical Historians' Organization, Inc.

street and the air was acrid with the smell of sweat. On the sidewalk I nudged my way between shoulders and signs, taking nearly twenty minutes to reach an area closer to the end of the block. The energy of the rally seemed to emanate from around a driveway leading to a legislative building. People squeezed onto concrete platforms near the building; three men sharing the space of one small square. Around ten o'clock, police began pushing rows of metal barriers toward the interior of the side-walk against protesters' bodies. The protest would last late into the night and repeat over the next several days. An opposition to fascism emerged as a prominent theme of the protest. Protesters carried signs saying "anti-fascist" and "no fascism." Some signs depicted Prime Minister Abe Shinzo[1] with a Hitler-style mustache. Numerous calls that cycled during the rally repeatedly invoked the anti-fascist sentiments of the protest: "Fascism wo yurusuna" (Don't permit fascism!) and "Fascism wa hantai" (Against fascism!).

I had not set out to study anti-fascism in Japan. Rather, these themes emerged from my ethnography of a nationwide antiracism movement that had taken its roots in the political aftermath of the 2011 Fukushima nuclear disaster. Over twenty-four months between 2014 and 2017, I followed several antiracism social movement organizations in Tokyo and Osaka at protests, at social gatherings, and during lobbying efforts. At the same time, to gain a sense of the broader nexus of social movements in Japan, I observed overlapping scenes of collective action, including antinuclear activism, labor organizing, and antiwar protests. In addition to sharing members, these demonstrations—while explicitly organized as "single issue" protests—often included anti-fascist messages. Most conspicuously, antiracist activists protested against hate speech while wearing clothing that featured antifa slogans, seemingly equivocating the two causes. They also organized social events around the theme of fighting against fascism and produced antifa cultural objects. As I continued with my fieldwork, fascism and its opposition had marked themselves as issues I could not ignore.

In his book *Anti-fascism in Britain*, historian Nigel Copsey disentangles anti-fascism from acts of protest and the structures of organizations, instead offering a definition of the phenomenon as "a thought, an attitude or feeling of hostility towards fascist ideology."[2] This broadened definition encourages us to evaluate anti-fascism as more than a single movement, but rather as a politics born out of ongoing negotiations, competing interests, and conflictual approaches. Similarly, contemporary antifa in Japan comprises a mix of political standpoints—at times, consisting of collaborations among left, liberal, and right-wing activists. In this inter-vention, I begin with this consideration of the variation within anti-fascism to explore a particular segment of Japanese antifa that I call "liberal antifa."[3] Liberal antifa is a political approach that simultaneously borrows from and distinguishes itself from traditional leftist antifa trajectories. Whereas global antifa has most fre-quently been described as leftist, communist, and working class,[4] liberal antifa in

Japan encompasses a broader spectrum of political positions. It is indeed adverse to articulating a coherent political ideology and instead seeks to be inclusive of allied participants—even if they diverge on other political stances. Activists within this camp do not always explicitly describe themselves as "liberal"—in fact, some identify as right wing. Yet I use this marker because "liberal" (*riboraru*) often functions as a way for contemporary activists to separate themselves from the vexed legacies of the Japanese New Left, a series of mobilizations that grew out of domestic antiwar politics as well as transnational civil rights.[5]

Many of the activists who would shepherd Japanese liberal antifa found their footing in the aftermath of the 2011 Fukushima nuclear disaster (3/11): a watershed moment that provided ordinary citizens with the impetus to reconstruct social movements as a mainstream, individualistic space.[6] In the words of Noma Yasumichi, an activist and founder of the Counter-Racist Action Collective:

> [The] 3/11 disaster woke up some long dormant Japanese people, but the movement was not recognized as an antifascism movement until Abe came back. Ordinary Japanese people took back general methods of protest like demonstrations and rallies after 3/11 and unconsciously prepared for [an] upcoming fascist government. Then it [fascism] actually came on and people were able to quickly resist it through an antifa movement.[7]

As ethnomusicologist Noriko Manabe points out in her writing on recent Japanese social movements, 3/11 was also crucial in centering music and culture in protests.[8] This integration of music, specifically punk and hip-hop, would lay the groundwork for the focus on cultural participation and consumption within liberal antifa communities.

In the following sections, I present a historical overview of the trajectories of anti-fascist politics in Japan. I argue that liberal antifa presents a departure from some of these histories by distinguishing itself from more leftist iterations of antifa that grew out of 1930s and postwar communist organizing. I analyze the ways that liberal antifa activists have framed the problem of fascism and how they have incorporated antifa into their everyday cultural practices. For liberal antifa, activists can collaborate regardless of their broader political views—as long as they agree in their opposition to fascism and racism. This includes the right wing, which encompasses a range of identifications—from Japanese nationalistic pride, a belief in the emperor as a deity, and anti-American patriotism. For liberal antifa, being right wing is not incommensurate with a desire to stand up for the dignities of marginalized people and an obligation to oppose political entities that seek to infringe on the rights of all people living in Japan.

In focusing on liberal antifa, this intervention does not aim to be a comprehensive view of anti-fascist politics in contemporary Japan. Indeed, in Japan there exist multiple leftist groups that practice a combination of drawing on antifa imagery and explicitly identifying as anti-fascist. In my fieldwork, I spent some time with groups that see themselves as descended from the New Left. The majority of the activists I worked with, however, eschewed an identification with leftist politics, even if they claimed the label of antifa. The analysis in this intervention relies on ethnographic observations of antiracist social movement collectives—namely, the Counter-Racist Action Collective (CRAC) and The Menfolk—and interviews with members of these groups. The informants quoted in this study were selected from the sixty individuals I interviewed for my larger study on contemporary antiracism in Japan. Although the topic of fascism came up organically in several of my initial interviews, it was usually not the main focus on my conversations. Thus, I chose some of my key informants—Noma Yasumichi, leader of CRAC; Takahashi Wakagi, formerly of Tokyo Democracy Crew and currently an immigrant rights activist; and Kimura Natsuki, artist and photographer of contemporary Japanese social movements—to answer more detailed questions about the sources and meanings of antifa within post-3/11 movements, particularly the antiracist movement.

Situating Antifa

Among liberal antifa, activists disagree about the histories of Japanese fascism—a disjuncture that reflects broader historical debates about Japan's histories of empire and militarism in the early twentieth century.[9] Noma Yasumichi claims that "most Japanese except right wingers" accepted that imperial Japan was fascist.[10] Activist Kimura Natsuki, on the other hand, draws distinctions between the fascists Hitler and Mussolini and the Japanese leaders Tojo and Hirohito. Rather than connecting Prime Minister Abe Shinzo to World War II Japanese leaders, he drew a comparison to Mussolini: "I call Abe a fascist now because I believe he's a dictator utilizing a modern form of what Mussolini came up with back in the day."[11]

The 1930s was a key period for political criticism and organizing against fascism within Japan, with Japanese intellectuals regularly discussing and critiquing fascism in their academic writings.[12] The growing opposition to fascism overlapped with economic critiques, with anti-fascist activists often participating in labor unions.[13] Anti-fascist organizing took on a variety of forms; some veered toward the left while other intellectuals felt that activists should be "liberal, antifascist reformers instead of Marxist revolutionaries."[14] Criticism of fascism also took place within religious spaces, particularly among Buddhists.[15] One significant anti-fascist initiative was the People's Front,[16] which appeared to be connected to anticapitalist movements of the same name that had begun proliferating transnationally during this period. Despite its location within transnational anti-fascist politics, however, Japanese activists complained of limited support from abroad, an absence that prevented the formation of a more robust domestic opposition to fascism.[17] From the 1930s and into the war period, government suppression of anti-fascism included outlawing the Japan Communist Party and the Japan Socialist Party,[18] arrests of activists, the banning of anti-fascist publications such as the People's Library,[19] and harassment of writers.

The restructuring of the Japanese state into a constitutional monarchy following its defeat during World War II laid the groundwork for renewed recognition of anti-fascist critics, including those affiliated with the Japan Communist Party.[20] In the postwar period, the People's Front and the Japan Communist Party pushed forth agendas of economic redistribution and prosecution of war criminals.[21] Antifa organizations that had existed in Tokyo and Kyoto in the 1930s would eventually pave the way for the emergence of the Association of Democratic Scientists in the mid-1940s, a collective that culled from various scientific disciplines to promote democratic values.[22] Another organization was Zengakuren, which pledged to oppose fascism and imperialism.[23] Anti-fascist activists occupied a precarious political position amid the US occupation, which lasted from the end of the war until early 1952, given the United States' active monitoring of communist activities.[24] In the 1950s, following the occupation, activists were highly critical of Kishi Nobusuke's ascent to the position of prime minister, authoring antifa criticisms in political cartoons and other media. Kishi was a political leader who had played a central role within Japan's imperial expansion in the lead-up to World War II and was later imprisoned as a Class A war criminal.[25]

New Left movements in Japan emerged in the period after the occupation, leading to student, antiwar, and labor movements. The Japanese New Left adopted Western norms and split from the traditional Left, which was communist. One of the most profound periods involved mass protests against the renewal of the Treaty of Mutual Cooperation and Security between the United States and Japan, known as Anpo, in 1960. Clashes between activists and political authorities featured prominently. The legacy of these movements has been most aligned with antiwar politics, though anti-fascist rhetoric appeared within these discourses. Intellectuals such as Muto Ichiyo, founder of the English-language magazine *AMPO*, criticized what he observed as "democratic fascism."[26] Muto's critique, alongside disapproval of Kishi, laid the groundwork for identifying fascist tendencies within Japan's explicitly democratic structure.

Amid this surge in leftist protests, ongoing conflicts with police elicited a backlash to these movements. The death of Kanba Michiko, a young female college student, during a protest in front of the National Diet in Tokyo on June 15, 1960, shocked the nation and further polarized opinions between leftists and those supportive of the state. The cause of Kanba's death was disputed, as people remained divided about whether police or fellow demonstrators had killed her.[27] Another significant moment came in 1972, when the communist group United Red Army occupied a lodge in Nagano Prefecture, taking the wife of the lodge owner hostage. The hostage crisis resulted in a ten-day standoff with police that ended after police captured the United Red Army members and rescued the hostage. Two police officers were killed in the process. Police violence was rooted as much in the notion of "security" for the Japanese state as in Cold War politics. As Deokhyo Choi points out, Zainichi Korean activists were targeted for their involvements in antiwar demonstrations protesting the US presence in Korea.[28] Police also orchestrated violent crackdowns on Zainichi Korean protesters.[29]

The controversies surrounding the Japanese New Left stained subsequent waves of activism. As protests swelled in the aftermath of the 2011 Fukushima nuclear disaster, activists sought to distinguish themselves from traditional leftist movements. As Takahashi Wakagi put it, "In order to counter Abe's 'fascism,' we compared ourselves with the popular fronts of the 1930s in which radical communists chose to collaborate with reformist socialists to counter the fascists. By this comparison, we attempted to present our movements as something different from the radical leftist movements originating in the '60s."[30] In this way, liberal antifa activists, rather than identifying with radical leftism, embraced the ideas of pragmatism and multipartisan coalition building.

Liberal antifa drew influence from the cultural practices of protests in the 1990s and 2000s, a movement that similarly bore complex relationships to radical politics. In Japan, the 1990s are typically understood as a "lost decade," both with regard to economic decline following the bursting of the country's bubble economy and in relation to political activism. This period, however, witnessed a new articulation of youth movements.[31] Distinct from the New Left, these youth movements responded to broader patterns of neoliberalization. They centered on young people living amid economic precarity, with many of them lacking regular employment.[32] At the same time, they dovetailed with more radical anti-globalization trends that were spreading across the globe in the wake of the 1999 WTO Seattle protests.[33] In Japan, precariat movements of the 1990s would lead to antiwar protests in the 2000s, particularly following the country's deployment of troops to Iraq in 2003. In 2008, activists staged a large protest against the G8 summit in Toyako, collaborating with foreigners and activists across the globe.[34] According to Noma, a number of the activists involved with these anti-globalization movements identified as antifascist anarchists. Antifa activists involved with the Black Helmet collective appeared at protests "dressed in black costumes, raising red/black bisected flags or circle-A anarchist symbols."[35]

In parallel to these protests, youth movements also sought to create alternative modes of economic and social participation. For instance, the anarchist collective Amateur's Riot created cafés and recycle shops. As one aspect of cultural participation, music played an important role in the construction of both protests and community more generally. One of the central innovations of movements within this period was the "sound demo," protests that incorporated musical performance such as live DJs and rap.[36] According to media and literature scholars Sharon

Hayashi and Anne McKnight, sound demos trace back to early 2003, growing out of protest to the Iraq War. Many of these sound demos functioned in conversation with transnational music influences, incorporating English alongside Japanese[37] and explicitly borrowing from the model of the UK's protest dance collective Reclaim the Streets.[38]

Activists also articulated a range of positions in bringing together music subculture and politics to critique neoliberalism. At times, music subcultures enabled activists to bridge complex perspectives, such as the prominent case of Amamiya Karin, who engaged with youth precariat movements while joining a right-wing "nationalistic punk rock" band.[39] Amamiya describes how the band's focus on "Japanese pride"—combined with the thrill of performance—was compelling during a period in which she felt lost and disenfranchised by her economic suffering. Music was particularly significant in social movements after the Fukushima nuclear disaster.[40] Punk rock often blurred antinuclear and anti-capitalist sentiments alongside a "complicated mix of political alienation."[41] In addition to antinuclear sound demos, punk appeared at major festivals such as Project Fukushima in 2011. This event included a number of major musicians, including Ōtomo Yoshihide and Endo Michirōichi of the flamboyant punk band The Stalin.[42]

While liberal antifa activists were generally separate from earlier iterations of antifa, the two segments saw some overlap, particularly with public-facing musicians. One example of this was ECD, an influential rapper who participated in anti-Iraq protests and later became a prominent figure in post-3/11 antinuclear movements.[43] Still, activists describe disjunctures between the two camps. As Noma puts it, "Most of the current antifa activists protesting far-right or Abe government actually don't know these pre-3/11 antifas. On the other hand, these pre-3/11 people sometimes hate newer people as not being left-, anti-capitalist-, or anti-imperialist enough."[44] Although 3/11 generated anti-capitalist sentiments and organizing around labor rights, for liberal antifa it also presented a new opportunity to disentangle social movements from the grasp of traditional leftist movements.

"By Any Means Necessary": Protest Framing

Antiracist activists credit the introduction of antifa framing in 2013 to journalist Sei Yoshiaki. Noma describes initial resistance to the label of antifa because it "sounds like we are extreme left or anarchists with black flags."[45] Sei, however, was interested in the culture of "antifa ultras" that had grown out of European football culture. He printed out hoodies emblazoned with ANTIFA and distributed them to other antiracist activists. Antifa's embeddedness in popular culture created multiple entry points for the activists who would become liberal antifa. Noma recalls being amused by the sight of self-avowed right-wing antiracist activists wearing antifa apparel.

Rather than critiquing right-wing ideology as a whole, liberal antifa activists specifically defined fascism through their rejection of Prime Minister Abe Shinzo.

As Takahashi Wakagi, a core member of CRAC and former leader of Tokyo Democracy Crew puts it:

When [Tokyo Democracy Crew] organized the first street demonstration
calling out Abe as fascist, we meant Abe does not belong to democracy. He was
elected, but we knew he would operate outside the norms of democracy. In
fact, his clique took over the LDP with the help of strong lobbyist groups
inspired by religions such as Nippon Kaigi or Seicho no Ie. He is also against
democratic and parliamentary procedures as evidenced by the way he pushed
through the State Secrecy Bill, etc.[46]

Another activist, Kimura Natsuki, noted for his photography of post-3/11 social movements, stated, "I'm scared because democracy is dying here and Abe may kill it without letting loose guys wearing brown uniforms."[47] For Kimura, Abe's fascism was an authoritarian encroachment on democracy with a polite image. Asō Tarō, deputy prime minister of Japan and minister of finance, also featured within Kimura's critique. Asō infamously suggested that the Liberal Democratic Party should consider borrowing techniques used by the Nazis, and that Hitler's "result" was not good even if his motive was correct.

    The term *fascism* offers a method for activists to articulate the connections between populist expressions of racism and state encroachments on democracy. By critiquing the state as fascist, activists articulate how they feel ignored, neglected, and disempowered by the state. Antifa functions as a framing method that comments simultaneously on the explicit racism associated with groups such as Zaitokukai, an organization that has been notorious for staging anti-Korean hate speech demonstrations, and state-level changes to reinterpret the constitution to allow for increased militarization. Antifa activists interpret multiple changes happening at once, including the Abe administration's changes to the structure of democracy, Abe ignoring the demands of antinuclear activists, and Abe simultaneously enabling the damage of hate speech.

    On September 11, 2011, in response to the Fukushima nuclear meltdown earlier that year, a group of antinuclear activists installed white tents in front of the Ministry of Economy, Trade and Industry (METI). The tents, covered with slogans such as "DON'T FORGET FUKUSHIMA," were connected to the weekly Friday night antinuclear rallies in front of the prime minister's residence and National Diet. Their positioning in front of METI not only highlighted the political crisis of nuclear power but also pointed to an anti-capitalist critique of the economic logics that prioritized prosperity over social and physical safety. The encampment soon became mired in a legal battle with the city. In the summer of 2016, antinuclear activists were ordered to evacuate the site; however, they continued to preserve the tents and participate in the weekly Friday rallies. Such acts of defiance attracted the ire of ultranationalist groups. In early August 2016, Zaitokukai announced its plans to protest the encampment on the fourteenth of the month. In a digital announcement it warned that "anti-Japanese left-wing people" would be coming to the tent.

Zaitokukai's framing of antinuclear activists as "anti-Japanese" is, in fact, contrary to how progressive activists describe themselves, as concerned citizens of the nation and protectors of Japanese democracy.[48] Progressive activists began circulating Zaitokukai's announcement, urging each other to show up and provide support for the tent. On the afternoon of August 14, 2016, a mix of activists appeared at the tents. They ranged from Tan Po Po Sya, a leftist environmental organization that grew out of the response to the 1987 Chernobyl disaster, to CRAC. As promised, the progressive activists were greeted by Zaitokukai members who circled the corner in cars and repeatedly entered the street in front of the tents to antagonize activists. As the rally and counterprotest waged on, members of Tan Po Po Sya—who were predominantly women and men in their sixties and seventies—stood in front of the tents in silence, many of them with observant, stoic facial expressions. CRAC members, on the other hand, had come prepared with bullhorns, amplifiers, and noise distortion machines. They aimed the noise distortion machines at Zaitokukai, rendering incomprehensible the ultranationalists' shouts.

Despite the rally's focus on nuclear power, the interactions between CRAC and Zaitokukai maps onto antifa and fascist camps, respectively. Even while expressing their opposition to antinuclear politics, ultranationalists directly invoke themes of militarism and imperial nostalgia. Networks such as CRAC describe these ultranationalists as "fascist." At the August 14 protest, right-wing men and women dressed in dark green jumpsuits that recalled World War II–era Japanese military uniforms. This symbolism was quickly detected by progressive activists who accused Zaitokukai members of "military cosplay." Right-wing activists also carried the imperial flag, a Japanese flag associated with World War II imperialism and militaristic nostalgia, which some progressive activists have described as a "Nazi flag."

That antiracist activists would show up to support an antinuclear encampment reflects the complex webs of mobilization that have emerged in the aftermath of 3/11. Activists, dissatisfied with the state's response to the disaster and its handling of information, interpret the disaster as evidence of the state's unresponsiveness to the needs of its people. Activists began conceptualizing their role as one of defending democracy, reclaiming it from the state as well as from ultranationalists. As Akira the Hustler, a gay artist and former sex worker put it: "I met Noma-san after 2011 at the TwitNoNukes antinuclear demonstration. TwitNoNukes—[I joined them because] it was rare for there to be a protest or organizing group and also I started thinking that it was relatively easy for Japan to become a totalitarian country. That it could very easily turn into a fascist country."[49] As Akira's statement demonstrates, 3/11 ushered in a crisis that made activists concerned that the country could go downhill and become one ruled by fascism. For Akira, this fear of fascism is linked to the notion that the government had stopped listening to the will of the people. This was both in relation to the question of nuclear power and safety but also the backlash to progressive movements that seemed to foment a surge in ultranationalism.

In 2013, following incidents such as a rally in Osaka where a teenage girl encouraged a crowd of ultranationalists to wage a "genocide" on the Korean neighborhood of Tsuruhashi, the problem of hate speech began drawing more attention. Zaitokukai had in previous years staged two major protests but in 2013 began regularly attacking Korean neighborhoods.[50] The antinuclear movement would turn out to be a gateway for activists to enter into the battle against hate speech. In early 2013, Noma—who had also been a leader in the antinuclear collective TwitNoNukes—put out a call over a blog, inviting people to join an all-male crew opposed to hate speech: Shibakitai. Alongside its rallies in Osaka, Zaitokukai's branch in Tokyo had begun regularly staging hate speech demonstrations in the Koreatown section of the city, Shin Ōkubo. Small in numbers, Shibakitai was unequipped to stop the hate speech demonstration in its entirety, so its members focused on Zaitokukai's walks through the narrow streets of Shin Ōkubo. During these walks (*osanpo*) members of Zaitokukai would harass shopkeepers and other denizens of Shin Ōkubo. Shibakitai's goal was to confront Zaitokukai directly, preventing and deflecting the harassment of ethnic Koreans.

Central to Shibakitai's organizing were the principles of "by any means necessary" and "make racists afraid again." Shibakitai activists also adopted other antifa verbiage, both in signs and in clothing. One of their favored expressions was "No pasaran," the classic Spanish antifa slogan. While Shibakitai operated a "by any means" approach to combating hate speech, other antiracist activists who would join the movement expressed their discomfort with physically oriented tactics. Activists such as Puraka-tai (Placard Group) focused instead on "nonviolent" methods of opposition. Avoiding physical skirmishes, they stood on the sidelines with antiracist signs. Although Puraka-tai was started by a man, Toshiki Kino, the group appealed to many women who were reluctant to become involved with physical confrontations. The group was significant in attracting more activists to the hate speech protests. By later in 2013, the Shin Ōkubo protest had grown to approximately a thousand counterprotesters and ushered in groups such as The Menfolk (Otoko Gumi), which also focused on physical confrontations. Alongside this growth, activists continued to use the linguistic and visual framing of antifa.

On November 29, 2015, at a protest in Omiya, a small city neighboring Tokyo, a cacophony of chants surrounded the streets and swallowed up the sound of the hate speech. Hate speech demonstrators walked slowly in the street, enveloped by hundreds of police officers in navy uniforms. They carried flags—contemporary Japanese flags and the controversial imperial flag. One hate speech demonstrator carried a sign: "Banish foreign criminals."

A man in a black leather jacket and black beanie cap held up a bullhorn creating a vacillating noise distortion. On his bullhorn was a sticker that read, "Rage Against Fascism," the name of an antifa punk party held annually. Another man held a bullhorn with two stickers: "This Machine Kills Fascists" and "Say no to H8." As the counterprotesters attempted to descend on the hate speech parade, they were pushed back by police officers who orchestrated a series of maneuvers to separate the two camps.

At the foot of a bridge, three police officers extended a rope to prevent counterprotesters—and unlucky pedestrians—from crossing. This group of protesters, rather than physically pushing back, waited behind the rope. They voiced their complaints verbally. While Shibakitai members often prepared for getting arrested, nonviolent protesters are typically reluctant to face direct confrontations with police. In large numbers, activists are willing to carry out certain activities that are, in the words of one activist, "in violation of the law," such as street sit-ins. However, as this incident with the rope reveals, protesters are often averse to challenging police authority in many other situations.

Ito Kenichiro, a scholar and activist, described "good" and "bad" police. Of the bad police, he observes, "They are horrible. They treat us as [a] public enemy." Good police on the other hand, "understand what we are doing." Ito elaborated on the relationship between protesters and the police:

They always try to outnumber us. Naturally it ends up too many police, and
less counter [protesters], much less racists and for the observer—the people
watching outside—they never know what's happening. Well, that's a good
thing—at the same time, if you look closely and if you take a picture you see it,
you see the police are protecting racists. It's also clear too. [For] Japanese
police [the] prime concern is order. They don't care about human rights; they
don't have this concept. That's the biggest issue. They never understand, this is
racism and antiracism, human rights violations—they see a violation of public
order, that's all.[51]

Political suppression and surveillance played a significant role in the attachment of stigma to the leftist traditions that continued on from the 1960s. Contemporary activists are willing to engage to some extent with police, but they can sometimes be physically stifled at protests. Instead—as the following section discusses in greater detail—sound and style become important as alternatives by which antifa activists can express their resistance without exposing themselves to physical risks.

In addition to CRAC, activists articulated liberal antifa through the group Tokyo Democracy Crew. Tokyo Democracy Crew is focused on the single issue of protecting democracy, a task that these activists believe requires the removal of the Abe administration. CRAC and Tokyo Democracy Crew, in particular, frequently collaborate, with participants overlapping in both groups. As Kobayashi Nao, an activist and graphic designer, put it: "'Let's go to battle with fascism and [this] neo-Nazi administration,' it's Tokyo Democracy Crew that's saying that."[52] As Kobayashi's words show, Tokyo Democracy Crew advances an antifa analysis of the Abe administration. Whereas both antiracism and antinuclear movements use antifa as one component of a critique of broader issues, Tokyo Democracy Crew frames protecting democracy as its central focus. Yet activists simultaneously draw distinctions and connections between multiple causes by, for instance, referencing antifa politics at counterprotests against hate speech or at antinuclear protests. Antifa framing is citational—creating conversations across different causes to develop a sense of a larger movement.

The citational politics of antifa are further evident in the methods activists use to analyze protest events. Activists not only invoke antifa in physical protests but ascribe to antifa politics in their coverage of events over social media. The following tweets are examples of these framings.

#Tokyo youngsters shouting #NoPasaran right now at 23:55 in front of the Diet bldg to protest new conspiracy bill. #Antifa #Public4Future[53]

#NoPasaran Happening now in Shinjuku, #Tokyo. A small racist group is totally covered by anti hate speech banners. No one can hear them beyond antifascists' chants. Awesome![54]

In Ginza, Tokyo. People chanting 'Down with Abe' march through the heart of Tokyo. #NoPasaran [Image of a red sign that says: "¡NOPASARAN! RAGE AGAINST FASCISM" "ABE IS OVER!"][55]

As the previous examples show, antifa functions both as a protest strategy and as a method of framing protest. In the early days of Shibakitai and The Menfolk, antifa operated to provide a logic for the concept of "by any means necessary," justifying the use of physical confrontations during and after hate speech demonstrations.[56] Yet the fluidity, and to some extent the undefined character, of the concept of antifa has enabled other "nonviolent" activists to make reference to it without resorting to physical confrontations. Rather than a strict ideology, antifa functions as an adaptive framing—an approach activists modify, for instance, in their conflicts with both hate speech demonstrators and state authority figures such as police.

Despite their connections and citational practices, antifa activists, and particularly Tokyo Democracy Crew, remain critical of far-left activism—even abroad. On April 15, 2018, Tokyo Democracy Crew tweeted that it was not only Trump that had colluded with Russians but that Russia had infiltrated and influenced "far leftist" groups such as Black Lives Matter and other "minority movements" in an effort to defeat Hillary Clinton. Tokyo Democracy Crew was identifying its position as liberal, rather than leftist. As Takahashi Wakagi, a former Tokyo Democracy Crew leader, put it, "TDC folks know what they are doing: during the last US presidential election, they vilified Black Lives Matter and Bernie Sanders and emphasized that their US counterpart is Hillary."[57] This identification with liberalism and rejection of leftism reflects divides among social movements. It has caused conflicts between new leftists as well as within the movement. Takahashi is emphatic that he left Tokyo Democracy Crew after the summer of 2015 due to his disagreements with the group.

Liberal antifa practices politicized strategies of ambivalence to reconcile its difficult relationship to New Left politics. Such an ambivalence grows out of activists' sense of the urgency of the post-3/11 political crisis. Activists felt that remaining nonaligned—in terms of left versus right—would facilitate the growth of social movements in this period. They also felt that culture was an important method to create further bridges and was powerful in cultivating opportunities for "ordinary Japanese" to restructure their everyday involvement with politics. By reconstructing social movements as experiential and aesthetically driven, these activists created multiple entry points for people to participate in political communities. Music, food, and fashion feature prominently within these constructions.

Liberal antifa activists' emphasis on culture—and reluctance to locate their placement amid a political spectrum—reflects their ambivalence and, sometimes, hostility to the politics of the Japanese New Left. Histories of political suppression of leftist social movements—and their consequent framing as dangerous, violent, and undesirable—is significant in the aesthetic formation of antifa. Just as antifa, which borrows heavily from punk music and culture, envisions itself as dissent against a cultural status quo, liberal antifa situates itself as a temporal disruption—a new alternative to fraught lineages of protest in Japan.

Cultures of Japanese Antifa

In *"There Ain't No Black in the Union Jack,"* Paul Gilroy famously describes the overlaps between antifa politics and antiracism in London in the 1970s.[58] He argues that through their shared overlaps in music subcultures, the two movements of people were able to come together. This also happened in part because of the racism of a popular punk group, The National Front. Gilroy argues that through the development of cultural spaces, people are able to build solidarity with each other across multiple lines. Liberal antifa in Japan is rooted in a similar kind of cultural signification, a fact blatantly acknowledged in materials produced by movement activists. In 2018, Noma published a book on Shibakitai, detailing the origins and philosophies of the movement. Discussing when he first heard about The National Front's song "Power in the Darkness," Noma explains the role of music in shaping the group: "Shibakitai is a group primarily of men in their thirties through fifties, many who have deep connections to subculture. Dependent on age, the artists [that activists are interested in] differ but many are influenced by punk/new wave, rap/hip hop, and techno and house music from the 70s to 90s—and from these influences they perhaps unconsciously picked up an antiracist stance."[59] The role of music and sub-cultures would not only guide Shibakitai but also CRAC and other activist mobilizations affiliated with Japanese liberal antifa.

This section describes the ways that activists construct liberal antifa as a site of cultural signification and its embodiment as a strategy of ambivalence. In the following discussion of food, fashion, music, and art, I show that liberal antifa operates simultaneously as a venue for socialization and a site of consumption. For this group of activists, antifa is a method by which activists develop an ambience of community, community that is loose and individualistic, constructed through affective ties rather than strictly organized. Antifa as an experiential site, moreover, appeals to activists because it enables them to resist the structures of hierarchical organizing that typify traditional leftist social movement groups. It is through such informal spaces of consumption and experience that activists are able to create a sense of community while rejecting membership in a singular organization.

Nabeyoko Dougenbozu is a small ramen shop in Nakano, a subcity within the Tokyo metropolis. I first visited the shop in March 2015, at the urging of activists who had talked up the quality of the ramen. In late June 2016, the exterior of the restaurant was painted in anticipation of the upcoming July elections: black letters over a white background spelling out "7.10 STOP FASCISM." An icon of a hand was affixed, placing a ballot into a slot. A cat drifted under a speech bubble that commanded, "GO VOTE." The signage reflected the activities under way within activist communities: groups of volunteers were assembling after work on weekdays, canvassing neighborhoods in Tokyo with flyers and pamphlets, and sometimes taking trucks on the road. The activists were focused on the reelection of Arita Yoshifu, a member of the Upper House in Japan's bicameral legislature. As the politician who led the passage of Japan's legal ban of hate speech in May 2016, Arita is revered among some activists as an indispensable figure within the country's antiracism movement.

The inside of Dougenbouzu is narrow, with an L-shaped counter seating around ten visitors. There is a series of antinuclear posters on the walls throughout the restaurant, including one of John Lennon and Yoko Ono, saying "War Is Over If You Want It." That day, radio in the background played coverage of a baseball game. Chikahiro, the owner of Dougenbouzu, is well known as a fan of the team the Hiroshima Carps. I was at the restaurant with Harumi, an activist involved with both antinuclear and antiracism scenes. Harumi and I had recently made a habit of getting together for ramen on Friday nights after attending the antinuclear rally in front of the prime minister's office. Harumi was intrigued by a new option among the shop's seasonal ramen offerings, one inspired by and made in the style of Taiwanese noodle soup. As Harumi and I went to the ticket vending machine to order our ramen, we ran into Minoru, a core member of Tokyo Democracy Crew and CRAC. Minoru said hello to me and commented that he had heard that I recently began volunteering at the office of the Kawasaki Citizen's Network. Then he introduced me to the man sitting next to him. After these greetings, Minoru returned to his conversation with his friend. We did not talk after that.

The ramen shop is a place where one is likely to run into other activists from the movement. Yet the rhythm and pace of these chance meetings are shaped by the object being consumed, ramen. Interactions tend to be brief, as is the amount of time it takes to finish a bowl of ramen. It did not take very long for Harumi and I to finish our ramen and, after our second glass of water after the meal, we decided to leave. As we got up, the person sitting next to her, a man with glasses and floppy hair, chatted up Harumi. They talked about a documentary that he had worked on, a film about Endo Michiro, a Japanese socialist punk. Endo, who died in May 2019, was the front man of The Stalin, which was infamous for stunts such as throwing a pig's head into the audience. As Harumi and I left the restaurant, we discussed Endo as well as Harumi's self-identification as a punk.

Dougenbouzu is unique, but it is not the only place where activists can connect food and politics. Another is a beloved pork bun stand in Osaka that is open for only several hours every weekend, across the street from a youth hostel also frequented by members of the antiracism movement. The owner of the pork bun stand—affectionately nicknamed "Mr. Pork Bun"—describes his clientele, "Antiracism and anti-fascism are there, but I don't say anything about it to my customers. More or less, people who know are the people who know." In this way, for Mr. Pork Bun, being part of antifa in these spaces of consumption is something that is shared on an unspoken basis, unlike Dougenbouzu, where politics are explicitly stated.

Dougenbouzu also represents the convergence of different segments of liberal antifa. In this case, food also functions as a venue by which activists engage with art. In February 2016, CRAC organized *Gunfire*, an exhibition celebrating the book launch of *Trigger*, activist Shimazaki Rody's photography of the movement.[60] The promotions for the exhibit claimed, "Actors, tattoo artists, foreigners, victims, punks, rudies, protesters, students and more. . . . The people captured by Shimazaki force us to reaffirm and attest the present state of our country, a state in which we have all lived together for the 5 years since the 3.11 tragedy." On our visit to the shop that week, Harumi told me about a discount. Customers who mentioned visiting *Gunfire* would receive a free egg for their ramen. In addition to the egg discount, flyers for Shimazaki's exhibit were available.

In addition to Shimazaki, another artist is Takekawa Nobuaki, a visual artist who frequently exhibits in the Tokyo area. One example of Takekawa's sculpture, *Imprisoned, Jailbreak*, is a hanger with baseball bats of multiple colors with spikes (fig. 1). The bats are colored silver, red, black, gold, and blue. At the top of the hanger is a head cast in silver-colored metal, shaped like a horned ogre. The art is a reference to the traditional holiday, *setsubun*, celebrated each year on February 3, marking the transition from winter to spring. During the holiday, adults and children partake in different traditional activities, such as throwing beans and eating

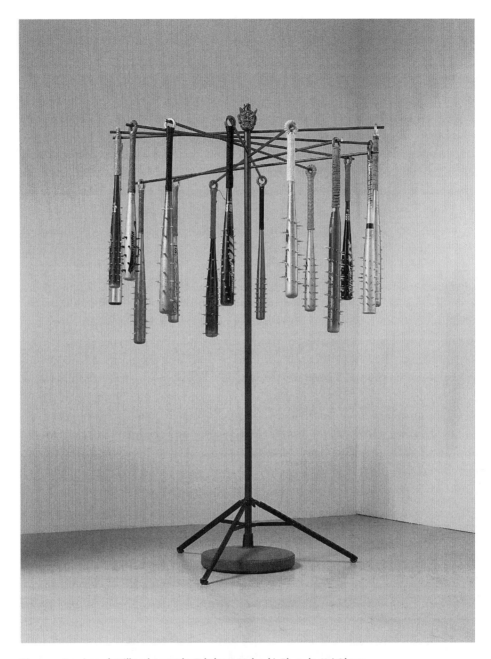

Figure 1. *Imprisoned, Jailbreak* (2013) by Takekawa Nobuaki. Photo by Kei Okana.

long sushi, to get rid of evil spirits and invite good fortune. The spiked bat, called *kanabo*, is a traditional weapon used to drive out demons. Takekawa's work integrates traditional and contemporary elements, and this piece is a commentary on racists as a source of "evil" in the country, a force that needs to actively be driven out. Embracing this theme, the CRAC Twitter account posted a picture of the piece

HOME > WEAR > Tee: TOKYO AGAINST FASCISM（ホワイト）

LOGIN

Tee: TOKYO AGAINST FASCISM（ホワ
イト）

¥2,000 税込

ⓘ 送料についてはこちら

S　　　✉ 再入荷お知らせ

M　　　✉ 再入荷お知らせ

L　　　✉ 再入荷お知らせ

XL　　　✉ 再入荷お知らせ

XXL　　　✉ 再入荷お知らせ

♡ お気に入りに追加

Figure 2. An activist models a Tokyo Against Fascism T-shirt for the Counter-Racist Action Collective (CRAC) online shop. Photos by Rody Shimazaki.

with the caption: "We SJWs would keep beating up fascists with these PC bats." In their words, they reclaim common English-language terms used to critique activists, such as "social justice warriors" and "political correctness."

Japan's liberal antifa community is also concerned with fashion. Dougen-bouzu is another example of this, selling T-shirts for two thousand yen. The T-shirts, black and white, mimic the logo of New York City's famed CBGB venue and boast the slogan: "DGBZ & ANTIFA Nabeyoko Against Fascism." Nabeyoko refers to the subneighborhood in Tokyo where the ramen shop is located. Another source of fashion is the CRAC website, which sells a range of products such as T-shirts, hoodies, hats, and jewelry. CRAC chooses members of the activist community, particularly ethnic minorities, to model the apparel. In one series of images on the website, a man sports "Tokyo Against Fascism" attire (fig. 2). Wearing a dark beanie, he opens his zip-up pullover to reveal a white "Tokyo Against Fascism" T-shirt. The shirt has black text with "AGAINST" written in white text with a red block behind it. The model lifts his face up and stares at the camera with a confrontational facial expression. In another series of images, a woman with ear-length bobbed hair models "No pasaran" sweatshirts of two colors—white with a black bar of white text and black with white text (fig. 3). The first image is a close-up, with her face cut off above her pink glossed lips. In the second photo she is sitting on a silver ladder. She is wearing red flat sneakers and covering her lap with her hands. Her bare legs are extended, and it is hard to tell if she is wearing shorts. Her eyes are obscured by a black hat tilted downward; the hat also reads "No pasaran."

Hoodie: Nopasaran 2015 Pullover (white)   Hoodie: Nopasaran 2015 Pullover (black)

SOLD OUT   SOLD OUT

Figure 3. An activist models the 2015 Nopasaran pullover for the Counter-Racist Action Collective (CRAC) online shop. Photos by Rody Shimazaki.

Music also plays a significant role in the formation of liberal antifa cultures. One slogan that activists use is "Strictly Antifascist. Music Is the Weapon of the Future." However, whereas antifa fashion and food are aimed toward popularizing the fight against fascism, music offers a medium for activists to engage with each other in subcultures. For Japanese liberal antifa, music is specifically targeted toward activists interested in punk music and rap—an echo of what Gilroy describes in the 1970s London antiracist scenes.

One of the regular events that is held on a nearly annual basis is Rage Against Fascism, a music party that pays homage to American political rock band Rage Against the Machine. On December 26, 2016, the event was held at Earthdom, a basement venue in Tokyo that appeared to look intentionally dilapidated. Above the main stage, silver masking tape hung off the ceiling. The entire room was dark except for the lit stage, which was painted black. Facing the stage, people danced and took photos on their phones. One person dove into the mass of people and began crowd-surfing. Behind the dense crowd, a woman sold fabric dolls at a table in the back of the room. She explained that they were made by grandmothers from Fukushima.

Down a dark hallway, adjacent to a heavy black door that opens into a smaller room at the venue, was an exhibit of Shimazaki's black-and-white photographs. They hung underneath a reindeer head made of paper with blood coming out of its neck. Most of the photographs came from Shimazaki's collection titled "TATTOO." One photo was of a bespectacled man, squinting in pain while a tattoo artist sketches outlines on his round belly. Another featured a man standing in a deserted street. His back facing the camera, he is nude except for his *fundoshi*, a thong-like traditional Japanese undergarment. His entire body is covered in tattoos. In Japan, tattoos are frequently a subject of a social stigma for their cultural association with organized crime. People with tattoos are often prohibited from certain spaces, such as public baths.

In the main room, Akuryo was on stage. Akuryo is a skinny man, frequently sporting a baseball cap and glasses. He is involved in the overlapping antinuclear, antiracism, and antifa scenes and performs at activist events at venues and parades. Before he began rapping his famous song, "Flatline," he said, "this is fighting music." He commenced performing the song:

Strike 'em out Late at night Antifa dancin'
Punchline liberates the world from fuckin' implications
Sexism Racism Handicaps . . . Tear down these walls
Party night!
Flatline
I'll stop the racism
And kick and smash the cocksuckers addicted to hatred.[61]

The song depicted the conflict between antifa activists and racists as a physical confrontation, invoking the explicit imagery of violence. In one line, Akuryo described eating the racists up, putting "salt on the guts." For the rapper, the problem of racism is one to be dealt with without "leniency," and activists must use any means possible to fight against hate speech. The image of confrontations also occurs alongside reference to masculinity. Without explicitly situating itself as a movement of men, antifa battles with racists, and fascists are gendered as masculine—a theme present not only in Akuryo's song but throughout its construction as tough and confrontational. Aside from violent imagery, Akuryo also constructed antifa as a space of pleasure, one inviting dancing and partying. Antifa was simultaneously a space for direct confrontations and one in which activists converge and share in social interactions.

The politics of music is not only in the lyrics or even the presence of sound,[62] but also in the function of live performance as a shared, embodied experience. As Black Hawk Hancock and Michael J. Lorr point out, punk music is a sensory experience that—through activities such as moshing and diving—can operate as a "technology of the collective."[63] For Japanese antifa, punk has served as a way for activists to engage in collective identity formation. Moreover, by marking themselves as unruly and embracing outsider-ness, liberal antifa activists use culture to reject the mainstream body politics that continue to uphold racist and classist systems of exclusion. Yet these same activists are also ambivalent about appearing outside the mainstream and often seek methods to attract new audiences through popular consumption.

Conclusion

This intervention has explored the ways that Japanese activists construct the meanings of liberal antifa, interpreting it as a means of building cultural spaces and as a strategy of ambivalence. Activists have applied the concept of antifa to a framework of action that is fluid and adaptable to large-scale protests. At the same time that Japanese liberal antifa takes inspiration from global antifa cultures, it has predominantly departed from radical left politics, instead incorporating mainstream themes such as nationalism. What marks the subversive potential of liberal antifa are its cultural forms—particularly the movement's engagement with music subcultures. Through offering methods of cultural participation, activists are able to "embody" the dissenting politics of antifa. Liberal antifa, moreover, is marked by contradictions, simultaneously embedding itself within popular modes of consumption— such as food and fashion—and more narrowly targeting specialized audiences.

At the same time that liberal and leftist iterations of Japanese antifa diverge, both connect nuclear crisis and racism as acute problems that threaten democracy. Yet their methods of connecting these issues differ significantly. Although liberal antifa is citational, activists generally practice a "single issue" approach at street protests. Outside of protests, and particularly in the space of music, however, liberal antifa activists articulate the connections between multiple social problems. Within this conceptualization, the political response to the 2011 Fukushima nuclear disaster is central. The disaster was critical in both triggering mass mobilizations and cultivating political analysis of the relationship between the state and extremist civil society actors. Liberal antifa offers a framework for analyzing and interpreting the problem of hate speech, an extreme form of racism, as part of broader patterns of structural discrimination.

Although antifa has been effective in criticizing the Abe administration, it has also been met with limits. As a movement characterized predominantly by loose styles of organizing, antifa on its own has been insufficient for advancing structural changes. Rather, groups such as CRAC have opted to blend their antifa approach with more traditional legalistic strategies, such as lobbying and lawmaking, in order to accomplish their goals of addressing hate speech.

Liberal antifa has had a complicated relationship with questions of physical force and violence. Antifa activist groups such as Shibakitai have used tactics of physical intimidation to confront hate speech demonstrations, under the umbrella of the strategy "by any means necessary." Despite the use of this tactic, however, certain antifa activists have disavowed the notion that their actions constitute "violence." They have, instead, argued that their actions are technically "nonviolent," falling under the category of what they call "extreme pressure."[64] Different interpretations of antifa, moreover, assume contrastive stances on the strategy of "by any means necessary." Groups such as Puraka-tai have eschewed physically confrontational tactics and created space for nonconfrontational protest. Instead of following a strict interpretation of method, liberal antifa operates as a loose framework through which activists mobilize.

Japanese antifa, in both its liberal and leftist iterations, sheds light on the multiplicities within the formation of global antifa. Moreover, this case demonstrates how activists attempt to leverage culture to reconcile complex political interests. The contradictions and "vague" qualities of liberal antifa are central to its formation. Rather than resolving these contradictions, activists have adopted a strategy of ambivalence in constructing liberal antifa. This ambivalence is one that relies on antifa as a cultural strategy without explicitly articulating a cohesive ideology. At the same time that this strategy has created multiple entry points for participation, it has also weakened the power of antifa as a critical tool. In the refusal to explicitly identify its ideology, liberal antifa cannot avoid the shadow of the New Left on its politics.

Vivian Shaw is a College Fellow in the Department of Sociology at Harvard University, where she is also the lead researcher for the AAPI COVID-19 Project. She earned her PhD in sociology from the University of Texas at Austin. Her research interests focus on race and ethnicity, particularly in relation to questions of culture, social movements, and the environment.

Notes

I would like to thank the editors and three anonymous reviewers who helped shape this piece. Thanks especially to Jecca Namakkal, who offered thoughtful and insightful guidance through multiple drafts. I am also grateful for the feedback and support I received from David Slater and Anna Skarpelis. This research was supported by the National Science Foundation, the Japan Society for the Promotion of Science, Mitsubishi Caterpillar Forklift America Inc., the Kobe College Corporation Japan Education Exchange, and the Center for East Asian Studies at the University of Texas at Austin.

1. This intervention follows the convention of writing Japanese names, with the family name preceding the given name.
2. Copsey, *Anti-fascism in Britain*, xvii.
3. Olechnowicz writes about liberal anti-fascism in the British case ("Liberal Anti-fascism in the 1930s").
4. Renton, *Fascism, Anti-fascism, and Britain in the 1940s*.
5. This intervention focuses on liberal antifa while acknowledging the existence of more radical iterations of antifa within traditional leftist communities in Japan.
6. This is in distinction from traditional leftist activism, which has typically relied on regular membership and hierarchical organization styles.
7. Noma Yasumichi, personal communication to author, October 14, 2019; edited for clarity.
8. Manabe, *Revolution Will Not Be Televised*.
9. This debate about if Japan was fascist has been controversial, with scholars in the United States more reluctant to name Japan as fascist. In contrast, numerous Japanese scholars, led by political scientist Masao Maruyama, have been forthright in identifying Japan as fascist, influenced by their backgrounds in Marxist analysis and direct experiences of police and government repression. See Sottile, "Fascist Era"; Young, "When Fascism Met Empire"; Sakai, "Imperial Nationalism and the Comparative Perspective."
10. Noma, personal communication.

11. Kimura Natsuki, personal communication to author, October 13, 2019.

12. Hofmann, *Fascist Effect*; Willensky, "Japanese Fascism Revisited"; Sakai, "Positions and Positionalities"; Bronson, *One Hundred Million Philosophers*.

13. Katayama, "Is a Democratic Revolution Possible in Japan?"

14. Bronson, *One Hundred Million Philosophers*, 28.

15. Victoria, "Carry the Buddha Out into the Street!"

16. Dimitrov, "People's Front against Fascism and War"; Bronson, *One Hundred Million Philosophers*; Hofmann, "What's Left of the Right"; Takenaka, "Gender and Post-war Relief."

17. Komatsu and Scott, "Japanese Franctireur Talks with Gide and Malraux."

18. Najita, "Civil Society in Japan's Modernity."

19. Torrance, "People's Library."

20. The Japan Communist Party was legally permitted to reassemble after the war. See Koshiro, "Japan's World and World War II"; Koschmann, "Japan Communist Party and the Debate over Literary Strategy."

21. Takenaka, "Gender and Post-war Relief."

22. Bronson, *One Hundred Million Philosophers*; Nakajima, "Depoliticization or Americanization of Japanese Science Studies."

23. Andrews, *Dissenting Japan*; McCormack, "Student Left in Japan."

24. As Murakami Wood, Lyon, and Abe point out, in the transition from the US occupation to the establishment of a new constitution in 1952, the state was "able to legitimate its reassertion of its right to monitor and control political and subversive activity" ("Surveillance in Urban Japan," 554). See also Gayle, *Women's History and Local Community in Postwar Japan*; Yamamoto, *Grassroots Pacifism in Post-war Japan*.

25. During Kishi's tenure, intellectuals produced numerous political cartoons depicting the prime minister as a fascist. See Esselstrom, "1960 'Anpo' Struggle in *The People's Daily*."

26. McCormack, "Nineteen-Thirties Japan."

27. Schieder, "People's Police."

28. Choi, "Fighting the Korean War in Pacifist Japan."

29. Zainichi Koreans are one of the largest ethnic minorities in Japan, including migrants who came to Japan during the imperial era as well as newcomers.

30. Takahashi Wakagi, personal communication with author, October 13, 2019.

31. Cassegård, *Youth Movements, Trauma, and Alternative Space*; Cassegård, "Lovable Anarchism."

32. O'Day, "Differentiating SEALDs from Freeters, and Precariats."

33. Higuchi, "Global Activist Network Involving Asia."

34. Tominaga, "Social Movements and the Diffusion of Tactics and Repertoires"; Maeckelbergh, "'Don't Get Arrested!'"; Smith, "Facing the Nation."

35. Noma, personal communication.

36. Hayashi and McKnight, "Good-Bye Kitty, Hello War"; O'Day, "Differentiating SEALDs from Freeters, and Precariats"; Manabe, *Revolution Will Not Be Televised*; Higuchi, "Global Activist Network Involving Asia."

37. Hayashi and McKnight, "Good-Bye Kitty, Hello War."

38. Higuchi, "Global Activist Network Involving Asia."

39. Amamiya and Beck would later describe a complicated position of being "beyond" a right-left political binary ("Suffering Forces Us to Think beyond the Right-Left Barrier"). See also Driscoll, "Hyperneoliberalism"; Allison, "Ordinary Refugees."

40. Manabe, *Revolution Will Not Be Televised*.
41. Novak, "Project Fukushima!"
42. Novak, "Project Fukushima!"
43. Noma Yasumichi, interview with author, February 3, 2015. See also Manabe, *Revolution Will Not Be Televised*.
44. Noma, personal communication; edited for clarity.
45. Noma, personal communication.
46. Takahashi, personal communication.
47. Kimura, personal communication.
48. Shaw, "'We Are Already Living Together.'"
49. Akira the Hustler, interview with author, October 25, 2016.
50. Founded in 2006, Zaitokukai staged several infamous incidents in the following years. In 2009 the group organized a mass protest against a young Filipina whose parents were deported for overstaying their visas. In December of that year it targeted a North Korean Zainichi elementary school in Kyoto.
51. Ito Kenichiro, interview with author, April 5, 2016.
52. Kobayashi Nao, interview with author, November 20, 2016.
53. C.R.A.C., "Tokyo youngsters shouting #NoPasaran."
54. C.R.A.C., "NoPasaran Happening now in Shinjuku, #Tokyo."
55. C.R.A.C., "In Ginza, Tokyo."
56. Shaw, "'Extreme Pressure.'"
57. Takahashi, personal communication.
58. Gilroy, *"There Ain't No Black in the Union Jack."*
59. Noma, *Jitsu roku Reishisuto wo Shibakitai*.
60. Shimazaki and ECD, *Hikigane*.
61. Lyrics and English translations were obtained from the music video for "Flatline."
62. Bender, Corpis, and Walkowitz, "Editors' Introduction"; Nyong'o, "Do You Want Queer Theory (or Do You Want the Truth)?"; Kheshti, "On the Threshold of the Political."
63. Hancock and Lorr, "More than Just a Soundtrack."
64. Shaw, "'Extreme Pressure.'"

References

Akuryo. *Flatline*. YouTube, December 24, 2015. www.youtube.com/watch?v=DfJBVOhfZ4U.

Allison, Anne. "Ordinary Refugees: Social Precarity and Soul in Twenty-First Century Japan." *Anthropological Quarterly* 85, no. 2 (2012): 345–70.

Amamiya, Karin, and Jodie Beck. "Suffering Forces Us to Think beyond the Right-Left Barrier." *Mechademia* 5, no. 1 (2010): 251–65.

Andrews, William. *Dissenting Japan: A History of Japanese Radicalism and Counterculture, from 1945 to Fukushima*. London: Hurst, 2016.

Bender, Daniel, Duane J. Corpis, and Daniel J. Walkowitz. "Editors' Introduction: Sound Politics: Critically Listening to the Past." *Radical History Review*, no. 121 (2015): 1–7.

Bronson, Adam. *One Hundred Million Philosophers: Science of Thought and the Culture of Democracy in Postwar Japan*. Honolulu: University of Hawai'i Press, 2016.

Cassegård, Carl. "Lovable Anarchism: Campus Protest in Japan from the 1990s to Today." *Culture Unbound: Journal of Current Cultural Research* 6, no. 2 (2014): 361–82.

Cassegård, Carl. *Youth Movements, Trauma, and Alternative Space in Contemporary Japan*. Leiden: Brill, 2013.

Choi, Deokhyo. "Fighting the Korean War in Pacifist Japan: Korean and Japanese Leftist Solidarity and American Cold War Containment." *Critical Asian Studies* 49, no. 4 (2017): 546–68.

Copsey, Nigel. *Anti-fascism in Britain*. London: Routledge, 2016.

C.R.A.C. (@crajp). "In Ginza, Tokyo. People chanting 'Down with Abe' march through the heart of Tokyo. #NoPasaran." Twitter, February 22, 2019.

C.R.A.C. (@crajp). "NoPasaran Happening now in Shinjuku, #Tokyo. A small racist group is totally covered by anti hate speech banners. No one can hear them beyond antifascists' chants. Awesome!" Twitter, September 27, 2018.

C.R.A.C. (@crajp). "Tokyo youngsters shouting #NoPasaran right now at 23:55 in front of the Diet bldg to protest new conspiracy bill. #Antifa #Public4Future." Twitter, June 14, 2017.

Dimitrov, Georgi. "The People's Front against Fascism and War." *Pravda*, November 7, 1936.

Driscoll, Mark. "Hyperneoliberalism: Youth, Labor, and Militant Mice in Japan." *positions: east asia cultures critique* 23, no. 3 (2015): 545–64.

Esselstrom, Erik. "The 1960 'Anpo' Struggle in *The People's Daily*: Shaping Popular Chinese Perceptions of Japan during the Cold War." *Asia-Pacific Journal: Japan Focus*, no. 51 (2012). apjjf.org/2012/10/51/Erik-Esselstrom/3869/article.html.

Gayle, Curtis Anderson. *Women's History and Local Community in Postwar Japan*. Florence: Routledge, 2013.

Gilroy, Paul. *"There Ain't No Black in the Union Jack": The Cultural Politics of Race and Nation*. Abingdon: Routledge, 2013.

Hancock, Black Hawk, and Michael J. Lorr. "More than Just a Soundtrack: Toward a Technology of the Collective in Hardcore Punk." *Journal of Contemporary Ethnography* 42, no. 3 (2013): 320–46.

Hayashi, Sharon, and Anne McKnight. "Good-Bye Kitty, Hello War: The Tactics of Spectacle and New Youth Movements in Urban Japan." *positions: east asia cultures critique* 13, no. 1 (2005): 87–113.

Higuchi, Takuro. "Global Activist Network Involving Asia: Global Continuation and Evolution in Japan." *Inter-Asia Cultural Studies* 13, no. 3 (2012): 467–75.

Hofmann, Reto. *The Fascist Effect: Japan and Italy, 1915–1952*. Ithaca, NY: Cornell University Press, 2015.

Hofmann, Reto. "What's Left of the Right: Nabeyama Sadachika and Anti-communism in Transwar Japan, 1930–1960." *Journal of Asian Studies* (2019): 1–25.

Katayama, Koshi. "Is a Democratic Revolution Possible in Japan?" *Free World* 2 (1942): 128.

Kheshti, Roshanak. "On the Threshold of the Political: The Sonic Performativity of Rooftop Chanting in Iran." *Radical History Review*, no. 121 (2015): 51–70.

Komatsu, Kyo, and Midori H. Scott. "A Japanese Franctireur Talks with Gide and Malraux." *Centennial Review of Arts and Science* 4, no. 1 (1960): 115–43.

Koschmann, J. Victor. "The Japan Communist Party and the Debate over Literary Strategy under the Allied Occupation of Japan." In *Legacies and Ambiguities: Postwar Fiction and Culture in West Germany and Japan*, edited by Ernestine Schlant and J. Thomas Rimer, 163–86. Washington, DC: Woodrow Wilson International Center for Scholars, 1991.

Koshiro, Yukiko. "Japan's World and World War II." *Diplomatic History* 25, no. 3 (2001): 425–41.

Maeckelbergh, Marianne. "'Don't Get Arrested!': Trust, Miscommunication, and Repression at the 2008 Anti-G8 Mobilization in Japan." *PoLAR: Political and Legal Anthropology Review* 41, no. 1 (2018): 124–41.

Manabe, Noriko. *The Revolution Will Not Be Televised: Protest Music after Fukushima*. New York: Oxford University Press, 2015.

McCormack, Gavan. "Nineteen-Thirties Japan: Fascism?" *Bulletin of Concerned Asian Scholars* 14, no. 2 (1982): 20–32.

McCormack, Gavan. "The Student Left in Japan." *New Left Review*, no. 65 (1971): 37.

Murakami Wood, David, David Lyon, and Kiyoshi Abe. "Surveillance in Urban Japan: A Critical Introduction." *Urban Studies* 44, no. 3 (2007): 551–68.

Najita, Tetsuo. "Civil Society in Japan's Modernity—An Interpretive Overview." In *Civil Society, Religion, and the Nation: Modernization in Intercultural Context; Russia, Japan, Turkey*, edited by Gerrit Steunebrink and Evert van der Zweerde, 101–15. Amsterdam: Rodopi, 2004.

Nakajima, Hideto. "Depoliticization or Americanization of Japanese Science Studies." *Social Epistemology* 27, no. 2 (2013): 163–76.

Noma Yasumichi. *Jitsu roku Reishisuto wo Shibakitai (The True Story of Shibakitai)*. Tokyo: Kawade Shobō Shinsha, 2018.

Novak, David. "Project Fukushima! Performativity and the Politics of Festival in Post-3/11 Japan." *Anthropological Quarterly* 90, no. 1 (2017): 225–53.

Nyong'o, Tavia. "Do You Want Queer Theory (or Do You Want the Truth)? Intersections of Punk and Queer in the 1970s." *Radical History Review*, no. 100 (2008): 103–19.

O'Day, Robin. "Differentiating SEALDs from Freeters, and Precariats: The Politics of Youth Movements in Contemporary Japan." *Asia-Pacific Journal: Japan Focus*, no. 37 (2015). apjjf.org/-Robin-O_Day/4376.

Olechnowicz, Andrzej. "Liberal Anti-fascism in the 1930s: The Case of Sir Ernest Barker." *Albion* 36, no. 4 (2005): 636–60.

Renton, Dave. *Fascism, Anti-fascism, and Britain in the 1940s*. London: Palgrave Macmillan, 2016.

Sakai, Naoki. "Imperial Nationalism and the Comparative Perspective." *positions: east asia cultures critique* 17, no. 1 (2009): 159–205.

Sakai, Naoki. "Positions and Positionalities: After Two Decades." *positions: east asia cultures critique* 20, no. 1 (2012): 67–94.

Schieder, Chelsea Szendi. "The People's Police: The Tokyo Police Museum's Version of History." *Asia-Pacific Journal: Japan Focus*, no. 44 (2015). apjjf.org/-Chelsea-Szendi_Schieder/4394.

Shaw, Vivian. "'Extreme Pressure': Gendered Negotiations of Violence and Vulnerability in Japanese Antiracism Movements." *Critical Asian Studies* 52, no. 1 (2019): 109–26.

Shaw, Vivian. "'We Are Already Living Together': Race, Collective Struggle, and the Reawakened Nation in Post-3/11 Japan." In *Precarious Belongings: Affect and Nationalism in Asia*, edited by Chih-ming Wang and Daniel PS Goh, 59–76. Lanham, MD: Rowman and Littlefield, 2017.

Shimazaki, Rody, and ECD. *Hikigane (Trigger)*. Korokara, 2016. www.shashasha.co/en/book/hikigane.

Smith, Nathaniel M. "Facing the Nation: Sound, Fury, and Public Oratory among Japanese Right-Wing Groups." In *Sound, Space, and Sociality in Modern Japan*, edited by Joseph D. Hankins and Carolyn S. Stevens, 51–70. New York: Routledge, 2014.

Sottile, Joseph P. "The Fascist Era: Imperial Japan and the Axis Alliance in Historical Perspective." In *Japan in the Fascist Era*, edited by E. Bruce Reynolds, 1–48. New York: Palgrave Macmillan, 2004.

Takenaka, Akiko. "Gender and Post-war Relief: Support for War-Widowed Mothers in Occupied Japan (1945–1952)." *Gender and History* 28, no. 3 (2016): 775–93.

Tominaga, Kyoko. "Social Movements and the Diffusion of Tactics and Repertoires: Activists' Network in Anti-globalism Movement." *World Academy of Science, Engineering and Technology: International Journal of Social, Behavioral, Educational, Economic, Business and Industrial Engineering* 8, no. 6 (2014): 1783–89.

Torrance, Richard. "The People's Library: The Spirit of Prose Literature versus Fascism." In *The Culture of Japanese Fascism*, edited by Alan Tansman, 56–79. Durham, NC: Duke University Press, 2009.

Victoria, Brian Daizen. "Carry the Buddha Out into the Street! A Sliver of Buddhist Resistance to Japanese Militarism." In *Politics and Religion in Modern Japan: Red Sun, White Lotus*, edited by Roy Starrs, 143–61. New York: Palgrave Macmillan, 2011.

Willensky, Marcus. "Japanese Fascism Revisited." *Stanford Journal of East Asian Affairs* 5, no. 1 (2005): 58–77.

Yamamoto, Mari. *Grassroots Pacifism in Post-war Japan: The Rebirth of a Nation*. London: Routledge, 2004.

Young, Louise. "When Fascism Met Empire in Japanese-Occupied Manchuria." *Journal of Global History* 12, no. 2 (2017): 274–96.

Teaching *It Can't Happen Here* in the Trump Era

How to Rewrite Fascism

Giulia Riccò

In the dystopian 1935 novel *It Can't Happen Here*, Sinclair Lewis imagines what it would look like if fascism came to the United States. Given the premise of the novel, it is no surprise that this book reportedly sold out on Amazon after the 2016 US presidential election.

At the start of the work, Senator Berzelius "Buzz" Windrip, a charismatic and boastful politician (loosely based on former Louisiana governor and senator Huey Long) wins the Democratic primary against Franklin Delano Roosevelt and, in a surprising turn that leaves the country stunned, swiftly rises to the presidency. As Lewis tells it, the person most unsettled by Buzz's historic victory is the novel's protagonist, Doremus Jessup, who owns and edits a newspaper in a small Vermont town. The novel follows Doremus's journey, as well as that of his co-citizens, toward political resistance. At first, Doremus silently accepts the reactionary and obsolete policies enacted by Windrip. When Windrip directly hurts Doremus's family, however, the latter's only possible reaction is to resist. From the novel's beginning and in contraposition to Doremus, Lewis introduces the character of Shad Ledue, the Jessups' gardener and handyman. Throughout the novel, we witness Shad's social and economic ascension, concurrent with and dependent on Doremus's precipitous fall into disgrace.

Radical History Review

Issue 138 (October 2020)   DOI 10.1215/01636545-8359566

© 2020 by MARHO: The Radical Historians' Organization, Inc.

I teach Sinclair Lewis's *It Can't Happen Here* in my upper-level undergraduate seminar called Global Fascism: Legitimizing State Violence across the Atlantic. I have taught this class at Duke University in the Spring 2019 term and most recently in Fall 2019 at the University of Michigan. Students' reactions ranged from outright shock and fear to bewilderment and incredulity. Most of the students were surprised that they had never encountered the novel before. And while *It Can't Happen Here* is a richly productive text for anybody interested in teaching fascism, the work requires pedagogical caution, as students tend to find it overwhelming, especially in the post-2016-election era. In this short essay, I will consider how best to teach students to read a novel that, though originally intended as a satirical take on the political situation of the United States and the world in the interwar period, has now become unnervingly relevant and prescient. Besides the specific case of *It Can't Happen Here*, the use of novels to tackle historical questions, due to fiction's untimely present, allows students to draw connections between disparate moments, thus stressing the importance of historical knowledge.

First, students need context for the novel—not just about the United States in the 1930s but also about the ways in which fascism can come to power. That is why it is important to arrive at *It Can't Happen Here* after having read with students both primary and secondary sources on fascism. In the first half of my course, students spend time familiarizing themselves with theorists such as Gustave Le Bon and Georges Sorel, whose ideas about crowd psychology and the ethics of violence, respectively, amply influenced fascist ideology. We also dwell at length on Italian primary sources (at least those available in English), such as the neo-idealist works of Giovanni Gentile. Having explored the generating ideas and historical circumstances of the rise of fascism in Europe, specifically in Italy, students can then engage with secondary readings on fascism, which include the work of important scholars such as Emilio Gentile, Zeev Sternhell, and Roger Griffin, among others.[1] The idea that Emilio Gentile puts forth in his article "Fascism and the Italian Road to Totalitarianism" (2008) about the nature of the fascist regime as a laboratory helps students to accept the fact that a strict definition of fascism cannot really exist. Students must acknowledge the eclectic nature of fascist ideology and its constant need for reinvention—or, as Antonio Gramsci said, of crisis—in order to be ready to engage productively in discussion about *It Can't Happen Here*.[2]

Through this first stage of reading and discussion, by the time the students have nearly arrived at reading Lewis's novel, they have become familiar with fascist theories and practices as they unfolded in Italy, Spain, Portugal, Brazil, and Argentina. More importantly, they have also become aware of the differences, not just the similarities, among the fascist movements and regimes in these countries. They are now ready to tackle the question of fascism in the United States. To offer a historical frame for *It Can't Happen Here*, we read two chapters from *Fear Itself* by Ira Katznelson, namely the introduction and the chapter titled "Pilot, Senator, and Judge," and a chapter from Nancy McLean's book *Behind the Mask of Chivalry: The Making of the Second Ku Klux Klan*.[3]

Once we start reading *It Can't Happen Here*, however, class discussion focuses only on the novel and the questions it raises about complicity, the duty to resist, and the precarious position of minorities during authoritarian uprisings. Students are often very passionate in their responses and interactions, and if, up to that point, Trumpism has not yet entered the classroom (at least not explicitly), during these meetings it is often all we talk about. As instructors, especially when we occupy tenuous positions within academia, it can be challenging to direct these meetings so that everyone's voice is heard equally; comments often range from insights regarding the reading itself to preoccupied reflections on the current political situation. For me, a woman and an immigrant who obviously has both a personal stake and a political stance in this conversation (denying it would be quite absurd), managing to navigate students' different stances—a phenomenon that undeniably exists, especially at public institutions—is always difficult. In order to better contain these dynamics, I designed a writing exercise that has proven effective in keeping students focused on the novel while enabling them to comment on the current political situation.

As a second teaching technique for this novel, then, I ask the students to choose a passage or a character from *It Can't Happen Here* and rewrite it according to what they know today. I instruct them to use their knowledge from the class to craft a sharp narrative that satirizes peculiar moments in today's politics, as Lewis does in his original work. I also offer them several ways in which they can create such a narrative: develop the perspective of a single character in the story, invent a new character, or talk about a particular moment in history.

This assignment is particularly powerful because literature affords us the possibility of moving between the past and the present more freely than historical sources permit. It is precisely in the malleability of fiction writing that students can negotiate the continuities and legacies of fascism in our current political moment. I am copying here excerpts from three brilliant, albeit different, ways in which students have tackled this assignment.[4]

The first example is a direct rewriting of "The Fifteen Points of Victory for the Forgotten Men,"[5] Windrip's campaign proclamation, as it would look in 2019. I am retaining the original text as well (in italics) to emphasize the current dramatic relevance of *It Can't Happen Here*.

(2) The President shall appoint a commission, equally divided between manual workers, employers, and representatives of the Public, to determine which Labor Unions are qualified to represent the Workers; and report to the Executive, for legal action, all pretended labor organizations, whether "Company Unions," or "Red Unions," controlled by Communists and the

so-called "Third International." The duly recognized Unions shall be constituted Bureaus of the Government, with power of decision in all labor disputes. Later, the same investigation and official recognition shall be extended to farm organizations. In this elevation of the position of the Worker, it shall be emphasized that the League of Forgotten Men is the chief bulwark against the menace of destructive and un-American Radicalism.

(2) The President shall appoint a commission, equally divided between manual workers, employers, and representatives of the Public, to determine what is necessary to ensure pointless Labor Union strikes do not interfere with workers' need to earn wages. These strikes, organized by selfish socialists who would rather complain than do the work necessary to help their family and their country, merely prevent the worker from providing their country and their family with the fruits of their labor. In this elevation of the position of the Worker, it shall be emphasized that this League of Forgotten Men is the chief bulwark against the menace of destructive and un-American socialism.

(4) *Believing that only under God Almighty, to Whom we render all homage, do we Americans hold our vast Power, we shall guarantee to all persons absolute freedom of religious worship, provided, however, that no atheist, agnostic, believer in Black Magic, nor any Jew who shall refuse to swear allegiance to the New Testament, nor any person of any faith who refuses to take the Pledge to the Flag, shall be permitted to hold any public office or to practice as a teacher, professor, lawyer, judge, or as a physician, except in the category of Obstetrics.*

(4) Our Founding Fathers guaranteed all people the absolute freedom of religious worship, which has come under fire in recent years. Under this administration, no person will be forced to violate their religious principles to partake in any part of the wedding of homosexual individuals in any way, nor will any person be allowed to violate the sanctity of life. Furthermore, disrespecting our National Anthem or Pledge of Allegiance in any manner should never be tolerated.

(9) *We cannot too strongly condemn the un-Christian attitude of certain otherwise progressive nations in their discriminations against the Jews, who have been among the strongest supporters of the League, and who will continue to prosper and to be recognized as fully Americanized, though only so long as they continue to support our ideals.*

(9) We strongly condemn so-called "progressive nations" for their tolerance of radical Islam, a violent religion that hates the United States and threatens the world order with terrorism and bloodshed. All relevant foreign and domestic policy needs to counter Islam's evil ideals.

The next two examples speak to each other but differ somewhat from the above student's approach. While in the case above, the rewrite is directly informed by current political debates around labor unions and religious freedom, the following rewrites take a more holistic approach in representing the Trumpian reality of our everyday lives. They still engage with both the novel and today's politics, but in the first case, the student chose to create a new character, a protester at one of Windrip's rallies, while in the second case, the student repurposed the Doremus–Shad relationship in an office setting. The following are excerpts from the students' essays.

Doremus wasn't sure who possessed the voice powerful enough to distract the Minute Men in their tracks. He came to realize that the disorganized M.M. forces were equally unsure about the exact identity of the female voice. The M.M. assumed she was a planned performer, about to recite a flowery, glory-voiced song or poem in praise of Buzz Windrip, so the troops smacked the few stray Jeffersonians who continued to speak over her into quiet submission. The room sank into docile silence, obeying the M.M.'s commands to turn all attention toward the stage. The crowd waited, impatiently anticipating the woman's words, which was deemed more important than their prolific bickering. At the front of the room, a brown-skinned, relatively voluptuous young woman stood in a respectable, knee-length dress. The dark-haired siren who held the attention of the rally's attendees occupied center stage. She projected her voice with the podium's microphone, hijacking the spotlight intended for the champion of the Forgotten Man.

"Everyone!" she repeated, piercing through the building's atmosphere with a high-pitched, yet self-assured voice, "In a few minutes you will hear from Buzz Windrip. I'm sorry, but I want to make sure you know who *exactly* this so-called champion really is. I'm sorry, but he is not what he seems to be at first glance. He doesn't care about you, he doesn't care about anyone. He will use you and throw you out like a piece of garbage.

"This is my story. My name is Gloria. I met Buzz Windrip at a friend's house almost five years ago. Together, we had a few drinks and got to talking. I'm sure you can imagine, I thought he was charming. I had only just arrived in America, and I didn't have many friends. I was staying with my sister, so he offered to walk me home, very gentlemanly, when the night was over. I trusted him, so when we arrived at my place . . . "

She stopped, hearing the crowd start to murmur. Doremus paused, sensing the restlessness of her audience.

Gloria trembled and continued, "You all need to know, Buzz hurt me . . . Buzz *raped* me. A rapist *cannot* be president."

The crowd erupted into screams of confusion and protest. The Minute Men, realizing Gloria was not a planned performer, and that she was *not* going to lead a cheerful song in praise of their future leader, invaded the stage. One M.M. smacked the mic away from Gloria's mouth and another seized her by the hair. She screamed, squirmed, twisting with all her might to free herself from his tortuous grip. . . . Doremus, more nauseated, feeling more helpless than ever, thought he might never see the woman again.

After some time, Gloria was pushed back onto the stage by the M.M., to Doremus's surprise. Trembling, Gloria approached the microphone and quickly whispered, "I'm sorry, I made a mistake by telling that story. What happened that night was my fault. I was flirtatious, it was my fault . . . and . . . and," her voice cracked, "vote for Buzz Windrip."

She collapsed onto the floor, as if physically pained by her words of affirmation for Windrip's candidacy. However, the outburst of the female accuser was soon forgotten by the attendees, almost as quickly as a Sunday sermon.

. . . . .

"Good morning!" Doremus called as he walked into the office, nodding at Shad. Shad nodded in return, keeping his eyes on his computer screen. The smell of mint strengthened as Doremus stopped by his desk. "What are you working on today?"

"Numbers from last week's sales," said Shad.

Doremus leaned over him. Shad's hand clenched around the mouse. "And you feel confident about working with this?" The real question was, *Do you think you're smart enough to do this?*

Shad squeezed the mouse again, urgently. As a boss, Doremus was as condescending as he was nosy, and he was easily the worst part of Shad's already dreadful nine-to-five. Every morning, he strolled into the office and interrogated his employees to make himself feel better. *Can you handle this, Mr. Ledue? Are you smart like me, Mr. Ledue? Did you graduate with a feminist studies degree and a minor in bullshit from a useless liberal college like me, Mr. Ledue?* Forty-seven years old and here he was, being treated like he was dumb as dirt.

"I can handle it, boss," Shad said instead.

It was enough to satisfy Doremus, who left the room full of cubicles to enter his own office. Shad had been there a few times; he remembered the diplomas mounted on the wall, the supple leather chair. The view of the entire city.

Shad picked up a cup of coffee that he had brewed in the office himself. He took a sip and swallowed, let its acid make a home. This time, it tasted like envy, sweet and hot.

. . .

People like Lorinda made him sick. It was easy for her to sit in her office, crying about Assyrians or whatever and demanding people do something about it. Meanwhile she ignored people in the same room as her who were struggling to make ends meet.

"Do you disagree?" Lorinda shot back immediately.

"No," Shad said carefully, taking a bite of his sandwich. "Why worry about dying people thousands of miles away from us? Don't we have our own problems?"

"What could be worse than letting those poor, innocent people die?"

What, indeed? Shad thought. Every conversation in the office confirmed what he already knew—that people like Doremus and Lorinda would never understand people like him, that people like Doremus and Lorinda would never care about people like him. To them he was more stupid, and more worthless, than a dead Syrian child.

"Couple of things," Shad said with a noncommittal shrug of his shoulders, and the conversation ended there. . . .

The next day, he knew what he had to do. Shad had thought about it for a while, not sure if he was willing to, but now it was not a matter of *want*. It was a matter of *need*. He was being offered a way out, and if he didn't take it, he was as stupid as Doremus thought he was. His hands gripped the steering wheel, sweaty, as he veered into the parking lot. He looked nervously over his shoulder. There was no one he knew around—good.

Even as he walked into the building, trying to make himself appear as small as possible, he knew what he had to do. The more he looked around, the more he saw people like him. The other Shad Ledues, escaping their nine-to-fives, unseen and unheard in their button-downs and khakis. The other Shad Ledues, tired of listening to their whiny wives and whiny governments. Tired of being abandoned by the country they had built.

The fear from this morning had melted away. The stakes were too high, the importance of winning too great. For once, he felt needed, wanted. He had been called on, after all. He looked at the men around him and knew they were smiling at him. If all went right, well, he'd be the one laughing at Lorinda and Doremus and Emma now!

Shad Ledue turned in his ballot.

Rewriting a passage from *It Can't Happen Here* becomes a therapeutic as well as a pedagogical process in that students can think through the Trumpism plaguing their worlds while putting it productively in conversation with the novel and the class discussion of interwar fascism. While the novel in itself fosters incredibly engaging discussions, the accompanying writing exercise allows students to gather their thoughts and beliefs in a more structured and creative way. (I do dedicate a class to workshopping some pieces of the texts in smaller groups, so students have a sense of what the assignment may look like.) More importantly, the assignment enables the participation of every student, including those who may not feel comfortable speaking about these issues openly. In that vein, the third example I offered above was written by a student who was shy and preferred not to speak in front of classmates.

Given the rise of extreme right-wing politicians throughout the world, the rewriting can also apply to a reality other than that of the United States. Interestingly, an international student from Colombia did the assignment with her own country in mind and wrote a touching "conversion" story based on the rise of fascism in Colombia, reaffirming the idea grounding the class itself: that fascism is indeed a global ideology.

Giulia Riccò is assistant professor of Italian in the Department of Romance Languages and Literatures at the University of Michigan. Her research and teaching interests include Italian and Brazilian literature and culture, fascism, and migration. Giulia's book manuscript, tentatively titled "Under the Auspices of Dante: Italianità in São Paulo, Brazil," explores the ways in which Italian and Brazilian nationalisms have informed each other. Her articles have appeared in *Forum Italicum*, *Cultural Dynamics*, and *Mester*.

Notes

1. These are the texts I use in my class to introduce fascism and fascist studies: Gustave Le Bon, *The Crowd: A Study of the Popular Mind* (1895); Georges Sorel, *Reflections on Violence* (1908); Giovanni Gentile, "The Manifesto of the Fascist Intellectuals" (1925) and "The Philosophic Basis of Fascism" (1928); Emilio Gentile, "Fascism as a Political Religion" (1990) and "Fascism and the Italian Road to Totalitarianism"; Zeev Sternhell, "How to Think about Fascism and Its Ideology" (2008); Roger Griffin, *Fascism* (2018); and excerpts from Hannah Arendt, *The Origins of Totalitarianism* (1948). We normally read them side by side with the following films: *1900* by Bernardo Bertolucci (1976) and *Vincere* by Marco Bellocchio (2009).
2. Gramsci, *L'ordine nuovo (1919–1920)*.
3. Katznelson, *Fear Itself*; MacLean, *Beyond the Mask of Chivalry*.
4. Students have consented to the use of their assignments in this piece.
5. Lewis, *It Can't Happen Here*, 61.

References

Gentile, Emilio. "Fascism and the Italian Road to Totalitarianism." *Constellations* 15, no. 3 (2008): 291–302.

Gramsci, Antonio. *L'ordine nuovo (1919–1920)*. Torino: Einaudi, 1995.

Katznelson, Ira. *Fear Itself: The New Deal and the Origins of Our Time*. New York: Liveright, 2013.

Lewis, Sinclair. *It Can't Happen Here*. New York: Penguin, 2014.

MacLean, Nancy. *Beyond the Mask of Chivalry: The Making of the Second Ku Klux Klan*. New York: Oxford University Press, 1995.

Anti-fascism in the Archive

Interference Archive's Collaboration
with no. *NOT EVER.*

*Jan Descartes, Michele Hardesty, Jen Hoyer,
Maggie Schreiner, and Brooke Shuman*

In the late summer of 2017, a member of the Seattle-based collaborative If You Don't They Will (IYDTW) stopped by Interference Archive (IA), a community archive of social movement cultural production in Brooklyn, New York. If You Don't They Will provides concrete and creative tools for countering white nationalism through a cultural lens. This includes creating spaces to generate visions, desires, incantations, actions, memes, and dreams for the kinds of worlds we want to live in.[1] The visitor asked the volunteer staffer if IA had any materials on "anti-fascist organizing." Back in Seattle, she explained, IYDTW had an installation on display, a "living archive" focused on oral interviews with community members who organized in the Pacific Northwest during the 1980s and 1990s to counter a coordinated effort, led by Richard Butler's neo-Nazi Aryan Nations, to establish a "white homeland" in the Pacific Northwest.[2] With its installation, titled no. *NOT EVER.*, IYDTW was using its collection of stories from the 1980s and 1990s to create what it called a "multi-media, inter-disciplinary, immersive workshop." The point was to make visible "rural, working class activist organizing strategies," and to activate new organizing against white nationalism in the current moment.[3] On that late July day, the staffer and the member of IYDTW talked about what it would be like to bring the installation to Brooklyn, and specifically how IA's

Radical History Review
Issue 138 (October 2020)   DOI 10.1215/01636545-8359580
© 2020 by MARHO: The Radical Historians' Organization, Inc.

Figure 1. no. *NOT EVER.* pocket guide. Design by Karen M. Chappell.

collections of movement posters, periodicals, buttons, and ephemera could provide it with a print culture supplement.

Less than two weeks later, on August 12, 2017, the Unite the Right rally drew large numbers from the white supremacist far right to Charlottesville, Virginia, an event punctuated by the vicious beating of DeAndre Harris and the murder of Heather Heyer.[4] The next day, the same IA staffer pulled out the documents she'd shared with IYDTW—Anti-Racist Action zines, newsletters from an Ohio group in the 1980s called Those United to Fight Fascism (TUFF), and issues of the *Black Panther* on the United Front Against Fascism—and this time posted them on social media to pay tribute to those who had engaged in these struggles in decades past. Not long after the catastrophe in Charlottesville, the IA podcast interviewed the Seattle collective. The rise in white extremism in the shadow of Trump's election was heavy on everyone's minds.[5] The need for an exhibition on anti-fascism at Interference Archive felt urgent, and our serendipitous encounter with IYDTW made it possible to create one more quickly.

no. *NOT EVER.* opened at Interference Archive in January 2018. It featured IYDTW's original installation contextualized with print culture from the IA collection, mostly ranging from the 1960s to the present. Creating this collaborative exhibition presented several challenges and opportunities, among them how to create a cohesive show with hybrid elements, how to create digital and physical safety for visitors and volunteers in a new storefront space, and how to foreground training and organizing through workshops.

Figure 2. Social media event page for the "Digital Activism and Antifa" panel event. Image courtesy of Jan Descartes.

Curatorial Process

The interviews documented in no. *NOT EVER.* chronicled how communities in the Pacific Northwest responded to an unprecedented influx of white nationalist groups in the 1980s and 1990s by forming a network of ad hoc nonprofits and research teams. During our initial conversations, IYDTW explained that "the goal is for viewers to enter into the space and feel like they are part of a conversation, and leave feeling like they too have the skills, the imagination, and the capacity to say 'no. *NOT EVER.*' to white nationalism in their particular context."[6] IYDTW categorized the interviews into three themes: cultural organizing, research, and free speech/no platforming. Each set of interviews is accompanied by resource cards that give definitions and prompts to help viewers envision how they would join the fight against white nationalism. The installation also includes an interactive time line and map, and a picnic table that symbolizes the conversations at the heart of community organizing against fascism.

We placed IYDTW's interactive installation at the front of the IA space and created six clusters of archival materials in the back: four displays of documents on the themes of cultural organizing, research, free speech/no platforming, and anti-fascism in the United States; a selection of related books; and a flat file containing even more documents that we couldn't fit on the walls. The decision to carry over IYDTW's central themes of cultural organizing, research, and free speech/no platforming allowed us to create a strong link between the place- and time-specific nature of the original no. *NOT EVER.* exhibition, and the work and collections of Interference Archive. We saw how the many movement organizations represented in our archive used the same methods—of cultural organizing, research, and no platforming—to identify and confront white supremacist groups.

Cultural organizing was a major focus of IYDTW, which reminds us, "All social movements use cultural organizing, including white nationalism."[7] Culture and cultural spaces create community, build connections between people, and advance shared ideas. White power bands attempt to infiltrate subcultural scenes, such as punk and "hardcore," in order to gain a more mainstream audience for their political message. Such infiltration was documented in *Soundtracks to the White Revolution: White Supremacist Assaults on Youth Subculture*, a 1999 catalog of white supremacist punk from the Center for New Community and Northwest Coalition for Human Dignity, which we included in our exhibition.[8] We also included examples of how anti-fascists must be prepared to thoughtfully confront white nationalism in our cultural spaces, while also using cultural tools to build community, create space for conversation, and bring energy and creativity to political organizing. This meant including materials from Rock Against Racism, an international campaign founded in England in 1976, and the US-based Anti-Racist Action, which built a culture of antiracism through punk shows, T-shirts, stickers, patches, and zines during the 1980s and 1990s.

Figure 3. Documents of Antifascism—"Research" Section, Interference Archive. Photo by Jen Hoyer.

For the theme of research, we highlighted how anti-fascist grassroots organizations and progressive nonprofits have learned to identify white nationalists for what they are and disseminate information on how to spot them. For example, we included the poster "Know Your Hate Symbols," a taxonomy of neo-Nazi and white supremacist imagery that might turn up in neighborhoods, campuses, and event spaces. We also included reports from nonprofits and national organizations like the Southern Poverty Law Center and the Institute for Southern Studies, which monitor and report on Aryan Nations, the Ku Klux Klan, and other white nationalist groups. These national nonprofits have the resources to collect data and inform the public, but as one activist in no. *NOT EVER.* says, "they need eyes and ears" to observe and expose locally organized white nationalists.

The concept of no platforming is encapsulated in Anti-Racist Action's first point of unity, "We go where they go. Whenever fascists are organizing or active in public, we're there. We don't believe in ignoring them or staying away from them. Never let the Nazis have the street!"[9] This basic principle specifically refers to denying fascists the opportunity to present their views or engage in publicly protected speech or debate. The materials we found in the collection used direct action as a tactic to deny fascists a platform: these included efforts of German anti-fascists to stop Nazi marches, and the efforts of Antifa Sacramento and By Any Means Necessary to shut down a neo-Nazi rally at the Sacramento capitol building in June 2016.

As we pulled materials from our collections, another question arose, sparked by the documents themselves: What does it mean to talk about fascism in the United States? To answer that question, we assembled a collection of documents that showed how activists on the Left from a wide political spectrum have answered this question since the 1960s. Some of their references point to European fascism of the 1930s and 1940s, but just as frequently they relate to a history of US repression, white supremacy, and white nationalist terror that predates Hitler and Mussolini. Anti-fascists seek to limit the power of white nationalist groups, and some activists point a spotlight at white supremacy itself as the root of fascism. Activists also draw attention to the cyclical nature of upsurges in white nationalist violence, which often accompany repressive backlash against radical movements, communities of color, Jewish communities, immigrants, women, and LGBTQIA+ communities. For example, the Black Panther Party's 1969 call for a United Front Against Fascism came in the face of increased surveillance, infiltration, and police violence, as well as assassination and incarceration of its organizers.[10] Jews for Racial and Economic Justice's 2017 booklet *Understanding Antisemitism: An Offering to Our Movement* addresses the rise of anti-Semitism in the wake of Trump's election, while reminding us that "an effect of antisemitism has been to distract and divide powerful movements for justice and equity, preserving oppressive systems and benefitting ruling elites."[11]

In order to make as many materials available for browsing and research as possible, we organized additional documents in an open-access flat file drawer,

Figure 4. A selection of anti-fascist buttons from the 1930s to the present. From Documents of Antifascism—"Fascism in the U.S.?" Section, Interference Archive. Photo by Brooke Shuman.

complete with a finding aid. Anyone visiting IA was free to explore the contents of this drawer, and it served as a bridge of sorts between the exhibition and the full open-stacks archival collection, among which no. *NOT EVER.* was distributed (making the Brooklyn installation very different from the white-wall gallery where it had been previously installed in Seattle). Elsewhere in the exhibition, we displayed a curated selection of books that had aided our process and could serve as further reading for visitors.

While researching relevant material in Interference Archive's collections, we uncovered two fascist items: a comic book and a flyer. We knew that we were absolutely opposed to exhibiting fascist items, in keeping with the no-platform approach in our exhibition. Yet these materials were relevant in another way: fascists often

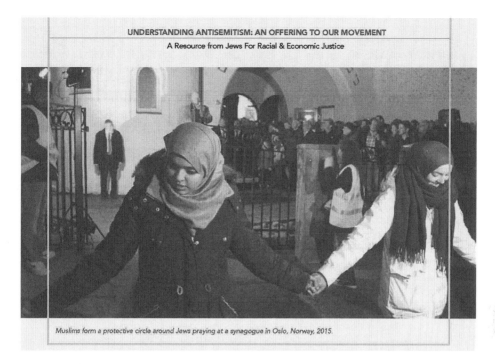

UNDERSTANDING ANTISEMITISM: AN OFFERING TO OUR MOVEMENT

A Resource from Jews For Racial & Economic Justice

Muslims form a protective circle around Jews praying at a synagogue in Oslo, Norway, 2015.

Figure 5. *Understanding Antisemitism: An Offering to Our Movement*, 2017. Lead authors: Leo Ferguson, Dove Kent, and Keren Soffer Sharon. Design: Leo Ferguson. From Documents of Antifascism—"Fascism in the U.S.?" Section, Interference Archive. Image courtesy of Jews for Racial and Economic Justice.

mimic subcultural styles and infiltrate subcultural spaces, looking to recruit adherents. These materials spoke to that process, and they were examples of the kinds of white nationalist cultural production that anti-fascists need to be prepared to confront and dismantle. We decided to include these items in a clearly labeled folder in the flat-file drawer of additional documents. In this way, visitors did not encounter these fascist items unexpectedly, yet, providing critical access to these materials highlighted our themes of anti-fascist research into fascist and white nationalist cultural organizing practices.

Addressing Security Concerns

The IA working group collaborating to bring no. *NOT EVER.* to Interference Archive also grappled with the security implications of exhibiting explicitly anti-fascist material in early 2018. To that end, two members of the exhibition working group met with New York City–based Cypurr Collective (cypurr.nyc) to discuss potential digital and physical security concerns. In many ways, we did the most tangible and straightforward tasks: we systematically strengthened the passwords to all our accounts, we transitioned from having a paper sign-up sheet for our email list to

Figure 6. *ARA News.* Anti-Racist Action, Columbus, Ohio, January and December 1998. *ARA News* provided news and context for current organizing, including details about important antiracist cultural events. Documents of Antifascism—Research Section, Interference Archive. Image courtesy of Anti-Racist Action/Josh McPhee.

having a tablet for sign-ups, which protected the identities and contact information of visitors to our space, and we created some basic emergency protocols for volunteers. These tasks helped us establish basic safety procedures that did not rely on the police and could work in a dispersed, all-volunteer space.

We also made a significant policy change that was driven directly by the needs of the exhibition. When no. *NOT EVER.* had been exhibited in Seattle, IYDTW had a policy of no photography or video to protect the activists in the videos. If their faces and testimonies appeared online, they could be matched to names, and the individuals then subjected to harassment, as many had been in the 1980s and 1990s. We decided to take a similar approach at Interference Archive: we allowed photos of documents but not of the videos, and reminded visitors to ask for consent before photographing other people in the space; this was the first time that Interference Archive had prohibited photography in our space.

Fortunately, we did not face any white supremacist threats during the exhibition; however, our abundance of caution may also have led us to under-promote the exhibition. The longer-term work would involve building more connections and stronger, anti-oppressive relationships within the dispersed volunteer collective, in the neighborhood, and among community and political organizations with which we are allied in the city and beyond.

Figure 7. *ARA Research Bulletin*, Chicago Anti-Racist Action, No. 1, May 2001. Publications like *ARA Research Bulletin* documented white nationalist groups and anti-fascist organizing. Documents of Antifascism—Research Section, Interference Archive. Image courtesy of Anti-Racist Action/Josh McPhee.

Programming

The Seattle group designed a series of workshops in conjunction with the exhibition, creating a bridge for visitors between the stories of those who organized in their communities against white nationalists and the work that anti-fascist organizers must do now to "disrupt, defuse, and compete" with fascists.[12] While we initially hoped for a weekend-long "train-the-trainer" session for local organizers to learn the specific education techniques developed by IYDTW, financial and other obstacles prevented us from making it a reality.

Instead, we built our own programming into the three-month run of the exhibition. The programming decisions intentionally reflected the exhibition's goal of empowering people to say no to white nationalism. Each workshop or discussion hopefully gave each participant the feeling when they left that they are a part of the conversation, and that individuals can and should participate locally in antifascism and anti–white nationalist work.

The variety of programming was intended to meet participants where they were in the conversation. There was a film screening of *ANTIFA*, directed by Brandon Jourdan and Marianne Maeckelbergh, with a guest speaker, anti-fascist activist Daryle Lamont Jenkins. Pop Gym, a Brooklyn-based nonprofit, facilitated a de-escalation workshop and a self-defense workshop where participants could learn basic tools for confronting white supremacy. The Antifa Discussion Series had a session titled "Community Resistance to White Nationalism," which created a safer space where newcomers to anti-fascism could work through their ideas. As anti-fascist community organizing grew in the 2000s to include the digital realm, we organized a panel discussion titled "Digital Activism and Antifa," followed by hands-on workshops and discussions. Panelists represented five projects in digital antifacist education, cultural organizing, and no platforming. Cypurr Collective introduced their education and digital activism; Metropolitan Anarchist Coordinating Council (MACC)'s No Platform For Fascism spoke about their YouTube plug-in, which empowered individuals to take down white supremacist content in directed campaigns; the Cutealism project presented their political digital propaganda tools; and Emily Crose discussed her project, NEMESIS, which tracks white nationalist symbolism on the internet. Programming throughout the entire exhibition brought people into the exhibition space of Interference Archive, allowed folks to engage with the material, and then quickly applied that information to various iterations of resistance in which individuals can participate.

Conclusion

The exhibit no. *NOT EVER.* at Interference Archive in early 2018 represented a full circle from that initial visit by a member of IYDTW. It presented a chapter in the history of organizing against white nationalism in the Pacific Northwest to a new audience, and gave visitors the opportunity to record and discuss their own

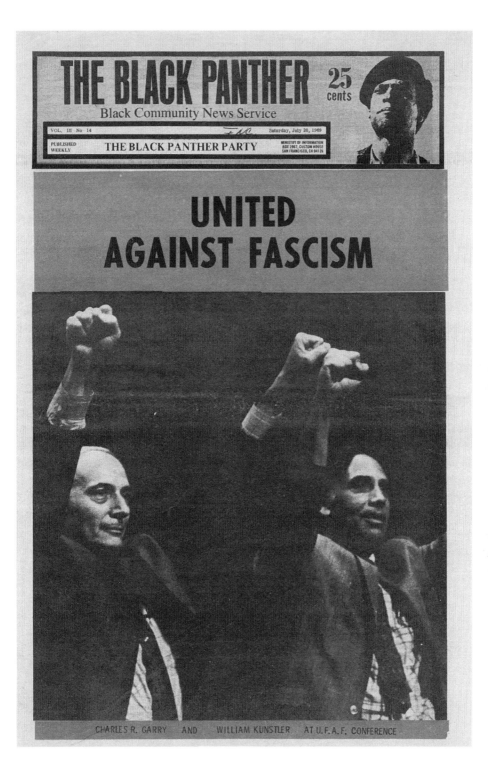

Figure 8. *The Black Panther*, Vol. 3, No. 14, July 26, 1969. Photo by Stephen Shames. From Documents of Antifascism—"Fascism in the U.S.?" Section, Interference Archive. Image courtesy of the Black Panther Party.

knowledge and experience of white nationalist activity and to strategize about how to confront it. At a moment in time when the media discourse around antifa was limited and panicked, no. *NOT EVER.* and IA's exhibition was expansive and risk taking. There were some challenges in collaborating from a distance, especially when our organizations have different strengths (IYDTW's installation focused on curated workshops, which were hard for us to reproduce; IA is known for its focus on graphics and print culture, which helped make the pocket guide popular).[13] And the exhibition came full circle in other ways: some visitors recognized their own activist work on the walls. Some used our IA materials for their own research, including the author of one of the books we used as a source. IYDTW has used this experience to help shape no. *NOT EVER.* as a traveling exhibition. For IA, we have created a finding aid (interferencearchive.org/wp-content/uploads/Documents-of-Antifascism-at -Interference-Archive.pdf) that makes it easier to locate materials that were in the exhibition. By combining our archives and our archival approaches, IA and IYDTW were able to give voice to organizers and activists who have been united in the fight against fascism.

Interference Archive is an open-stacks archive and community space in Brooklyn, New York. Founded in 2011, our collection contains the cultural production of social movements around the world: stickers, pamphlets, T-shirts, posters, magazines, and more. We believe that this history of people organizing for change belongs to everyone and can play a critical role in current and future social movements, and so we dedicate our labor to caring for this collection, keeping our doors open for the public to come in and look through these materials, and planning events and exhibitions that engage our community with the ideas and ideologies represented in our archive. Interference Archive is volunteer run and is supported financially through a community-based sustainer program.

Notes

1.   If You Don't They Will: www.ifyoudonttheywill.com. The website can be accessed at web.archive.org/web/20191030002748/https://nonononotever.com.
2.   Butler and others referred to this project of local infiltration and settlement as the "Northwest Territorial Imperative." Southern Poverty Law Center, "Richard Butler."
3.   Interference Archive, "Installation Proposal: Interference Archive."
4.   Shapira, "Ex-White Nationalist Found Guilty"; Katz and Stockman, "James Fields Guilty of First-Degree Murder."
5.   Interference Archive, "Anti-fascists in the Pacific Northwest."
6.   Personal communication, August 4, 2017.
7.   If You Don't They Will, no. *NOT EVER.* pocket guide.
8.   Burghart, *Soundtracks to the White Revolution.*
9.   Anti-Racist Action, "ARA Points of Unity."
10.   These connections were informed also by Christopher Vials's *Haunted by Hitler.*
11.   Ferguson, Kent, and Sharon, *Understanding Antisemitism.*
12.   The terminology "disrupt, defuse, and compete" comes from Nakagawa and Ramos, "What Time Is It?" IYDTW's workshops have grown in part out of Cristien Storm's

previous work with Home Alive, a self-defense organization founded in 1993. For more details on Storm's approach, see Storm, *Empowered Boundaries*.

13. IYDTW was featured on "Not All White People," an episode of the CNN show *United Shades of America with W. Kamau Bell* that aired on May 5, 2019, where the pocket guide was also the star.

CURATED SPACES provides a focus on visual culture in relation to social, historical, or political subject matter.

References

Anti-Racist Action. "ARA Points of Unity." 48o Anti-Racist Action, n.d. 48oara.blackblogs.org /ara-points-of-unity.

Burghart, Devin. *Soundtracks to the White Revolution: White Supremacist Assaults on Youth Subculture*. Chicago: Center for New Community, 1999.

Ferguson, Leo, Dove Kent, and Keren Soffer Sharon. *Understanding Antisemitism: An Offering to Our Movement.* Jews for Racial and Economic Justice, November 2017. jfrej.org/wp -content/uploads/2018/04/JFREJ-Understanding-Antisemitism-November-2017-v1-3-2 .pdf.

If You Don't They Will. no. *NOT EVER*. Pocket guide, designed by Karen M. Chappell. n.d.

Interference Archive. "Anti-fascists in the Pacific Northwest." *Audio Interference* (podcast), no. 41 (2017). archive.org/details/AudioInterference41.

Interference Archive. "Installation Proposal: Interference Archive." If You Don't They Will, 2017.

Katz, Jonathan M., and Farah Stockman. "James Fields Guilty of First-Degree Murder in Death of Heather Heyer." *New York Times*, December 8, 2018. www.nytimes.com/2018/12/07/us /james-fields-trial-charlottesville-verdict.html.

Nakagawa, Scot, and Tarso Luís Ramos. "What Time Is It? Why We Can't Ignore the Momentum of the Right." Political Research Associates, July 14, 2016. politicalresearch.org.

"Not All White People." *United Shades of America with W. Kamau Bell*, Season 4, Episode 2. CNN, May 5, 2019.

Shapira, Ian. "Ex-White Nationalist Found Guilty in Beating of Black Man in Charlottesville Parking Garage." *Washington Post*, February 8, 2019. www.washingtonpost.com/local/ex -white-nationalist-found-guilty-in-beating-black-man-in-charlottesville-parking-garage /2019/02/08/f701706c-2b0a-11e9-984d-9b8fba003e81_story.html.

Southern Poverty Law Center. "Richard Butler." www.splcenter.org/fighting-hate/extremist-files /individual/richard-butler.

Storm, Cristien. *Empowered Boundaries: Speaking Truth, Setting Boundaries, and Inspiring Social Change*. Berkeley, CA: North Atlantic Books, 2018.

Vials, Christopher. *Haunted by Hitler: Liberals, the Left, and the Fight against Fascism in the United States*. Amherst: University of Massachusetts Press, 2014.

Keep up to date on new scholarship

Issue alerts are a great way to stay current on all the cutting-edge scholarship from your favorite Duke University Press journals. This free service delivers tables of contents directly to your inbox, informing you of the latest groundbreaking work as soon as it is published.

To sign up for issue alerts:

1. Visit **dukeu.press/register** and register for an account. You do not need to provide a customer number.

2. After registering, visit **dukeu.press/alerts**.

3. Go to "Latest Issue Alerts" and click on "Add Alerts."

4. Select as many publications as you would like from the pop-up window and click "Add Alerts."

read.dukeupress.edu/journals

Meridians

feminism, race, transnationalism

Meridians, an interdisciplinary feminist journal, provides a forum for the finest scholarship and creative work by and about women of color in U.S. and international contexts. The journal engages the complexity of debates around feminism, race, and transnationalism in a dialogue across ethnic, national, and disciplinary boundaries. Meridians publishes work that makes scholarship, poetry, fiction, and memoir by and about women of color central to history, economics, politics, geography, class, sexuality, and culture. The journal provokes the critical interrogation of the terms used to shape activist agendas, theoretical paradigms, and political coalitions.

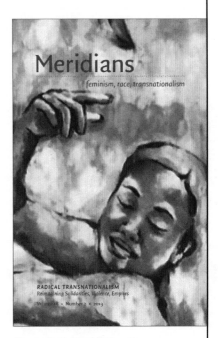

Ginetta E. B. Candelario, editor